THIS IS YOUR **PASSBOOK®** FOR ...

AUTO MECHANIC

NATIONAL LEARNING CORPORATION®

passbooks.com

PASSBOOK® SERIES

THE *PASSBOOK® SERIES* has been created to prepare applicants and candidates for the ultimate academic battlefield – the examination room.

At some time in our lives, each and every one of us may be required to take an examination – for validation, matriculation, admission, qualification, registration, certification, or licensure.

Based on the assumption that every applicant or candidate has met the basic formal educational standards, has taken the required number of courses, and read the necessary texts, the *PASSBOOK® SERIES* furnishes the one special preparation which may assure passing with confidence, instead of failing with insecurity. Examination questions – together with answers – are furnished as the basic vehicle for study so that the mysteries of the examination and its compounding difficulties may be eliminated or diminished by a sure method.

This book is meant to help you pass your examination provided that you qualify and are serious in your objective.

The entire field is reviewed through the huge store of content information which is succinctly presented through a provocative and challenging approach – the question-and-answer method.

A climate of success is established by furnishing the correct answers at the end of each test.

You soon learn to recognize types of questions, forms of questions, and patterns of questioning. You may even begin to anticipate expected outcomes.

You perceive that many questions are repeated or adapted so that you can gain acute insights, which may enable you to score many sure points.

You learn how to confront new questions, or types of questions, and to attack them confidently and work out the correct answers.

You note objectives and emphases, and recognize pitfalls and dangers, so that you may make positive educational adjustments.

Moreover, you are kept fully informed in relation to new concepts, methods, practices, and directions in the field.

You discover that you arre actually taking the examination all the time: you are preparing for the examination by "taking" an examination, not by reading extraneous and/or supererogatory textbooks.

In short, this PASSBOOK®, used directedly, should be an important factor in helping you to pass your test.

AUTO MECHANIC

JOB DESCRIPTION
Under supervision, overhauls, repairs and maintains engines and component assemblies used in automotive, construction and special equipment powered by internal combustion engines; performs related work.

EXAMPLES OF TYPICAL TASKS
Acts as a "trouble shooter" in determining mechanical and electrical defects. Makes minor repairs and adjustments in the field so that a vehicle may be returned to the garage or repair shop under its own power. Overhauls and makes repairs to internal combustion engines, brake systems, transmission and ignition systems, rear ends, differential assemblies and fuel systems. Aligns wheels and repairs steering equipment. Relines and adjusts brakes and clutches. May transmit orders to other journeymen as directed. May supervise machinist helpers, senior automotive servicemen, automotive servicemen and other personnel as directed. Trains assigned machinist helpers, senior automotive servicemen, automotive servicemen, or other related personnel in the performance of various maintenance and/or repair tasks. May make minor auto body repairs. May prepare reports and orders; maintain records and inventories of supplies and materials. May operate motor vehicle or equipment in the performance of assigned duties

SCOPE OF THE EXAMINATION
The multiple-choice test may include questions on the operating principles of internal combustion automotive components such as engines, transmissions, clutches, brakes, wheels, tires; trouble shooting and repair of motor vehicle components, accessories and systems; tools, safety, basic mathematics, reading comprehension, materials and electricity; shop equipment and shop techniques commonly used in effecting overhaul and reconstruction of automotive components; and other related areas.

―――

HOW TO TAKE A TEST

I. YOU MUST PASS AN EXAMINATION

A. *WHAT EVERY CANDIDATE SHOULD KNOW*

Examination applicants often ask us for help in preparing for the written test. What can I study in advance? What kinds of questions will be asked? How will the test be given? How will the papers be graded?

As an applicant for a civil service examination, you may be wondering about some of these things. Our purpose here is to suggest effective methods of advance study and to describe civil service examinations.

Your chances for success on this examination can be increased if you know how to prepare. Those "pre-examination jitters" can be reduced if you know what to expect. You can even experience an adventure in good citizenship if you know why civil service exams are given.

B. *WHY ARE CIVIL SERVICE EXAMINATIONS GIVEN?*

Civil service examinations are important to you in two ways. As a citizen, you want public jobs filled by employees who know how to do their work. As a job seeker, you want a fair chance to compete for that job on an equal footing with other candidates. The best-known means of accomplishing this two-fold goal is the competitive examination.

Exams are widely publicized throughout the nation. They may be administered for jobs in federal, state, city, municipal, town or village governments or agencies.

Any citizen may apply, with some limitations, such as the age or residence of applicants. Your experience and education may be reviewed to see whether you meet the requirements for the particular examination. When these requirements exist, they are reasonable and applied consistently to all applicants. Thus, a competitive examination may cause you some uneasiness now, but it is your privilege and safeguard.

C. *HOW ARE CIVIL SERVICE EXAMS DEVELOPED?*

Examinations are carefully written by trained technicians who are specialists in the field known as "psychological measurement," in consultation with recognized authorities in the field of work that the test will cover. These experts recommend the subject matter areas or skills to be tested; only those knowledges or skills important to your success on the job are included. The most reliable books and source materials available are used as references. Together, the experts and technicians judge the difficulty level of the questions.

Test technicians know how to phrase questions so that the problem is clearly stated. Their ethics do not permit "trick" or "catch" questions. Questions may have been tried out on sample groups, or subjected to statistical analysis, to determine their usefulness.

Written tests are often used in combination with performance tests, ratings of training and experience, and oral interviews. All of these measures combine to form the best-known means of finding the right person for the right job.

II. HOW TO PASS THE WRITTEN TEST

A. NATURE OF THE EXAMINATION

To prepare intelligently for civil service examinations, you should know how they differ from school examinations you have taken. In school you were assigned certain definite pages to read or subjects to cover. The examination questions were quite detailed and usually emphasized memory. Civil service exams, on the other hand, try to discover your present ability to perform the duties of a position, plus your potentiality to learn these duties. In other words, a civil service exam attempts to predict how successful you will be. Questions cover such a broad area that they cannot be as minute and detailed as school exam questions.

In the public service similar kinds of work, or positions, are grouped together in one "class." This process is known as *position-classification*. All the positions in a class are paid according to the salary range for that class. One class title covers all of these positions, and they are all tested by the same examination.

B. FOUR BASIC STEPS

1) Study the announcement

How, then, can you know what subjects to study? Our best answer is: "Learn as much as possible about the class of positions for which you've applied." The exam will test the knowledge, skills and abilities needed to do the work.

Your most valuable source of information about the position you want is the official exam announcement. This announcement lists the training and experience qualifications. Check these standards and apply only if you come reasonably close to meeting them.

The brief description of the position in the examination announcement offers some clues to the subjects which will be tested. Think about the job itself. Review the duties in your mind. Can you perform them, or are there some in which you are rusty? Fill in the blank spots in your preparation.

Many jurisdictions preview the written test in the exam announcement by including a section called "Knowledge and Abilities Required," "Scope of the Examination," or some similar heading. Here you will find out specifically what fields will be tested.

2) Review your own background

Once you learn in general what the position is all about, and what you need to know to do the work, ask yourself which subjects you already know fairly well and which need improvement. You may wonder whether to concentrate on improving your strong areas or on building some background in your fields of weakness. When the announcement has specified "some knowledge" or "considerable knowledge," or has used adjectives like "beginning principles of..." or "advanced ... methods," you can get a clue as to the number and difficulty of questions to be asked in any given field. More questions, and hence broader coverage, would be included for those subjects which are more important in the work. Now weigh your strengths and weaknesses against the job requirements and prepare accordingly.

3) Determine the level of the position

Another way to tell how intensively you should prepare is to understand the level of the job for which you are applying. Is it the entering level? In other words, is this the position in which beginners in a field of work are hired? Or is it an intermediate or advanced level? Sometimes this is indicated by such words as "Junior" or "Senior" in the class title. Other jurisdictions use Roman numerals to designate the level – Clerk I, Clerk II, for example. The word "Supervisor" sometimes appears in the title. If the level is not indicated by the title, check the description of duties. Will you be working under very close supervision, or will you have responsibility for independent decisions in this work?

4) Choose appropriate study materials

Now that you know the subjects to be examined and the relative amount of each subject to be covered, you can choose suitable study materials. For beginning level jobs, or even advanced ones, if you have a pronounced weakness in some aspect of your training, read a modern, standard textbook in that field. Be sure it is up to date and has general coverage. Such books are normally available at your library, and the librarian will be glad to help you locate one. For entry-level positions, questions of appropriate difficulty are chosen – neither highly advanced questions, nor those too simple. Such questions require careful thought but not advanced training.

If the position for which you are applying is technical or advanced, you will read more advanced, specialized material. If you are already familiar with the basic principles of your field, elementary textbooks would waste your time. Concentrate on advanced textbooks and technical periodicals. Think through the concepts and review difficult problems in your field.

These are all general sources. You can get more ideas on your own initiative, following these leads. For example, training manuals and publications of the government agency which employs workers in your field can be useful, particularly for technical and professional positions. A letter or visit to the government department involved may result in more specific study suggestions, and certainly will provide you with a more definite idea of the exact nature of the position you are seeking.

III. KINDS OF TESTS

Tests are used for purposes other than measuring knowledge and ability to perform specified duties. For some positions, it is equally important to test ability to make adjustments to new situations or to profit from training. In others, basic mental abilities not dependent on information are essential. Questions which test these things may not appear as pertinent to the duties of the position as those which test for knowledge and information. Yet they are often highly important parts of a fair examination. For very general questions, it is almost impossible to help you direct your study efforts. What we can do is to point out some of the more common of these general abilities needed in public service positions and describe some typical questions.

1) General information

Broad, general information has been found useful for predicting job success in some kinds of work. This is tested in a variety of ways, from vocabulary lists to questions about current events. Basic background in some field of work, such as sociology or economics, may be sampled in a group of questions. Often these are principles which have become familiar to most persons through exposure rather than through formal training. It is difficult to advise you how to study for these questions; being alert to the world around you is our best suggestion.

2) Verbal ability

An example of an ability needed in many positions is verbal or language ability. Verbal ability is, in brief, the ability to use and understand words. Vocabulary and grammar tests are typical measures of this ability. Reading comprehension or paragraph interpretation questions are common in many kinds of civil service tests. You are given a paragraph of written material and asked to find its central meaning.

3) Numerical ability

Number skills can be tested by the familiar arithmetic problem, by checking paired lists of numbers to see which are alike and which are different, or by interpreting charts and graphs. In the latter test, a graph may be printed in the test booklet which you are asked to use as the basis for answering questions.

4) Observation

A popular test for law-enforcement positions is the observation test. A picture is shown to you for several minutes, then taken away. Questions about the picture test your ability to observe both details and larger elements.

5) Following directions

In many positions in the public service, the employee must be able to carry out written instructions dependably and accurately. You may be given a chart with several columns, each column listing a variety of information. The questions require you to carry out directions involving the information given in the chart.

6) Skills and aptitudes

Performance tests effectively measure some manual skills and aptitudes. When the skill is one in which you are trained, such as typing or shorthand, you can practice. These tests are often very much like those given in business school or high school courses. For many of the other skills and aptitudes, however, no short-time preparation can be made. Skills and abilities natural to you or that you have developed throughout your lifetime are being tested.

Many of the general questions just described provide all the data needed to answer the questions and ask you to use your reasoning ability to find the answers. Your best preparation for these tests, as well as for tests of facts and ideas, is to be at your physical and mental best. You, no doubt, have your own methods of getting into an exam-taking mood and keeping "in shape." The next section lists some ideas on this subject.

IV. KINDS OF QUESTIONS

Only rarely is the "essay" question, which you answer in narrative form, used in civil service tests. Civil service tests are usually of the short-answer type. Full instructions for answering these questions will be given to you at the examination. But in case this is your first experience with short-answer questions and separate answer sheets, here is what you need to know:

1) Multiple-choice Questions

Most popular of the short-answer questions is the "multiple choice" or "best answer" question. It can be used, for example, to test for factual knowledge, ability to solve problems or judgment in meeting situations found at work.

A multiple-choice question is normally one of three types—

- It can begin with an incomplete statement followed by several possible endings. You are to find the one ending which *best* completes the statement, although some of the others may not be entirely wrong.
- It can also be a complete statement in the form of a question which is answered by choosing one of the statements listed.
- It can be in the form of a problem – again you select the best answer.

Here is an example of a multiple-choice question with a discussion which should give you some clues as to the method for choosing the right answer:

When an employee has a complaint about his assignment, the action which will *best* help him overcome his difficulty is to
   A. discuss his difficulty with his coworkers
   B. take the problem to the head of the organization
   C. take the problem to the person who gave him the assignment
   D. say nothing to anyone about his complaint

In answering this question, you should study each of the choices to find which is best. Consider choice "A" – Certainly an employee may discuss his complaint with fellow employees, but no change or improvement can result, and the complaint remains unresolved. Choice "B" is a poor choice since the head of the organization probably does not know what assignment you have been given, and taking your problem to him is known as "going over the head" of the supervisor. The supervisor, or person who made the assignment, is the person who can clarify it or correct any injustice. Choice "C" is, therefore, correct. To say nothing, as in choice "D," is unwise. Supervisors have and interest in knowing the problems employees are facing, and the employee is seeking a solution to his problem.

2) True/False Questions

The "true/false" or "right/wrong" form of question is sometimes used. Here a complete statement is given. Your job is to decide whether the statement is right or wrong.

SAMPLE: A roaming cell-phone call to a nearby city costs less than a non-roaming call to a distant city.

This statement is wrong, or false, since roaming calls are more expensive.
This is not a complete list of all possible question forms, although most of the others are variations of these common types. You will always get complete directions for

answering questions. Be sure you understand *how* to mark your answers – ask questions until you do.

V. RECORDING YOUR ANSWERS

Computer terminals are used more and more today for many different kinds of exams.

For an examination with very few applicants, you may be told to record your answers in the test booklet itself. Separate answer sheets are much more common. If this separate answer sheet is to be scored by machine – and this is often the case – it is highly important that you mark your answers correctly in order to get credit.

An electronic scoring machine is often used in civil service offices because of the speed with which papers can be scored. Machine-scored answer sheets must be marked with a pencil, which will be given to you. This pencil has a high graphite content which responds to the electronic scoring machine. As a matter of fact, stray dots may register as answers, so do not let your pencil rest on the answer sheet while you are pondering the correct answer. Also, if your pencil lead breaks or is otherwise defective, ask for another.

Since the answer sheet will be dropped in a slot in the scoring machine, be careful not to bend the corners or get the paper crumpled.

The answer sheet normally has five vertical columns of numbers, with 30 numbers to a column. These numbers correspond to the question numbers in your test booklet. After each number, going across the page are four or five pairs of dotted lines. These short dotted lines have small letters or numbers above them. The first two pairs may also have a "T" or "F" above the letters. This indicates that the first two pairs only are to be used if the questions are of the true-false type. If the questions are multiple choice, disregard the "T" and "F" and pay attention only to the small letters or numbers.

Answer your questions in the manner of the sample that follows:

32. The largest city in the United States is
    A. Washington, D.C.
    B. New York City
    C. Chicago
    D. Detroit
    E. San Francisco

1) Choose the answer you think is best. (New York City is the largest, so "B" is correct.)
2) Find the row of dotted lines numbered the same as the question you are answering. (Find row number 32)
3) Find the pair of dotted lines corresponding to the answer. (Find the pair of lines under the mark "B.")
4) Make a solid black mark between the dotted lines.

VI. BEFORE THE TEST

Common sense will help you find procedures to follow to get ready for an examination. Too many of us, however, overlook these sensible measures. Indeed, nervousness and fatigue have been found to be the most serious reasons why applicants fail to do their best on civil service tests. Here is a list of reminders:

- Begin your preparation early – Don't wait until the last minute to go scurrying around for books and materials or to find out what the position is all about.
- Prepare continuously – An hour a night for a week is better than an all-night cram session. This has been definitely established. What is more, a night a week for a month will return better dividends than crowding your study into a shorter period of time.
- Locate the place of the exam – You have been sent a notice telling you when and where to report for the examination. If the location is in a different town or otherwise unfamiliar to you, it would be well to inquire the best route and learn something about the building.
- Relax the night before the test – Allow your mind to rest. Do not study at all that night. Plan some mild recreation or diversion; then go to bed early and get a good night's sleep.
- Get up early enough to make a leisurely trip to the place for the test – This way unforeseen events, traffic snarls, unfamiliar buildings, etc. will not upset you.
- Dress comfortably – A written test is not a fashion show. You will be known by number and not by name, so wear something comfortable.
- Leave excess paraphernalia at home – Shopping bags and odd bundles will get in your way. You need bring only the items mentioned in the official notice you received; usually everything you need is provided. Do not bring reference books to the exam. They will only confuse those last minutes and be taken away from you when in the test room.
- Arrive somewhat ahead of time – If because of transportation schedules you must get there very early, bring a newspaper or magazine to take your mind off yourself while waiting.
- Locate the examination room – When you have found the proper room, you will be directed to the seat or part of the room where you will sit. Sometimes you are given a sheet of instructions to read while you are waiting. Do not fill out any forms until you are told to do so; just read them and be prepared.
- Relax and prepare to listen to the instructions
- If you have any physical problem that may keep you from doing your best, be sure to tell the test administrator. If you are sick or in poor health, you really cannot do your best on the exam. You can come back and take the test some other time.

VII. AT THE TEST

The day of the test is here and you have the test booklet in your hand. The temptation to get going is very strong. Caution! There is more to success than knowing the right answers. You must know how to identify your papers and understand variations in the type of short-answer question used in this particular examination. Follow these suggestions for maximum results from your efforts:

1) Cooperate with the monitor

The test administrator has a duty to create a situation in which you can be as much at ease as possible. He will give instructions, tell you when to begin, check to see that you are marking your answer sheet correctly, and so on. He is not there to guard you, although he will see that your competitors do not take unfair advantage. He wants to help you do your best.

2) Listen to all instructions

Don't jump the gun! Wait until you understand all directions. In most civil service tests you get more time than you need to answer the questions. So don't be in a hurry. Read each word of instructions until you clearly understand the meaning. Study the examples, listen to all announcements and follow directions. Ask questions if you do not understand what to do.

3) Identify your papers

Civil service exams are usually identified by number only. You will be assigned a number; you must not put your name on your test papers. Be sure to copy your number correctly. Since more than one exam may be given, copy your exact examination title.

4) Plan your time

Unless you are told that a test is a "speed" or "rate of work" test, speed itself is usually not important. Time enough to answer all the questions will be provided, but this does not mean that you have all day. An overall time limit has been set. Divide the total time (in minutes) by the number of questions to determine the approximate time you have for each question.

5) Do not linger over difficult questions

If you come across a difficult question, mark it with a paper clip (useful to have along) and come back to it when you have been through the booklet. One caution if you do this – be sure to skip a number on your answer sheet as well. Check often to be sure that you have not lost your place and that you are marking in the row numbered the same as the question you are answering.

6) Read the questions

Be sure you know what the question asks! Many capable people are unsuccessful because they failed to *read* the questions correctly.

7) Answer all questions

Unless you have been instructed that a penalty will be deducted for incorrect answers, it is better to guess than to omit a question.

8) Speed tests

It is often better NOT to guess on speed tests. It has been found that on timed tests people are tempted to spend the last few seconds before time is called in marking answers at random – without even reading them – in the hope of picking up a few extra points. To discourage this practice, the instructions may warn you that your score will be "corrected" for guessing. That is, a penalty will be applied. The incorrect answers will be deducted from the correct ones, or some other penalty formula will be used.

9) Review your answers

If you finish before time is called, go back to the questions you guessed or omitted to give them further thought. Review other answers if you have time.

10) Return your test materials

If you are ready to leave before others have finished or time is called, take ALL your materials to the monitor and leave quietly. Never take any test material with you. The monitor can discover whose papers are not complete, and taking a test booklet may be grounds for disqualification.

VIII. EXAMINATION TECHNIQUES

1) Read the general instructions carefully. These are usually printed on the first page of the exam booklet. As a rule, these instructions refer to the timing of the examination; the fact that you should not start work until the signal and must stop work at a signal, etc. If there are any *special* instructions, such as a choice of questions to be answered, make sure that you note this instruction carefully.

2) When you are ready to start work on the examination, that is as soon as the signal has been given, read the instructions to each question booklet, underline any key words or phrases, such as *least, best, outline, describe* and the like. In this way you will tend to answer as requested rather than discover on reviewing your paper that you *listed without describing*, that you selected the *worst* choice rather than the *best* choice, etc.

3) If the examination is of the objective or multiple-choice type – that is, each question will also give a series of possible answers: A, B, C or D, and you are called upon to select the best answer and write the letter next to that answer on your answer paper – it is advisable to start answering each question in turn. There may be anywhere from 50 to 100 such questions in the three or four hours allotted and you can see how much time would be taken if you read through all the questions before beginning to answer any. Furthermore, if you come across a question or group of questions which you know would be difficult to answer, it would undoubtedly affect your handling of all the other questions.

4) If the examination is of the essay type and contains but a few questions, it is a moot point as to whether you should read all the questions before starting to answer any one. Of course, if you are given a choice – say five out of seven and the like – then it is essential to read all the questions so you can eliminate the two that are most difficult. If, however, you are asked to answer all the questions, there may be danger in trying to answer the easiest one first because you may find that you will spend too much time on it. The best technique is to answer the first question, then proceed to the second, etc.

5) Time your answers. Before the exam begins, write down the time it started, then add the time allowed for the examination and write down the time it must be completed, then divide the time available somewhat as follows:

- If 3-1/2 hours are allowed, that would be 210 minutes. If you have 80 objective-type questions, that would be an average of 2-1/2 minutes per question. Allow yourself no more than 2 minutes per question, or a total of 160 minutes, which will permit about 50 minutes to review.
- If for the time allotment of 210 minutes there are 7 essay questions to answer, that would average about 30 minutes a question. Give yourself only 25 minutes per question so that you have about 35 minutes to review.

6) The most important instruction is to *read each question* and make sure you know what is wanted. The second most important instruction is to *time yourself properly* so that you answer every question. The third most important instruction is to *answer every question*. Guess if you have to but include something for each question. Remember that you will receive no credit for a blank and will probably receive some credit if you write something in answer to an essay question. If you guess a letter – say "B" for a multiple-choice question – you may have guessed right. If you leave a blank as an answer to a multiple-choice question, the examiners may respect your feelings but it will not add a point to your score. Some exams may penalize you for wrong answers, so in such cases *only*, you may not want to guess unless you have some basis for your answer.

7) Suggestions
   a. Objective-type questions
      1. Examine the question booklet for proper sequence of pages and questions
      2. Read all instructions carefully
      3. Skip any question which seems too difficult; return to it after all other questions have been answered
      4. Apportion your time properly; do not spend too much time on any single question or group of questions
      5. Note and underline key words – *all, most, fewest, least, best, worst, same, opposite*, etc.
      6. Pay particular attention to negatives
      7. Note unusual option, e.g., unduly long, short, complex, different or similar in content to the body of the question
      8. Observe the use of "hedging" words – *probably, may, most likely*, etc.
      9. Make sure that your answer is put next to the same number as the question
      10. Do not second-guess unless you have good reason to believe the second answer is definitely more correct
      11. Cross out original answer if you decide another answer is more accurate; do not erase until you are ready to hand your paper in
      12. Answer all questions; guess unless instructed otherwise
      13. Leave time for review

   b. Essay questions
      1. Read each question carefully
      2. Determine exactly what is wanted. Underline key words or phrases.
      3. Decide on outline or paragraph answer

4. Include many different points and elements unless asked to develop any one or two points or elements
5. Show impartiality by giving pros and cons unless directed to select one side only
6. Make and write down any assumptions you find necessary to answer the questions
7. Watch your English, grammar, punctuation and choice of words
8. Time your answers; don't crowd material

8) Answering the essay question

Most essay questions can be answered by framing the specific response around several key words or ideas. Here are a few such key words or ideas:

M's: manpower, materials, methods, money, management
P's: purpose, program, policy, plan, procedure, practice, problems, pitfalls, personnel, public relations
    a. Six basic steps in handling problems:
        1. Preliminary plan and background development
        2. Collect information, data and facts
        3. Analyze and interpret information, data and facts
        4. Analyze and develop solutions as well as make recommendations
        5. Prepare report and sell recommendations
        6. Install recommendations and follow up effectiveness

    b. Pitfalls to avoid
        1. *Taking things for granted* – A statement of the situation does not necessarily imply that each of the elements is necessarily true; for example, a complaint may be invalid and biased so that all that can be taken for granted is that a complaint has been registered
        2. *Considering only one side of a situation* – Wherever possible, indicate several alternatives and then point out the reasons you selected the best one
        3. *Failing to indicate follow up* – Whenever your answer indicates action on your part, make certain that you will take proper follow-up action to see how successful your recommendations, procedures or actions turn out to be
        4. *Taking too long in answering any single question* – Remember to time your answers properly

IX. AFTER THE TEST

Scoring procedures differ in detail among civil service jurisdictions although the general principles are the same. Whether the papers are hand-scored or graded by machine we have described, they are nearly always graded by number. That is, the person who marks the paper knows only the number – never the name – of the applicant. Not until all the papers have been graded will they be matched with names. If other tests, such as training and experience or oral interview ratings have been given, scores will be combined. Different parts of the examination usually have different weights. For example, the written test might count 60 percent of the final grade, and a rating of training and experience 40 percent. In many jurisdictions, veterans will have a certain number of points added to their grades.

After the final grade has been determined, the names are placed in grade order and an eligible list is established. There are various methods for resolving ties between those who get the same final grade – probably the most common is to place first the name of the person whose application was received first. Job offers are made from the eligible list in the order the names appear on it. You will be notified of your grade and your rank as soon as all these computations have been made. This will be done as rapidly as possible.

People who are found to meet the requirements in the announcement are called "eligibles." Their names are put on a list of eligible candidates. An eligible's chances of getting a job depend on how high he stands on this list and how fast agencies are filling jobs from the list.

When a job is to be filled from a list of eligibles, the agency asks for the names of people on the list of eligibles for that job. When the civil service commission receives this request, it sends to the agency the names of the three people highest on this list. Or, if the job to be filled has specialized requirements, the office sends the agency the names of the top three persons who meet these requirements from the general list.

The appointing officer makes a choice from among the three people whose names were sent to him. If the selected person accepts the appointment, the names of the others are put back on the list to be considered for future openings.

That is the rule in hiring from all kinds of eligible lists, whether they are for typist, carpenter, chemist, or something else. For every vacancy, the appointing officer has his choice of any one of the top three eligibles on the list. This explains why the person whose name is on top of the list sometimes does not get an appointment when some of the persons lower on the list do. If the appointing officer chooses the second or third eligible, the No. 1 eligible does not get a job at once, but stays on the list until he is appointed or the list is terminated.

X. HOW TO PASS THE INTERVIEW TEST

The examination for which you applied requires an oral interview test. You have already taken the written test and you are now being called for the interview test – the final part of the formal examination.

You may think that it is not possible to prepare for an interview test and that there are no procedures to follow during an interview. Our purpose is to point out some things you can do in advance that will help you and some good rules to follow and pitfalls to avoid while you are being interviewed.

What is an interview supposed to test?

The written examination is designed to test the technical knowledge and competence of the candidate; the oral is designed to evaluate intangible qualities, not readily measured otherwise, and to establish a list showing the relative fitness of each candidate – as measured against his competitors – for the position sought. Scoring is not on the basis of "right" and "wrong," but on a sliding scale of values ranging from "not passable" to "outstanding." As a matter of fact, it is possible to achieve a relatively low score without a single "incorrect" answer because of evident weakness in the qualities being measured.

Occasionally, an examination may consist entirely of an oral test – either an individual or a group oral. In such cases, information is sought concerning the technical knowledges and abilities of the candidate, since there has been no written examination for this purpose. More commonly, however, an oral test is used to supplement a written examination.

Who conducts interviews?

The composition of oral boards varies among different jurisdictions. In nearly all, a representative of the personnel department serves as chairman. One of the members of the board may be a representative of the department in which the candidate would work. In some cases, "outside experts" are used, and, frequently, a businessman or some other representative of the general public is asked to serve. Labor and management or other special groups may be represented. The aim is to secure the services of experts in the appropriate field.

However the board is composed, it is a good idea (and not at all improper or unethical) to ascertain in advance of the interview who the members are and what groups they represent. When you are introduced to them, you will have some idea of their backgrounds and interests, and at least you will not stutter and stammer over their names.

What should be done before the interview?

While knowledge about the board members is useful and takes some of the surprise element out of the interview, there is other preparation which is more substantive. It *is* possible to prepare for an oral interview – in several ways:

1) Keep a copy of your application and review it carefully before the interview

This may be the only document before the oral board, and the starting point of the interview. Know what education and experience you have listed there, and the sequence and dates of all of it. Sometimes the board will ask you to review the highlights of your experience for them; you should not have to hem and haw doing it.

2) Study the class specification and the examination announcement

Usually, the oral board has one or both of these to guide them. The qualities, characteristics or knowledges required by the position sought are stated in these documents. They offer valuable clues as to the nature of the oral interview. For example, if the job involves supervisory responsibilities, the announcement will usually indicate that knowledge of modern supervisory methods and the qualifications of the candidate as a supervisor will be tested. If so, you can expect such questions, frequently in the form of a hypothetical situation which you are expected to solve. NEVER go into an oral without knowledge of the duties and responsibilities of the job you seek.

3) Think through each qualification required

Try to visualize the kind of questions you would ask if you were a board member. How well could you answer them? Try especially to appraise your own knowledge and background in each area, *measured against the job sought*, and identify any areas in which you are weak. Be critical and realistic – do not flatter yourself.

4) Do some general reading in areas in which you feel you may be weak

For example, if the job involves supervision and your past experience has NOT, some general reading in supervisory methods and practices, particularly in the field of human relations, might be useful. Do NOT study agency procedures or detailed manuals. The oral board will be testing your understanding and capacity, not your memory.

5) Get a good night's sleep and watch your general health and mental attitude

You will want a clear head at the interview. Take care of a cold or any other minor ailment, and of course, no hangovers.

What should be done on the day of the interview?

Now comes the day of the interview itself. Give yourself plenty of time to get there. Plan to arrive somewhat ahead of the scheduled time, particularly if your appointment is in the fore part of the day. If a previous candidate fails to appear, the board might be ready for you a bit early. By early afternoon an oral board is almost invariably behind schedule if there are many candidates, and you may have to wait. Take along a book or magazine to read, or your application to review, but leave any extraneous material in the waiting room when you go in for your interview. In any event, relax and compose yourself.

The matter of dress is important. The board is forming impressions about you – from your experience, your manners, your attitude, and your appearance. Give your personal appearance careful attention. Dress your best, but not your flashiest. Choose conservative, appropriate clothing, and be sure it is immaculate. This is a business interview, and your appearance should indicate that you regard it as such. Besides, being well groomed and properly dressed will help boost your confidence.

Sooner or later, someone will call your name and escort you into the interview room. *This is it.* From here on you are on your own. It is too late for any more preparation. But remember, you asked for this opportunity to prove your fitness, and you are here because your request was granted.

What happens when you go in?

The usual sequence of events will be as follows: The clerk (who is often the board stenographer) will introduce you to the chairman of the oral board, who will introduce you to the other members of the board. Acknowledge the introductions before you sit down. Do not be surprised if you find a microphone facing you or a stenotypist sitting by. Oral interviews are usually recorded in the event of an appeal or other review.

Usually the chairman of the board will open the interview by reviewing the highlights of your education and work experience from your application – primarily for the benefit of the other members of the board, as well as to get the material into the record. Do not interrupt or comment unless there is an error or significant misinterpretation; if that is the case, do not hesitate. But do not quibble about insignificant matters. Also, he will usually ask you some question about your education, experience or your present job – partly to get you to start talking and to establish the interviewing "rapport." He may start the actual questioning, or turn it over to one of the other members. Frequently, each member undertakes the questioning on a particular area, one in which he is perhaps most competent, so you can expect each member to participate in the examination. Because time is limited, you may also expect some rather abrupt switches in the direction the questioning takes, so do not be upset by it. Normally, a board member will not pursue a single line of questioning unless he discovers a particular strength or weakness.

After each member has participated, the chairman will usually ask whether any member has any further questions, then will ask you if you have anything you wish to add. Unless you are expecting this question, it may floor you. Worse, it may start you off on an extended, extemporaneous speech. The board is not usually seeking more information. The question is principally to offer you a last opportunity to present further qualifications or to indicate that you have nothing to add. So, if you feel that a significant qualification or characteristic has been overlooked, it is proper to point it out in a sentence or so. Do not compliment the board on the thoroughness of their examination – they have been sketchy, and you know it. If you wish, merely say, "No thank you, I have nothing further to add." This is a point where you can "talk yourself out" of a good impression or fail to present an important bit of information. Remember, *you close the interview yourself.*

The chairman will then say, "That is all, Mr. _____, thank you." Do not be startled; the interview is over, and quicker than you think. Thank him, gather your belongings and take your leave. Save your sigh of relief for the other side of the door.

How to put your best foot forward

Throughout this entire process, you may feel that the board individually and collectively is trying to pierce your defenses, seek out your hidden weaknesses and embarrass and confuse you. Actually, this is not true. They are obliged to make an appraisal of your qualifications for the job you are seeking, and they want to see you in your best light. Remember, they must interview all candidates and a non-cooperative candidate may become a failure in spite of their best efforts to bring out his qualifications. Here are 15 suggestions that will help you:

1) Be natural – Keep your attitude confident, not cocky

If you are not confident that you can do the job, do not expect the board to be. Do not apologize for your weaknesses, try to bring out your strong points. The board is interested in a positive, not negative, presentation. Cockiness will antagonize any board member and make him wonder if you are covering up a weakness by a false show of strength.

2) Get comfortable, but don't lounge or sprawl

Sit erectly but not stiffly. A careless posture may lead the board to conclude that you are careless in other things, or at least that you are not impressed by the importance of the occasion. Either conclusion is natural, even if incorrect. Do not fuss with your clothing, a pencil or an ashtray. Your hands may occasionally be useful to emphasize a point; do not let them become a point of distraction.

3) Do not wisecrack or make small talk

This is a serious situation, and your attitude should show that you consider it as such. Further, the time of the board is limited – they do not want to waste it, and neither should you.

4) Do not exaggerate your experience or abilities

In the first place, from information in the application or other interviews and sources, the board may know more about you than you think. Secondly, you probably will not get away with it. An experienced board is rather adept at spotting such a situation, so do not take the chance.

5) If you know a board member, do not make a point of it, yet do not hide it

Certainly you are not fooling him, and probably not the other members of the board. Do not try to take advantage of your acquaintanceship – it will probably do you little good.

6) Do not dominate the interview

Let the board do that. They will give you the clues – do not assume that you have to do all the talking. Realize that the board has a number of questions to ask you, and do not try to take up all the interview time by showing off your extensive knowledge of the answer to the first one.

7) Be attentive

You only have 20 minutes or so, and you should keep your attention at its sharpest throughout. When a member is addressing a problem or question to you, give him your undivided attention. Address your reply principally to him, but do not exclude the other board members.

8) Do not interrupt

A board member may be stating a problem for you to analyze. He will ask you a question when the time comes. Let him state the problem, and wait for the question.

9) Make sure you understand the question

Do not try to answer until you are sure what the question is. If it is not clear, restate it in your own words or ask the board member to clarify it for you. However, do not haggle about minor elements.

10) Reply promptly but not hastily

A common entry on oral board rating sheets is "candidate responded readily," or "candidate hesitated in replies." Respond as promptly and quickly as you can, but do not jump to a hasty, ill-considered answer.

11) Do not be peremptory in your answers

A brief answer is proper – but do not fire your answer back. That is a losing game from your point of view. The board member can probably ask questions much faster than you can answer them.

12) Do not try to create the answer you think the board member wants

He is interested in what kind of mind you have and how it works – not in playing games. Furthermore, he can usually spot this practice and will actually grade you down on it.

13) Do not switch sides in your reply merely to agree with a board member

Frequently, a member will take a contrary position merely to draw you out and to see if you are willing and able to defend your point of view. Do not start a debate, yet do not surrender a good position. If a position is worth taking, it is worth defending.

14) Do not be afraid to admit an error in judgment if you are shown to be wrong

The board knows that you are forced to reply without any opportunity for careful consideration. Your answer may be demonstrably wrong. If so, admit it and get on with the interview.

15) Do not dwell at length on your present job

The opening question may relate to your present assignment. Answer the question but do not go into an extended discussion. You are being examined for a *new* job, not your present one. As a matter of fact, try to phrase ALL your answers in terms of the job for which you are being examined.

Basis of Rating

Probably you will forget most of these "do's" and "don'ts" when you walk into the oral interview room. Even remembering them all will not ensure you a passing grade. Perhaps you did not have the qualifications in the first place. But remembering them will help you to put your best foot forward, without treading on the toes of the board members.

Rumor and popular opinion to the contrary notwithstanding, an oral board wants you to make the best appearance possible. They know you are under pressure – but they also want to see how you respond to it as a guide to what your reaction would be under the pressures of the job you seek. They will be influenced by the degree of poise you display, the personal traits you show and the manner in which you respond.

ABOUT THIS BOOK

This book contains tests divided into Examination Sections. Go through each test, answering every question in the margin. At the end of each test look at the answer key and check your answers. On the ones you got wrong, look at the right answer choice and learn. Do not fill in the answers first. Do not memorize the questions and answers, but understand the answer and principles involved. On your test, the questions will likely be different from the samples. Questions are changed and new ones added. If you understand these past questions you should have success with any changes that arise. Tests may consist of several types of questions. We have additional books on each subject should more study be advisable or necessary for you. Finally, the more you study, the better prepared you will be. This book is intended to be the last thing you study before you walk into the examination room. Prior study of relevant texts is also recommended. NLC publishes some of these in our Fundamental Series. Knowledge and good sense are important factors in passing your exam. Good luck also helps. So now study this Passbook, absorb the material contained within and take that knowledge into the examination. Then do your best to pass that exam.

———

EXAMINATION SECTION

EXAMINATION SECTION
TEST 1

DIRECTIONS: Each question or incomplete statement is followed by several suggested answers or completions. Select the one that BEST answers the question or completes the statement. *PRINT THE LETTER OF THE CORRECT ANSWER IN THE SPACE AT THE RIGHT.*

1. Front stabilizer bars on automotive vehicles are set in such a manner that they   1.____

    A. apply force opposite to that of the springs when the springs are deflected equally
    B. normally connect to both lower control arms
    C. are adjustable in order to level the vehicle
    D. have one end attached to the lower control arm and the other end attached to the frame

2. Ignition point contact alignment is BEST adjusted by bending the   2.____

    A. movable point arm   B. pivot post
    C. breaker plate   D. stationary point bracket

3. When disc brake pads are retracted so as not to be touching the braking disc, the amount of retraction   3.____

    A. is affected by the piston return springs
    B. must be a minimum of 1/32 of an inch
    C. is affected by the piston seals
    D. is limited by the metering valve

4. A PROPERLY operating positive crankcase ventilation valve will   4.____

    A. control air flow as a direct function of engine speed
    B. increase air flow in direct proportion to the increase in manifold vacuum
    C. shut off air flow at high intake manifold vacuum
    D. reduce air flow at high intake manifold vacuum

5. The air-fuel ratio, by weight, in a properly functioning gasoline automotive engine is MOST NEARLY   5.____

    A. 15:1   B. 30:1   C. 600:1   D. 9000:1

6. Cam ground pistons are distinguished by   6.____

    A. being ground perfectly round
    B. having a larger diameter across the piston pin faces
    C. having a larger diameter parallel to the crankshaft centerline
    D. having a larger diameter perpendicular to the crankshaft centerline

7. In an automotive engine, the intake valves USUALLY open _____ TDC and close _____ BDC of the intake stroke.   7.____

    A. after; after   B. after; before
    C. before; before   D. before; after

8. In an automotive engine, the exhaust valves USUALLY open _____ BDC of the power stroke and _____ TDC of the intake stroke.

    A. after; before   B. before; before
    C. before; after   D. after; after

8.____

9. The PRIMARY function of a blower on a two-cycle diesel engine is to

    A. provide air for scavenging
    B. increase the compression ratio
    C. blow in the fuel-air mixture
    D. cool the oil after compression in the injector pump

9.____

10. Excessive free travel of the clutch pedal would be indicated if the

    A. transmission was hard to shift smoothly
    B. clutch slipped when fully engaged
    C. throwout bearing failed prematurely
    D. release levers were worn

10.____

11. Vacuum is usually referred to in inches of mercury.
The number of pounds per square inch pressure above zero (absolute pressure) of a 20 inch vacuum is MOST NEARLY

    A. 4.9   B. 7.4   C. 9.6   D. 11.8

11.____

12. Only a portion of the heat energy released by the gasoline in an automotive engine is transmitted to the wheels for driving purposes.
In an automobile in good condition and with an efficiently operating engine, this portion is MOST NEARLY

    A. 90%   B. 50%   C. 20%   D. 2%

12.____

13. An adjustment is made to the right front wheel of a vehicle equipped with shims at the junction of the upper suspension arm and the frame support by moving the upper suspension arm away from the frame a greater amount in the front than in the rear. This is done to

    A. increase the steering knuckle angle
    B. adjust the caster in a negative direction
    C. adjust the camber in a negative direction
    D. adjust the caster in a rotary direction

13.____

14. In an automotive rear axle in which the pinion gear engages the ring gear below the centerline of the axle, the cut of the pinion and ring gear is

    A. spiral bevel   B. spur bevel
    C. double helical   D. hypoid

14.____

15. Of the following statements concerning the operation in low gear of a fully synchronized (in forward gears) three-speed transmission, the one that is NOT correct is that

    A. both clutch sleeves must engage gears
    B. power is being transmitted through the countershaft gears
    C. one clutch sleeve must be engaged
    D. the reverse idler gear is being driven by a countershaft gear

15.____

Questions 16-17.

DIRECTIONS: Questions 16 and 17 are to be answered in accordance with the following paragraph.

Steam cleaners get their name from the fact that steam is used to generate pressure and is also a by-product of heating the cleaning solution. Steam itself has little cleaning power. It will melt some soils, but it does not dissolve them, break them up, or destroy their clinging power. Rather surprisingly, good machines generate as little steam as possible. Modern surface chemistry depends on a chemical solution to dissolve dirt, destroy its clinging power, and hold it in suspension. Steam actually hinders such a solution, but heat helps its physical and chemical action. Cleaning is most efficient when a hot solution reaches the work in heavy volume.

16. In accordance with the above paragraph, for MOST efficient cleaning,   16._____

    A. a heavy volume of steam is needed
    B. hot steam is needed to break up the soils
    C. steam is used to dissolve the surface dirt
    D. a hot chemical solution should always be used

17. With reference to the above paragraph, the steam in a steam cleaner is used to   17._____

    A. generate pressure
    B. create by-product chemicals
    C. slow down the chemical action of the cleaning solution
    D. dissolve accumulations of dirt

18. An electromechanical regulator for an automotive alternator differs from a DC generator in that the alternator regulator   18._____

    A. has a current regulator unit
    B. has a reverse current relay
    C. does not have a current regulator unit
    D. does not have a voltage regulator unit

19. Of the following statements concerning the charging of lead acid batteries, the one MOST NEARLY correct is that   19._____

    A. a fast charge (40-50 amp, 12V) can safely be used if the battery temperature does not exceed 185° F
    B. heavily sulphated batteries respond best to a slow charging rate
    C. a battery on trickle charge cannot be damaged by overcharging
    D. the higher the battery temperature, the smaller the charging current with constant applied voltage

20. The ignition points of a conventional ignition system are adjusted to increase the point gap.   20._____
This adjustment will

    A. increase the dwell angle
    B. retard the ignition timing

C. advance the ignition timing
D. decrease the dwell angle with no change in ignition timing

21. A single diaphragm distributor vacuum advance unit
21.____

    A. advances the spark under part throttle operation
    B. is connected to the intake manifold
    C. advances the spark in proportion to engine speed
    D. advances the spark during acceleration or full throttle operation

22. The part of a conventional ignition system that could properly be considered part of BOTH the primary and secondary circuits would be the
22.____

    A. condenser   B. distributor rotor
    C. coil   D. ignition points

23. As compared to a conventional type of spark plug, a resistor type of spark plug will
23.____

    A. reduce the inductive portion of the spark
    B. lengthen the capacitive portion of the spark
    C. require a higher voltage to function properly
    D. have an auxiliary air gap

24. If the criterion that limits the yearly major repair expenses to 30% of the current value of equipment were reduced to 15% and the depreciation rate of 20% of original cost each year were increased to 25%, the expenses for major repairs in a shop handling a constant flow of equipment of the same type and age would
24.____

    A. decrease   B. remain the same
    C. increase slightly   D. increase markedly

Question 25.

DIRECTIONS: Question 25 is to be answered in accordance with the following paragraph.

    The storage battery is a lead-acid, electrochemical device used for storing energy in its chemical form. The battery does not actually store electricity, but converts an electrical charge into chemical energy which is stored until the battery terminals are connected to a closed external circuit. When the circuit is closed, the chemical energy inside the battery is transformed back into electrical energy through a chemical action, and, as a result, current flows through the circuit.

25. According to the above paragraph, a lead-acid battery stores
25.____

    A. current   B. electricity
    C. electrical energy   D. chemical energy

26. A cam is to be fashioned from a circular disc with a hole drilled eccentrically on a diameter of the disc but perpendicularly to the surface of the disc. A keyed shaft is to be fitted into the hole so that the disc may be rotated in order to function as a cam.
If the disc is 5 inches in diameter and 1/2 inch thick and the hole is to be 1 inch in diameter, the distance from the center of the disc to the center of the hole to be drilled in order for the disc to act as a cam with a 2 inch lift should be _____ inch(es).
26.____

    A. 2   B. 1 1/2   C. 1   D. 1/2

27. Sparks and open flames should be kept away from batteries that are being charged because of the danger of explosion or fire resulting from the ignition of the generated _____ gas.

    A. fluorine   B. nitrogen   C. hydrogen   D. argon

27.____

28. Safety standards indicate that the use of any motor vehicle equipment having an obstructed view to the rear

    A. requires a reverse signal alarm audible above the surrounding noise level
    B. requires the use of two back-up lights of at least 45 watt capacity each
    C. requires the use of a safety contact alarm rear bumper audible above the surrounding noise level
    D. is prohibited

28.____

29. In the performance of a compression test, it is found that the addition of a tablespoon of SAE 40 motor oil causes no significant increase in the low compression pressure. The low compression pressure is most probably NOT caused by

    A. a broken piston   B. a leaking head gasket
    C. sticking valves   D. worn piston rings

29.____

30. Automotive exhaust gas analyzers, as generally used in emission control maintenance, will NORMALLY indicate the percentage of

    A. NO   B. SO_2 C. CO_2 D. CO

30.____

Questions 31-33.

DIRECTIONS: Questions 31 through 33 are to be answered in accordance with the information given below.

For most efficient utilization of funds and facilities, the rule has been established that the repair cost of a part cannot exceed 50% of the vendor's price for a new part and that a part cannot be made in-house if the cost would be more than 70% of the vendor's price for a new one.

You have found that the average removed sprocket shaft, as shown below, requires both bearing sections to be built up and remachined and one sprocket section to be built up and remachined. The foreman of the machine shop has given you the following information relative to the manufacture or repair of the shafts:

	Time	Rate
Weld 1 bearing section	*1.2 hours*	*$8/hr.*
Weld 1 keyway and sprocket section	*2.0 hours*	*$8/hr.*
Turn 1 bearing section	*0.6 hours*	*$8/hr.*
Turn 1 sprocket section	*0.7 hours*	*$8/hr.*
Cut 1 keyway	*0.5 hours*	*$8/hr.*

Purchasing has quoted shaft material at $12/ft. and new shafts at $160 each.

5

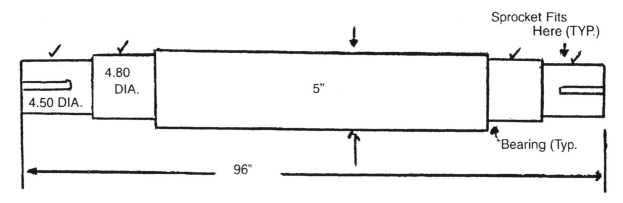

31. In accordance with the information given above, the cost for in-house manufacture of one shaft is

    A. $110.40   B. $112.00   C. $124.80   D. $132.60

31.____

32. In accordance with the information given above, the cost of in-house repair of one shaft is

    A. $68.40   B. $54.40   C. $30.40   D. $14.40

32.____

33. In accordance with the information given above, the PROPER procedure to follow, under the given rules, is to

    A. repair old shafts and buy new shafts
    B. repair old shafts and make new shafts
    C. make no repairs but make new shafts
    D. make no repairs but buy new shafts

33.____

34. The series of small vertical oscillations in the area of the center of a superimposed pattern on the screen of a properly adjusted oscilloscope showing the secondary circuit of a properly tuned automotive engine directly follows the instant at which the

    A. spark plugs fire   B. points open
    C. points close   D. coil starts to discharge

34.____

35. A rectangularly shaped repair facility for light trucks is 160 feet wide and 260 feet long. A 10 foot space is provided along each wall for benches and equipment. A 60 foot wide area in the middle of the floor is to remain clear for its entire 260 foot length. The entrance to the shop is at one end of this open area. Assuming that there are no columns to contend with, the MAXIMUM area available for parking of trucks is _____ square feet.

    A. 15,600   B. 19,200   C. 26,000   D. 41,600

35.____

36. A criterion is established that limits the yearly major repair expenses to 30% of the current value of the equipment. Equipment is depreciated at a rate of 20% of its original cost each year. A truck purchased on January 1, 2000 for $9,000 had a reconditioned engine installed in February 2003 at a total cost of $900.
The amount of money available for additional major repairs on this truck in 2003 was

    A. none   B. $180   C. $360   D. $720

36.____

37. Twenty fuel injectors are ordered for your shop by the purchasing department. The terms are list, less 30%, less 10%, less 5%.
If the list price of a fuel injector is $70 and all terms are met upon delivery, the charges to your budget will be

    A. $1359.60   B. $1085.40   C. $837.90   D. $630.80

7.____

38. The cylinders of an 8 cylinder automotive engine have a bore of 4 inches and the pistons have a stroke of 4 inches. If the clearance volume in each cylinder is 6.0 cubic inches, the cubic inch displacement of the engine is MOST NEARLY

    A. 306   B. 354   C. 402   D. 450

38.____

39. An automotive engine cylinder has a bore of 4 inches and its pistons have a stroke of 4 inches.
If the clearance volume in the cylinder is 6.0 cubic inches, the compression ratio is MOST NEARLY

    A. 10.62:1   B. 9.37:1   C. 8.37:1   D. 7.62:1

39.____

40. Of the following deficiencies found during the inspection of passenger car brakes for issuance of a State Certificate of Inspection, the one that would be cause for REJECTION of the car brakes is that

    A. there is less than 3/64 in. of lining remaining above the drum brake shoe lining rivet heads
    B. the master cylinder brake fluid level is anything less than full
    C. the brake drums have been found to be more than .020 inches oversize
    D. the brake pedal reserve is less than one-half the total possible travel

40.____

41. When checking a fuel pump for proper operation, it is ALWAYS necessary to

    A. connect a vacuum gage to the fuel line between the pump and the carburetor
    B. make the vacuum test before the pressure test
    C. set the gages at floor level to maintain a consistent reference point
    D. make a vacuum test if the pressure or volume test results are not up to specification

41.____

42. On a single cylinder 4 stroke cycle internal combustion engine equipped with a flywheel magneto, the ignition points open at the end of the _____ strokes.

    A. intake and the compression
    B. compression and the exhaust
    C. power and the compression
    D. intake and the power

42.____

43. An impulse coupling is MOST usually found in

    A. an automatic transmission
    B. a limited slip differential
    C. the front axle of 4 wheel drive vehicles
    D. a magneto

43.____

Questions 44-45.

DIRECTIONS: Questions 44 and 45 are to be answered in accordance with the following
paragraph.

*You have been instructed to expedite the fabrication of four special salt spreader trucks
using chassis that are available in the shop. All four trucks must be delivered before the
opening of business on December 1, 2015. Based on workload and available hours, the foreman of the body shop indicates that he could manufacture one complete salt spreader body
in five weeks, with one additional week required for mounting and securing each body to the
available chassis. No work could begin on the body until the engines and hydraulic components, which would have to be purchased, were available for use. The purchasing department has promised delivery of engines and hydraulic components three months after the
order is placed. (Assume that all months have four weeks and the same crew is doing the
assembling and manufacturing.)*

44.   With reference to the above paragraph, assuming that the purchasing department placed   44.____
the order at the beginning of the first week in February 2015 and ultimate delivery of the
engines and components was delayed by six weeks, the date of completion of the first
salt spreader truckwould be CLOSEST to the end of the _____ week in _____, 2015.

    A.   fourth; July   B.   second; August
    C.   fourth; August   D.   first; September

45.   With reference to the above paragraph, the LATEST date that the engines and associ-   45.____
ated hydraulic components could be requisitioned in order to meet the specified deadline
would be CLOSEST to the beginning of the _____ week in _____, 2015.

    A.   first; February   B.   first; March
    C.   third; March   D.   first; April

46.   In an OHV internal combustion engine, excessive inlet valve guide clearance manifests   46.____
itself initially by

    A.   lowered cylinder compression pressure
    B.   excessive oil consumption
    C.   increased manifold vacuum
    D.   fluffy black deposits on spark plugs

47.   One of your mechanics has performed an automotive fuel system test and reports a fuel   47.____
flow of 1/2 pint/minute at 500 rpm, a static fuel pump discharge pressure of 6 psi, and a
15 in.Hg vacuum at the pump inlet flex line.
These results should suggest to the mechanic that

    A.   the system was operating properly
    B.   he should check for a leaking pump inlet flex line
    C.   he should replace the defective fuel pump
    D.   check for a plugged inlet fuel line

48. An electrician is wiring a light switch on a light truck. The light switch will operate the following lamp bulbs:

Quantity	No.	Description	Current (each)
2	194	Marker	.3
3	67	Clearance	.4
2	1157	Stop/tail	2.1/ .6
2	1141	Front park	1.5
2	6012	Headlamp	4.2/3.4

The parking lamps are to be on when the headlamps are on.
If the permissible current capacities of wire are

16 gage	0 - 6 amp
14 gage	6 - 15 amp
12 gage	15 - 20 amp
10 gage	20 - 25 amp

the smallest size wire that the electrician should use to supply power to the switch would be a _____ gage wire.

   A. 16   B. 14   C. 12   D. 10

48.____

49. In an automotive cooling system, the bypass passage or bypass valve

   A. permits a small amount of coolant to pass around the thermostat to maintain circulation
   B. permits the circulation of coolant through the engine block when the thermostat is closed
   C. directly connects the pump inlet to the pump discharge to prevent cavitation in the pump
   D. prevents the coolant in the system from developing excessive pressure

49.____

50. When adjusting a recirculating ball worm-and-nut steering gear, it is IMPROPER procedure to

   A. remove the pitman arm before making adjustments
   B. loosen the lash adjustment before checking bearing preload
   C. make the pitman shaft gear over center adjustment with the steering wheel in the center of travel position
   D. adjust the bearing preload with the steering wheel in the center of travel position

50.____

KEY (CORRECT ANSWERS)

1. B	11. A	21. A	31. C	41. D
2. D	12. C	22. C	32. B	42. B
3. C	13. B	23. A	33. A	43. D
4. D	14. D	24. A	34. C	44. A
5. A	15. A	25. D	35. B	45. B
6. D	16. D	26. C	36. B	46. B
7. D	17. A	27. C	37. C	47. D
8. C	18. C	28. A	38. C	48. B
9. A	19. B	29. D	39. B	49. B
10. A	20. C	30. D	40. B	50. D

EXAMINATION SECTION
TEST 1

DIRECTIONS: Each question or incomplete statement is followed by several suggested answers or completions. Select the one that BEST answers the question or completes the statement. *PRINT THE LETTER OF THE CORRECT ANSWER IN THE SPACE AT THE RIGHT.*

1. If a gasoline engine cylinder is excessively worn, it will be found that the wear is practically always GREATEST   1.____

    A. at the top of the ring travel
    B. at the middle of the ring travel
    C. at the lowest ring travel
    D. where the cylinder is coolest

2. After boring or honing a worn gasoline engine cylinder, it is good practice to clean the grit out of the pores of the cast iron block.
In the absence of continuous cleaning facilities, this is done BEST by cleaning the cylinder with   2.____

    A. gasoline   B. hot water and soap
    C. benzine   D. kerosene and waste

3. One of the BEST ways to check the concentricity of the valve guide and valve seat is by the use of a(n)   3.____

    A. expanding reamer   B. dial indicator
    C. inside micrometer   D. bevel protractor

4. The thimble of a micrometer is slightly before the .475" graduation on the barrel.
If the thimble reading is between .018" and .019", and the reading on the vernier is .006", then the full opening is   4.____

    A. .4946"   B. .4696"   C. .4686"   D. .4936"

5. The sum of 9/16", 11/32", 15/64", and 1 3/32" is MOST NEARLY   5.____

    A. 2.234"   B. 2.134"   C. 2.334"   D. 2.214"

6. The diameter of a circle whose circumference is 14.5" is MOST NEARLY   6.____

    A. 4.62"   B. 4.81"   C. 4.72"   D. 4.51"

7. A *literate* worker is one who is MOST NEARLY   7.____

    A. unlearned   B. sinuous
    C. educated   D. impervious

8. If a mechanic is told that a certain repair job is *feasible,* this means it is MOST NEARLY   8.____

    A. laborious   B. moderate
    C. practicable   D. easy

9. A mechanic who is *dexterous* at his job is one who is MOST NEARLY   9.____

    A. proficient   B. devious   C. devoted   D. imparial

10. To obtain a certain type of fit, an intentional difference in the dimensions of the mating parts is usually specified on the blueprints.
This intentional difference is called

    A. allowance   B. tolerance   C. clearance   D. nominal

10._____

11. A micro-inch is

    A. an inch measured on a micrometer
    B. an inch measured with a microscope
    C. a ten-thousandth of an inch
    D. one-millionth of an inch

11._____

12. Assuming the bore of a gasoline engine cylinder measures 3 inches and the piston for this cylinder has a stroke of 4 inches, the piston displacement, in cubic inches per stroke of piston, will be MOST NEARLY

    A. 36   B. 48   C. 32   D. 28

12._____

13. If an engine cylinder should be worn in such a way that there is a taper of 0.008" from top to bottom, the piston ring and gap, when traveling up and down over this surface, will be opening and closing MOST NEARLY

    A. 0.008"   B. 0.016"   C. 0.020"   D. 0.024"

13._____

14. In freezing weather, a lead acid storage battery should NOT have a specific gravity reading

    A. above 1.250   B. above 1.235
    C. below 1.250   D. of 1.285

14._____

15. In servicing a worn and badly tapered gasoline engine cylinder that has quite a *step* at the bottom of the ring travel, it is BEST to

    A. start the honing in the unworn area below the ring travel
    B. start the honing in the center of the ring travel
    C. start the honing in the unworn area above the ring travel
    D. just fit an oversized piston for the top part of the cylinder

15._____

16. In a gasoline engine, if the distributor breaker points are replaced twice as often as the generator brushes, but the generator brushes are replaced one quarter as often as the spark plugs, then it is CORRECT to say that the spark plugs are replaced _____ as often as the distributor breaker points.

    A. twice   B. four times
    C. one-half   D. one-quarter

16._____

17. In the four stroke cycle gasoline engine, the sequence of the steps in each cylinder to complete a cycle is which one of the following?
Intake stroke,

    A. power stroke, compression stroke, exhaust stroke
    B. compression stroke, exhaust stroke, power stroke
    C. exhaust stroke, compression stroke, power stroke
    D. compression stroke, power stroke, exhaust stroke

17._____

18. The cutting edge of a cold chisel should be tempered at a temperature corresponding to   18.____
a color of

    A. blue   B. pale blue   C. light straw   D. purple

19. To properly service a clutch, the type that is commonly used on gasoline engines, it is   19.____
important that the face or frictional surface of the flywheel should run true within a tolerance of MOST NEARLY

    A. .006"   B. .012"   C. .018"   D. .025"

20. The BEST way to check a warped cylinder head is by means of a   20.____

    A. straight edge   B. surface gauge
    C. feeler gauge   D. dial indicator

21. Upon inspecting a cam ground piston skirt, while cold, it will be found that the skirt is   21.____
USUALLY

    A. circular in cross-section
    B. smaller in diameter than the piston head
    C. widest at wrist pin bosses
    D. oval in cross-section

22. If a transmission main drive gear, having 20 teeth, rotates at 450 R.P.M. and drives a   22.____
countershaft drive gear at 300 R.P.M., the TOTAL number of teeth on the countershaft
drive gear will be

    A. 30   B. 15   C. 25   D. 45

23. In reference to the piston, wrist pin, and connecting rod assembly of a gasoline engine, it   23.____
is NOT common practice to ever

    A. *fix* the pin to the piston by a set screw
    B. allow the pin to rotate in both the connecting rod and piston bosses
    C. anchor the pin to connecting rod
    D. use precision type split bearings at the wrist pin end of connecting rod

24. Upon dismantling a gasoline engine, it was found that the piston rings were stuck in the   24.____
grooves, not being free to rotate.
This was MOST likely caused by

    A. operating the engine with spark setting in advanced position
    B. the thermostat maintaining too low an engine temperature
    C. dirty or contaminated lubricating oil
    D. using the wrong type of spark plugs in the engine

25. Many gasoline engines today are being built with cylinder heads of cast aluminum alloy.   25.____
The reason for using aluminum is MAINLY because it

    A. is a better conductor of heat
    B. will not rust
    C. has less expansion per degree F. than cast iron
    D. is lighter in weight

26. A gasoline engine that utilizes a rocker arm for operating intake and exhaust valves is COMMONLY classified as a(n) _____ engine.   26._____

    A. *T*-head   B. *I*-head   C. *L*-head   D. 2 cam shaft

27. Assuming that a sliding gear transmission is so built that there is a gear ratio between the transmission main drive gear and the countershaft drive gear of 1.5 to 1, and, with gears shifted to low speed, there is an additional gear ratio between the countershaft low-speed gear and the low-and-reverse mainshaft gear of 1.5 to 1, then, for the propeller shaft to rotate 200 R.P.M., the crankshaft will have to rotate MOST NEARLY _____ R.P.M.   27._____

    A. 450   B. 600   C. 500   D. 300

28. Which one of the following statements concerning shop safety precautions would you select as being CORRECT?   28._____

    A. Starting a machine while it is being adjusted or repaired is a good practice.
    B. Guards may be removed by the operator to expedite the work.
    C. Gears, pulleys, and belts should be guarded to a height of 6 feet above the floor.
    D. Knowledge and care will not prevent most accidents.

29. The breaker points on a six lobe cam distributor are USUALLY brought and held together by means of a   29._____

    A. cam   B. spring   C. worm gear   D. timer

30. Pitted or burned distributor breaker points may BEST be refaced by using   30._____

    A. emery cloth   B. sandpaper
    C. an oil stone   D. a steel file

31. The piece of equipment commonly used on many gasoline engines that is composed of such parts as yokes, struts, release levers, pressure springs, and pilot bearing is MOST likely a   31._____

    A. clutch   B. transmission
    C. torque converter   D. differential

32. Upon installing a reconditioned clutch in a gasoline engine that uses a clutch foot pedal, the proper adjustment to make on the clutch pedal *free play* on most cars is MOST NEARLY   32._____

    A. 2"   B. 1"   C. 0.25"   D. none

33. A gasoline engine cylinder that is worn and has been found to have a taper of .012" can BEST be reconditioned before being placed into operation again by   33._____

    A. *replacing* the oil ring backed with an expander
    B. *replacing* the original oil ring with a very active one
    C. *reboring* or honing the cylinder and using an oversized piston
    D. *reboring* or honing the cylinder and using an undersized piston

34. In the S.A.E. Standard Series of Screw Threads, a screw size 7/16"-20 would be classified as   34._____

    A. NC   B. NF   C. EF   D. NS

35. In the 90° V-type eight cylinder gasoline engine, the number of *throws* or *cranks* on the crankshaft is USUALLY

    A. eight   B. six   C. four   D. two

35._____

36. Grinding and refinishing exhaust valves and seats on MOST gasoline engines should be done so that the seat angle (relative to the centerline passing through the valve guide) is USUALLY

    A. 60°   B. 25°   C. 35°   D. 45°

36._____

37. An automotive gasoline engine is being completely reconditioned, including the fitting of the valve stem in its guide.
In the absence of specific information from the manufacturer, the proper exhaust valve stem to guide clearance for MOST engines should be

    A. .003"   B. .010"   C. .018"   D. .030"

37._____

38. An instrument which can be used generally to measure inside and outside measurements without making any calculations is called a _____ caliper.

    A. Gear tooth   B. Vernier
    C. Telescoping   D. Micrometer

38._____

Questions 39-40.

DIRECTIONS: Questions 39 and 40 are based upon the following paragraph. Use only the information contained in this paragraph in answering these questions.

With the engine running at normal idling speed, and the engine hood open, attach the vacuum gauge to the intake manifold. The vacuum gauge should read about 18 to 21 inches, and the pointer should be steady. A needle fluctuating between 10 and 15 inches may indicate a defective cylinder-head, gasket or valve. An extremely low reading indicates a leak in the intake manifold or gaskets. Accelerate the engine with full throttle momentarily. Notice if the gauge indicator fails to drop to approximately 2 inches as the throttle is opened, and recoil to at least 24 inches as the throttle is closed. If so, this may be an indication of diluted oil, poor piston ring sealing, or an abnormal restriction in the exhaust, carburetor, or air cleaner. The above readings apply to sea level. There will be approximately 1 inch drop for each 1000 feet of altitude.

39. If a vacuum test is made on a properly operating engine at an altitude of 3000 feet, the vacuum gauge should read MOST NEARLY

    A. 12"   B. 15"   C. 13"   D. 24"

39._____

40. If a vacuum test is made on an engine which has an abnormal restriction in the exhaust, this will be evidenced by

    A. a leak in the intake manifold
    B. the gauge indicator failing to drop to approximately 3 inches on opening the throttle
    C. the gauge fluctuating around 12 inches
    D. a steady high gauge reading

40._____

41. The PROPER thing to do in checking the fuel pump of a gasoline engine which will NOT 41.____
start because of insufficient gas is to

    A. remove the pump from the engine in order to check
    B. disconnect the fuel line from the tank to the pump and run the pump
    C. disconnect the pump to the carburetor line and run the pump
    D. make sure that the external plugs over the pump valves are loosened before running the pump

42. It is a good policy to occasionally change the brake fluid in a hydraulic brake system. 42.____
However, before refilling with fresh brake fluid, it is advisable to flush out the system
with

    A. alcohol   B. kerosene   C. gasoline   D. a light oil

43. Battery hydrometers are calibrated to give the correct specific gravity readings of lead 43.____
acid storage batteries at a temperature of

    A. 70° F.   B. 80° F.   C. 32° F.   D. 60° F.

44. In a gasoline engine, if grease should leak into the cooling system by way of the water 44.____
pump and, in addition, combustion gases should leak into the coolant, a test of the coolant will be found MOST likely to be

    A. slightly alkaline   B. slightly acid
    C. strongly alkaline   D. free of foreign deposits

45. Reverse flushing of a clogged gasoline engine block and radiator cooling system is done 45.____
PROPERLY by

    A. not removing the thermostat out of the engine block
    B. connecting the flushing gun at the bottom of the engine block
    C. using air and water
    D. using low pressure steam

46. In an automotive gasoline engine water cooling system, the water distributing tube is 46.____
USUALLY found

    A. at the top of the radiator
    B. at the bottom of the radiator
    C. on top of the cylinder head
    D. in the engine block

47. When reference is made to the *compression ratio* of an automotive gasoline engine, this 47.____
is BEST described to be the

    A. volume above the piston at top dead center
    B. displacement volume as the piston moves down to bottom dead center
    C. total volume of a cylinder divided by its clearance volume
    D. displacement volume of a cylinder divided by its clearance volume

48. When the piston of a gasoline engine is said to be in *rock* position, it is meant that the   48._____

    A. piston has reached rock bottom of its stroke
    B. crankshaft cannot move without causing the piston to move
    C. crankshaft can move about $20°$ without causing the valves to open or close
    D. crankshaft can move about $15°$ without causing the piston to move up or down

49. Regarding the automatic transmission which today is very popular with most automobile   49._____
engines, the features that are found on MOST of the various transmission units are

    A. hydraulic controls
    B. full power automatic shifting planetaries
    C. double pinion planetary full torque shifts
    D. split torque fluid drives

50. An air leak between the intake manifold and the engine block can BEST be checked by   50._____

    A. Applying a soapy solution to each joint on the block
    B. applying a little gasoline at each manifold and block joint
    C. using a heavy oil at each joint in the block
    D. listening for the sucking sound of air entering the joint

---

KEY (CORRECT ANSWERS)

1. A	11. D	21. D	31. A	41. C
2. B	12. D	22. A	32. B	42. A
3. B	13. D	23. D	33. C	43. B
4. C	14. C	24. C	34. B	44. B
5. A	15. A	25. A	35. C	45. C
6. A	16. A	26. B	36. D	46. D
7. C	17. D	27. A	37. A	47. C
8. C	18. C	28. C	38. B	48. D
9. A	19. A	29. B	39. B	49. A
10. A	20. A	30. C	40. B	50. B

TEST 2

DIRECTIONS: Each question or incomplete statement is followed by several suggested answers or completions. Select the one that BEST answers the question or completes the statement. *PRINT THE LETTER OF THE CORRECT ANSWER IN THE SPACE AT THE RIGHT.*

1. The LEAST likely reason for a shunt generator to lose most of its residual magnetism is due to

    A. alternating current fed to the field winding
    B. too much vibration of generator
    C. excessive operating temperature
    D. the generator delivering too much current

1.____

2. In today's modern high compression engines, hard starting, rough running, and poor gas economy are LEAST likely to be due to the electrical system having

    A. high resistor plugs   B. cracked distributor cap
    C. worn insulation   D. fouled plugs

2.____

3. The method that is NOT used for detecting cracks that may exist in a gasoline engine block or head is by

    A. dye penetrants   B. pressure testing
    C. the sheradizing method   D. the magnetic method

3.____

4. Before making any front wheel alignment checks on a car, such as toe-in and camber, it is ADVISABLE to

    A. first make sure that the vehicle has no load in it
    B. jack up the front wheels so that they are free to turn
    C. inflate the tires to recommended pressure
    D. first check the wheel brakes

4.____

5. When replacing a new cylinder head gasket on a gasoline engine, it is good practice to tighten the cylinder head nuts with a torque wrench to a gauge reading, in foot pounds, of MOST NEARLY

    A. 60   B. 40   C. 90   D. 25

5.____

6. Assume that a carburetor has been reconditioned and the mechanic replaced the metering rod with one of a larger diameter than the original one.
On operating the carburetor, it is MOST likely that

    A. at idling, the engine would run at a higher speed
    B. the engine will receive a leaner mixture
    C. the carburetor would easily flood
    D. there will be very little noticeable difference in engine operation

6.____

7. A mechanic, running a test on a gasoline engine, has noted on the job sheet that the cam angle is 32 degrees.
From this information, it is evident that the mechanic is running a test on the

    A. cam shaft   B. ignition system
    C. front wheel   D. valve timing

7.____

8. An idler gear that is often found in a sliding gear transmission is used MAINLY   8.____

    A. when more power is desired
    B. when engine is idling and car is not in motion
    C. to reverse the direction of rotation
    D. to obtain a reduced gear speed

9. Assume that a compression test is made of a six-cylinder gasoline engine having a com-   9.____
pression ratio of 6.5 to 1. A reading of 95 lbs. was obtained for cylinders #1, #2, #4, and
#6, 52 lbs. for cylinder #3, and 72 lbs. for cylinder #5. Upon squirting engine oil into the
cylinder and rechecking pressures again, it was found that cylinder #5 read 93 lbs., and
cylinder #3 read 52 lbs.
From the above results, it is MOST probable that the

    A. exhaust valve on cylinder #5 does not seat properly
    B. cylinder #3 piston rings or cylinder are worn
    C. cylinder #5 piston rings are worn
    D. oil leaks past the cylinder #5 valve guides

10. In operating a gasoline engine using a manual gear shift, if it becomes difficult to shift,   10.____
especially into low gear, the trouble is MOST likely due to the

    A. clutch plate not burning
    B. clutch shaft splines tapering toward the end
    C. clutch facing being too dry
    D. clearance between the pressure plate and the flywheel being too great

11. In reference to the internal combustion engine, the term *mechanical efficiency* is fre-   11.____
quently used.
The meaning of this term is BEST defined as the

    A. thermal efficiency divided by the volumetric efficiency
    B. thermal efficiency multiplied by the volumetric efficiency
    C. indicated horsepower divided by the brake horsepower
    D. brake horsepower divided by the indicated horsepower

12. In calculating the *indicated* horsepower of a gasoline engine by means of a formula, the   12.____
item that is NOT considered in the calculations is USUALLY the

    A. number of power strokes per cycle
    B. pressure exerted on the piston during the power stroke
    C. diameter of the piston
    D. length of the piston

13. The type of gear drive that will operate MORE quietly under similar conditions in a differ-   13.____
ential unit is one consisting of a _____ gear.

    A. worm and
    B. drive pinion and spur bevel
    C. drive pinion and hypoid
    D. drive pinion and spiral-bevel

14. The differential of many trucks is very often made up of a worm and gear drive.   14._____
In reference to this type of drive, which one of the following statements is TRUE?

    A. The worm is usually made of bronze and the worm gear of steel.
    B. The rear worm bearing need not be very rugged since it takes very little thrust.
    C. This type of drive allows a large speed reduction.
    D. This type of drive is not recommended because the worm must be mounted on top of the worm gear.

15. It is common practice today for some manufacturers to make the outside surface of alu-   15._____
minum alloy pistons highly resistant to wear by

    A. spheroidizing   B. case hardening
    C. anodizing   D. annealing

16. The ease with which the front wheels of a car return to the straight-ahead position after   16._____
having completed a turn is due to the

    A. toe-in   B. side thrust   C. camber   D. caster

17. If you should be driving a truck downhill on a slippery road and the rear end of the truck   17._____
begins to skid to the right, it would be BEST for you to

    A. apply the brakes slowly and disengage the clutch
    B. let up on the gas pedal slowly and turn the wheels to the right
    C. turn the wheels to the right and disengage the clutch
    D. apply the brakes hard and turn the wheels to the left

18. If a *no load test* is made on the electric starting motor used on most passenger cars   18._____
today, it will be found that the number of amperes the motor would draw, at its rated
speed, is MOST NEARLY

    A. 70   B. 105   C. 210   D. 20

19. By the correct valve timing of a gasoline engine is meant the proper opening and closing   19._____
of valves with reference to the

    A. carburetor mixing jets   B. distributor setting
    C. position of piston   D. cylinder compression ratio

20. The *primary* ignition circuit of an automotive gasoline engine is composed of the battery,   20._____

    A. starting motor, generator, ignition coil, spark plugs
    B. ammeter, ignition coil, ignition switch, distributor rotor
    C. ammeter, ignition switch, ignition coil secondary winding
    D. ammeter, ignition switch, coil primary winding, breaker points

21. To increase the ampere-hour capacity of a lead-acid storage battery, it is necessary to   21._____
increase the

    A. number of cells
    B. amount of the electrolyte
    C. number of plates per cell
    D. voltage of the cells

22. Intake and exhaust manifolds, used on the present day gasoline engine, are designed   22._____
and built so that their walls come in contact with each other in order to

    A. prevent condensation of fuel vapor
    B. save space
    C. get better valve action
    D. reduce vaporization

23. By referring to the *torque* of a gasoline engine crankshaft is meant the   23._____

    A. ratio of crankshaft to rear axle
    B. horsepower developed at axles
    C. turning moment of the crankshaft
    D. permissible bend of flexibility in the crankshaft

24. Upon making a running test of the braking system of a car, it was found that the brake   24._____
drum on one of the wheels ran abnormally cool.
From this result, the auto mechanic will find that this is MOST likely due to

    A. worn brake lining
    B. a broken return spring
    C. the brake drum surface worn too smooth
    D. an inoperative brake

25. The factor that has no relation upon the determination of proper wheel alignment is   25._____

    A. pivot inclination   B. toe-out
    C. caster   D. drop-center rim

26. If a gasoline engine is continued in operation with the contact points of a reverse current   26._____
relay or *cut-out* being fused together, the result would MOST likely be to

    A. *run down* the battery
    B. reverse the current through the voltage coils
    C. demagnetize the relay iron core
    D. overcharge the battery

27. Starting motors that mesh directly with the flywheel gears and are used on most modern   27._____
cars today are designed to give an engine cranking speed, in R.P.M., of MOST NEARLY

    A. 150   B. 250   C. 350   D. 400

28. The type of electric starting motor used on most cars today, because of its high starting   28._____
torque, is USUALLY the _____ type.

    A. shunt wound   B. series wound
    C. compound wound   D. capacitor

29. If an engine, while running, has a noticeable piston slap, it is LIKELY that this is caused   29._____
by

    A. worn cylinder walls
    B. excessively advanced ignition timing
    C. worn main bearings
    D. worn end-thrust bearings

30. Vapor-lock in a gasoline engine is MOST likely due to 30._____

    A. an over-rich gas-air mixture
    B. fuel forming bubbles in the gas line
    C. a tear in the fuel pump diaphragm
    D. the carburetor being clogged with dirt

31. In starting on a cold day, the choke is pulled out. 31._____
The PRIMARY reason for this is that it

    A. allows more fuel to enter the carburetor enriching the mixture
    B. increases the amount of air in the carburetor
    C. reduces the amount of fuel entering the carburetor
    D. speeds up the supply of air and fuel to the motor

32. When driving at night toward another car, the CORRECT procedure as to lights is to put 32._____
on

    A. your high beams
    B. your low beams
    C. whatever lights the other driver uses
    D. your parking lights

33. The liquid in a battery in good condition is 33._____

    A. an acid solution   B. a caustic solution
    C. a salt water solution   D. water only

34. The ammeter of an automobile indicates the flow of electric current 34._____

    A. from the battery to the starting motor
    B. outside of the starting circuit
    C. to the lights
    D. to and from the storage battery

35. Manifolds are used to conduct 35._____

    A. gases out of an engine only
    B. gases into an engine only
    C. gases into or out of an engine
    D. heat into the piston

36. Of the following, the one NOT concerned with transmitting the driving power from the 36._____
engine to the driving wheels is the

    A. clutch   B. drive shaft
    C. flywheel   D. front axle

37. To prevent short circuits in the electrical system of a car, we use 37._____

    A. a layer of rust   B. insulation
    C. oil   D. water

38. An alert auto mechanic knows that if the center tread of the tires of a car show little wear while the outer edges show considerable wear, it is a sign of driving

    A. on over-inflated tires
    B. on properly inflated tires
    C. on under-inflated tires
    D. too fast for proper braking

38.____

39. The working parts of an engine are lubricated by

    A. grease in the transmission
    B. oil in the transmission
    C. oil from the carburetor
    D. oil in the crankcase

39.____

40. The water in the cooling system of a car should be

    A. acid   B. alkaline   C. neutral   D. salty

40.____

41. Of the following, the type of service that a mechanic should be personally concerned with is

    A. adjustment of small parts such as spark plugs
    B. daily inspection of vehicles for gas, oil, and water
    C. general overhauls of large unit assemblies
    D. replacement of unit assemblies such as fuel pumps

41.____

42. The part of a car which allows one wheel to go faster than the other in going around a corner is the

    A. brake   B. differential
    C. slip joint   D. universal joint

42.____

43. If the temperature gauge indicates the engine is getting overheated,

    A. allow it to cool down
    B. pour cold water in immediately
    C. pour hot water in immediately
    D. pour in a cooling antifreeze at once

43.____

44. The clutch pedal is being used properly when you

    A. press it down in order to change gears
    B. push it down to the floor going down hill
    C. rest your left foot on it
    D. use it only for emergencies

44.____

45. The part of an engine in which the gasoline and air burns is the

    A. camshaft   B. carburetor
    C. cylinder   D. piston

45.____

46. The part of an engine which mixes the gasoline with the air is the

    A. camshaft   B. carburetor
    C. cylinder   D. piston

46.____

47. The function of a generator in a car is to supply the 47.____

    A. ignition system with current
    B. lights with current
    C. battery with current to recharge it
    D. starting motor with current

48. The accelerator pedal is used for controlling the 48.____

    A. carburetor throttle   B. ignition system
    C. oil pressure   D. spark plug

49. Alcohol is put into the radiator of an automobile in cold weather because it _____ the _____ point of the mixture. 49.____

    A. *lowers;* boiling   B. *lowers;* freezing
    C. *raises;* boiling   D. *raises;* freezing

50. A good rule to follow when driving in winter when roads may be icy is to 50.____

    A. be prepared to come to a quick stop when the car starts to skid
    B. be sure of your brakes so you can come down hard on them
    C. keep your speed down and turn the wheels in the direction of any skid that may occur
    D. put the car in neutral and gently pat the brakes into position

---

KEY (CORRECT ANSWERS)

1.	D	11.	D	21.	C	31.	A	41.	B
2.	A	12.	D	22.	A	32.	B	42.	B
3.	C	13.	C	23.	C	33.	A	43.	A
4.	C	14.	C	24.	D	34.	D	44.	A
5.	A	15.	C	25.	D	35.	C	45.	C
6.	B	16.	D	26.	D	36.	D	46.	B
7.	B	17.	B	27.	A	37.	B	47.	C
8.	C	18.	A	28.	B	38.	C	48.	A
9.	C	19.	C	29.	A	39.	D	49.	B
10.	B	20.	D	30.	B	40.	C	50.	C

TEST 3

DIRECTIONS: Each question or incomplete statement is followed by several suggested answers or completions. Select the one that BEST answers the question or completes the statement. *PRINT THE LETTER OF THE CORRECT ANSWER IN THE SPACE AT THE RIGHT.*

1. A sudden falling back of about 5 points on a vacuum gauge with the engine running under 15 m.p.h. indicates

    A. a leaky manifold gasket
    B. loose or worn valve guides
    C. points are pitted
    D. a burned valve in one cylinder

1.____

2. When the vacuum gauge needle drifts regularly between 5 and 19, it means that

    A. the carburetor is poorly adjusted
    B. there is a compression leak between cylinders
    C. the exhaust system is clogged
    D. the ignition advance is incorrect

2.____

3. A bent steering arm will affect

    A. caster
    C. camber
    B. toe-out
    D. king pin inclination

3.____

4. When the accelerator is depressed quickly, the

    A. vacuum in the intake manifold increases
    B. vacuum in the intake manifold remains the same
    C. pressure in the float chamber increases
    D. pressure in the intake manifold increases

4.____

5. When an air cleaner has collected an excessive amount of road dust, the

    A. mixture becomes leaner
    B. compression pressure is increased
    C. volumetric efficiency increases
    D. mixture becomes richer

5.____

6. The full weight of the rear of a vehicle is carried by the axle shaft of a

    A. semi-floating axle
    C. three-quarter floating axle
    B. full floating axle
    D. jack shaft

6.____

7. Certain engines are designed with the spark plug port over the exhaust valve because

    A. this keeps spark plugs at proper temperature
    B. this design reduces detonation
    C. spark plugs last longer
    D. this prevents loss of power

7.____

8. The MAIN advantage of valve seat inserts is to   8._____

    A. reduce wear on the valve face
    B. reduce frequency of valve grinding
    C. keep clearance on valve more nearly constant
    D. increase the life of the valves

9. The harmonic balancer on a crankshaft is used   9._____

    A. as a flywheel
    B. to neutralize torsional crankshaft vibration
    C. to offset the weight of the flywheel
    D. to offset the weight of the connecting rods

10. Sealed clutch release bearings require   10._____

    A. cup grease   B. spicer grease
    C. engine oil   D. no grease

11. The pressure which forces the gas from the fuel pump to the carburetor is produced by   11._____

    A. the expanding action of the diaphragm spring
    B. the upstroke of the pump arm
    C. the vacuum created in the pump
    D. decreased pressure in the fuel bowl

12. A low reading on the oil gauge is a PROBABLE indication of   12._____

    A. high engine temperature   B. bearings too tight
    C. oil dilution   D. too heavy a grade of oil

13. Pressure plate springs are checked for   13._____

    A. number of coils   B. thickness of coils
    C. weight   D. height and pressure

14. Of the following, the CHIEF advantage of *over-drive* in modern transmissions is that it   14._____

    A. allows the engine to run slower at high car speeds
    B. allows the car to coast on hills
    C. requires less shifting
    D. provides greater power at high speeds

15. The oil circuit through a gear type oil pump is   15._____

    A. between the gear teeth
    B. over the gear teeth
    C. under the gear teeth
    D. between the gear teeth and pump housing

16. Good compression in an engine depends upon   16._____

    A. ignition timing
    B. carburetor adjustment
    C. type of gasoline used
    D. condition of rings and valves

17. The differential pinion gear meshes with the ring gear below the horizontal center line of the ring gear on a _____ gear.

    A. spiral bevel   B. hypoid
    C. spur   D. straight bevel

17._____

18. Heavy flank contact on teeth between drive pinion gear and ring gear will result in

    A. excessive play between gear teeth
    B. noisy gear operation
    C. broken drive pinion bearings
    D. excessive end play in differential case bearings

18._____

19. Back firing in the carburetor is caused by

    A. too rich a mixture
    B. excess oil in combustion chamber
    C. faulty fuel pump
    D. too lean a mixture

19._____

20. A worn metering pin will cause

    A. fast idle speed
    B. rich mixture under load
    C. leaner mixture under load
    D. engine stalling

20._____

21. Broken gear teeth on differential side gears will cause a

    A. squeak when the car is traveling in a straight ahead direction
    B. broken axle
    C. knock in rear end when car is making a turn
    D. loss of power

21._____

22. Excessive accumulation of soft carbon deposit on intake valve stems and under intake valve heads is an indication that the

    A. intake valve guides are worn
    B. carburetor is set too rich
    C. gasoline is stale
    D. spark is weak, causing poor compression

22._____

23. The MOST popular type of clutch used today in modern vehicles is the _____ clutch.

    A. wet   B. 3-plate
    C. multiple-disc   D. single plate

23._____

24. When a Timken bearing is used in a transmission, it is readily identified by

    A. its tapered rollers
    B. the concave races
    C. the barrel-shaped rollers
    D. an exclusive retainer design

24._____

25. The MOST common type of cooling system in use today is

    A. pump or pressure   B. splash and gravity
    C. radiator and fan   D. thermosyphon

25.____

26. Scoring of pistons and cylinder walls is caused by

    A. pistons fitting too loose
    B. infrequent oil changes
    C. high piston temperatures
    D. insufficient piston clearances

26.____

27. Regardless of the number of cylinders, the distributor of the magneto MUST always be driven at _____ speed.

    A. engine   B. one-half engine
    C. twice engine   D. constant

27.____

28. The capacity of a battery is determined by the

    A. rate at which a battery can be charged
    B. quantity of electrolyte the case can hold
    C. rate at which it can be discharged
    D. voltage of the battery

28.____

29. While driving along the road, all lights suddenly flare up and burn out because

    A. a fuse blew out
    B. a short circuit occurred in a lighting wire
    C. a wire became loose on the ground switch
    D. the battery cable broke off

29.____

30. A solenoid is often used to operate the

    A. generator   B. starter   C. battery   D. ignition

30.____

31. In a storage battery, the H_2SO_4 after reacting with the active material in the plates forms H_2O^4 in the electrolyte when

    A. a battery is discharging   B. it is being charged
    C. it is gassing   D. it is sulphated

31.____

32. Voltage and current regulators prevent

    A. overload of starter   B. static in radio
    C. spark plug failure   D. overcharging of battery

32.____

33. Batteries not in service will become discharged because of

    A. drop in specific gravity   B. open circuit
    C. lack of agitation   D. local action

33.____

34. Throwing of solder from generator commutator is caused USUALLY by

    A. poor insulation   B. overload
    C. underload   D. high tension current

34.____

35. A low generator output with a fully charged battery indicates   35.____

    A. worn or pitted vibrator points
    B. eroded battery terminals
    C. correct generator control
    D. the vibrator armature spring is too weak

36. Generator output control or regulation is based on controlling the   36.____

    A. armature magnetism   B. field current
    C. third brush   D. polarity

37. When an armature is revolved between the pole pieces of a growler, a heavy vibration is   37.____
caused by a _____ voltage current induced in a(n) _____ coil.

    A. *low;* open   B. *high;* open
    C. *high;* short-circuited   D. *low;* short-circuited

38. In shunt wound generators, full control of the generator output is obtained through the   38.____
use of

    A. third brush   B. current regulator
    C. voltage regulator   D. current and voltage regulator

39. The function of the cut-out relay in the battery generator circuit is to   39.____

    A. regulate the generator voltage
    B. regulate the generator amperage
    C. prevent the loss of battery current
    D. prevent the battery from being overcharged

40. A cracked distributor cap usually would cause misfiring because of   40.____

    A. poor contact   B. short circuit
    C. high resistance   D. overloading

41. In a sealed beam headlight, the   41.____

    A. lamp is sealed in the car fender
    B. light rays are sealed within the lamp
    C. lens and reflector are sealed together
    D. light beam is sealed in one direction on the road

42. The capacity of a storage battery is determined by the   42.____

    A. number of cells   B. composition of the case
    C. number of plates   D. shape of the battery

43. Armature *neutral point* is obtained by   43.____

    A. adjusting position of brushes
    B. neutralizing residual magnetism
    C. aligning the ignition contacts
    D. unmeshing the starter pinion gear

44. Cam angle is increased by 44.____

   A. increasing the point gap   B. decreasing the point gap
   C. centrifugal advance   D. greater advance

45. A shorted armature coil 45.____

   A. must be shellacked
   B. may be corrected by undercutting the commutator
   C. must have commutator refaced
   D. must be baked

46. A steady miss at all speeds is USUALLY caused by 46.____

   A. clogged low speed jet   B. low float level
   C. defective spark plug   D. poor condenser

47. When testing an armature, if the sawblade vibrates, it indicates that the armature is 47.____

   A. grounded   B. correct
   C. short-circuited   D. open-circuited

48. If an electric gasoline gauge registers full at all times, trouble is in the 48.____

   A. wire to the tank   B. line to the switch
   C. gasoline line   D. battery terminal

49. The Dyer Starter Drive 49.____

   A. is an over-running clutch drive
   B. works like the Bendix Drive
   C. rotates the starter pinion while it is moved towards the flywheel
   D. has a special gear reduction

50. The MOST accurate method used to time the ignition of an engine is by 50.____

   A. locating the piston position with a wire
   B. use of neon timing light
   C. watching for contact point opening
   D. watching valve position

KEY (CORRECT ANSWERS)

1.	D	11.	A	21.	C	31.	A	41.	C
2.	B	12.	C	22.	A	32.	D	42.	C
3.	B	13.	D	23.	D	33.	D	43.	A
4.	D	14.	A	24.	A	34.	B	44.	B
5.	D	15.	D	25.	A	35.	C	45.	B
6.	A	16.	D	26.	D	36.	B	46.	C
7.	B	17.	B	27.	B	37.	C	47.	C
8.	B	18.	B	28.	C	38.	D	48.	A
9.	B	19.	D	29.	D	39.	C	49.	C
10.	D	20.	B	30.	B	40.	B	50.	B

―――――

EXAMINATION SECTION
TEST 1

DIRECTIONS: Each question or incomplete statement is followed by several suggested
answers or completions. Select the one that BEST answers the question or
completes the statement. *PRINT THE LETTER OF THE CORRECT ANSWER
IN THE SPACE AT THE RIGHT.*

1.   Piston rings are used to   1.____

   A.   keep the piston from wearing
   B.   prevent leakage of gas into the crankcase
   C.   keep the cylinder walls smooth
   D.   reduce the friction between the cylinder walls and the piston

2.   By camber is meant the   2.____

   A.   forward tilt of the king pin
   B.   backward tilt of the king pin
   C.   outward tilt of the front wheels from the vertical
   D.   difference of the distance between the front wheels at the front and at the rear of
         the front wheels

3.   An engine develops more torque when the car is   3.____

   A.   rounding a curve   B.   going down a hill
   C.   in low speed   D.   in high speed

4.   When the brakes of a car squeak as they are applied, the PROBABLE cause is the fact   4.____
     that the brake

   A.   linings are dry
   B.   linings are wet
   C.   pedal is out of adjustment
   D.   shoes are warped

5.   A compression test of all cylinders in an automobile engine is made PRIMARILY to   5.____

   A.   check uniformity among the cylinders
   B.   obtain the highest reading possible
   C.   check on the specified compression ratio
   D.   check the cylinder bore condition

6.   Valve springs are used to   6.____

   A.   open the valves   B.   keep the valves open
   C.   open and close the valves   D.   close the valves

7.   A common cause of an over-rich carburetor mixture is a   7.____

   A.   dirty air cleaner
   B.   leaking intake valve in the fuel pump
   C.   low float level in the carburetor
   D.   late spark timing

8. The pin that transmits power from the piston to the connecting rod is called the _____ pin.   8._____

    A. king   B. wrist   C. connecting rod   D. taper

9. Spark plugs that foul because of excessive carbon formation produced by slow speed engine operation can be corrected by   9._____

    A. installing spark plugs of a higher heat range
    B. advancing the ignition timing
    C. lowering the carburetor fuel level
    D. adjusting the manifold heat control valve

10. In a six-cylinder engine, the cranks on the crankshaft are set apart _____ degrees.   10._____

    A. 30   B. 45   C. 120   D. 60

11. A carburetor that causes hard starting when the engine is hot may be corrected by   11._____

    A. the installation of an accelerator pump piston
    B. an anti-percolating valve
    C. installing a new high speed jet
    D. adjustment of the throttle valve set screw

12. A dragging of the brakes at one wheel may be caused by   12._____

    A. excessive grease on the lining
    B. a clogged brake line
    C. insufficient fluid in the master cylinder
    D. a leaking wheel cylinder

13. Toe-in of front wheels is necessary to   13._____

    A. offset the drag created by the caster angle
    B. compensate for the decrease in the king pin inclination
    C. produce easy recovery to a straight ahead position after turning a corner
    D. overcome the run-out due to the camber angle

14. A manifold heat control valve that is sticking in the *open* position will cause   14._____

    A. sluggish engine operation when cold
    B. hard starting when the engine is hot
    C. vapor lock
    D. a substantial increase in fuel consumption

15. A vacuum gauge shows a normal engine condition when   15._____

    A. the reading indicates a fluctuation between 15 and 17 inches of mercury
    B. there is a steady reading of 17 to 21 inches of mercury
    C. there is an intermittent reading of 16 to 18 inches of mercury
    D. there is a steady reading of 16 inches of mercury

16. A cam ground piston means that it   16._____

    A. is elliptical in shape   B. uses no piston rings
    C. has no wrist pin   D. has a complex head formation

17. Accurate spacing of the distributor points is accomplished with the use of a   17.____

    A.   flat thickness gauge   B.   round thickness gauge
    C.   syncroscope   D.   dial indicator

18. Hydraulic brake liquid leaking at the rubber boot at the end of a master cylinder USU-ALLY indicates   18.____

    A.   a faulty check valve
    B.   that the master cylinder has been overfilled
    C.   leakage at the primary cup
    D.   leakage at the master cylinder cup washer

19. Light detonation or spark knock that occurs when accelerating with a fully opened throttle on a hard pull indicates that   19.____

    A.   the spark is too far advanced
    B.   the spark is too far retarded
    C.   the condition is normal
    D.   a low grade of fuel is being used

20. Breaker points in service for some time may appear dull and gray upon inspection. This condition is   20.____

    A.   due to a high battery voltage
    B.   due to improper condenser capacity
    C.   a normal condition
    D.   due to a high resistance in the primary circuit

21. When a conventional automobile transmission is in neutral position, with the clutch engaged and the engine running,   21.____

    A.   both the countershaft and the clutch shaft are turning
    B.   only the countershaft is turning
    C.   only the clutch shaft is turning
    D.   only the reverse idler shaft is turning

22. The condenser in the electrical system of an automobile is used to   22.____

    A.   increase the spark at the distributor points
    B.   retard the ignition timing
    C.   reduce arcing at the breaker points
    D.   complete the primary circuit

23. Positive camber in the front wheels tends to   23.____

    A.   overcome the effect of *toe-in*
    B.   overcome the effect of *toe-out*
    C.   overcome the effect of caster
    D.   center the weight of the vehicle on the large inner wheel cearing

24. Hypoid rear ends should be lubricated with a(n)   24.____

    A.   aluminum soap grease   B.   fibrous grease
    C.   low pressure lubricant   D.   extreme pressure lubricant

25. The MAIN advantage of hydraulic brake systems is that they   25.____

    A. do not wear out the linings as rapidly as mechanical brakes do
    B. apply uniform pressure to each set of wheel brakes
    C. stop the automobile more quickly
    D. do not require adjustment

26. The purpose of an overdrive unit on an automobile is to   26.____

    A. increase the speed of an engine in relation to the speed of the wheels
    B. simplify shifting
    C. increase the speed of the wheels in relation to the speed of the engine
    D. aid in braking the speed of the car when descending hills

27. The S.A.E. number of a lubricant indicates its   27.____

    A. tar content   B. flash point
    C. viscosity   D. acid content

28. *Hot, cold,* or *standard* spark plugs are distinguishable by the   28.____

    A. shape and length of the lower porcelain insulator
    B. overall length of the plug
    C. diameter of the shell
    D. thickness of the shell

29. The amount of fuel mixture that can be drawn into a cylinder depends upon the   29.____

    A. displacement of the piston
    B. combustion chamber area
    C. spark timing
    D. speed of the fuel pump

30. To adjust the valves of an automobile engine, it is necessary to have the piston on   30.____

    A. bottom dead center
    B. top dead center
    C. intake stroke
    D. top dead center compression stroke

31. The backing plate on all automobiles is used PRIMARILY to   31.____

    A. retain the axle in the housing
    B. keep water from entering the brake mechanism
    C. provide a support for the brake shoes
    D. aid in stopping the automobile

32. The Hotchkiss type of rear-end drive uses   32.____

    A. two radius rods, sometimes attached to the front ends of the rear housing and to the upper face of the car's frame
    B. the two rear springs to absorb the rear-end torque and to transmit the driving thrust to the frame of the car
    C. two angle irons shaped like the letter *V,* reinforced with a cross rod
    D. a metal casing around the driveshaft

33. The camshaft of a four-stroke cycle engine rotates at   33.____

    A. crankshaft speed
    B. one-half crankshaft speed
    C. one-quarter crankshaft speed
    D. twice crankshaft speed

34. Looking in the direction in which a current flows through a conductor, the magnetic field   34.____
surrounding it always travels in a(n) _____ direction.

    A. alternating   B. anti-clockwise
    C. southerly   D. clockwise

35. Contact point spring pressure should be set at _____ ounces.   35.____

    A. 6 to 10   B. 17 to 21   C. 31 to 35   D. 36 to 40

36. The resistance of a suppressor may be measured by a(n)   36.____

    A. voltmeter   B. ohmmeter
    C. watt meter   D. inductance meter

37. The capacity of a condenser is generally measured in   37.____

    A. microfarads   B. farads   C. milliamps   D. ohms

38. Breaker points of a six cylinder engine should be set at   38.____

    A. .018   B. .0018   C. .180   D. 1.80

39. A fuse is placed in the lighting circuit to prevent   39.____

    A. short circuit   B. horn from blowing
    C. damage to wiring   D. overload of generator

40. The voltage of a battery is determined by   40.____

    A. the number of plates in each cell
    B. adding a stronger acid solution to the electrolyte
    C. connecting more cells in parallel
    D. connecting more cells in series

41. The blood vessels that carry blood toward the heart are the   41.____

    A. arteries   B. capillaries
    C. corpuscles   D. veins

42. If an artery has been cut, you could tell by the   42.____

    A. quick clotting of the blood
    B. Rh factor of the blood
    C. slow, steady flow of blood
    D. spurting of the blood

43. The BEST material to be used directly over a wound or burn is   43.____

    A. absorbent cotton   B. adhesive tape
    C. sterile gauze   D. a tourniquet

44. Aromatic spirits of ammonia is used as a(n)   44.____

    A. antidote for arsenic poisoning
    B. stimulant
    C. sedative drug
    D. sterilizing solution

45. A compound fracture is one in which   45.____

    A. broken bones protrude through the skin
    B. bones are broken and shattered
    C. a large bone and its adjoining smaller bones are broken
    D. two or more bones are broken

Questions 46-50.

DIRECTIONS: Each of Questions 46 to 50 consists of a group of four words. Examine each
group carefully, then in the space at the right print the letter
    A - if only one word in the group is spelled correctly
    B - if two words in the group are spelled correctly
    C - if three words in the group are spelled correctly
    D - if all four words in the group are spelled correctly

46. Wendsday, particular, similar, hunderd   46.____

47. realize, judgment, opportunities, consistent   47.____

48. equel, principle, assistense, commitee   48.____

49. simultaneous, privilege, advise, ocassionaly   49.____

50. necissery, official, Febuary, distence   50.____

KEY (CORRECT ANSWERS)

1.	B	11.	B	21.	A	31.	C	41.	D
2.	C	12.	B	22.	C	32.	B	42.	D
3.	C	13.	D	23.	D	33.	B	43.	C
4.	D	14.	A	24.	D	34.	D	44.	B
5.	A	15.	B	25.	B	35.	B	45.	A
6.	D	16.	A	26.	C	36.	B	46.	B
7.	A	17.	D	27.	C	37.	A	47.	D
8.	B	18.	D	28.	A	38.	A	48.	A
9.	A	19.	C	29.	A	39.	C	49.	C
10.	C	20.	C	30.	D	40.	D	50.	A

TEST 2

DIRECTIONS: Each question consists of a statement. You are to indicate whether the statement is TRUE (T) or FALSE (F). *PRINT THE LETTER OF THE CORRECT ANSWER IN THE SPACE AT THE RIGHT.*

1. The starting of an engine is NOT affected by a sticking automatic choke.

    1.____

2. To aid the starting of an overchoked engine, it is necessary to crank the engine with the throttle wide open to help clear the cylinders of raw gasoline.

    2.____

3. The oil pressure gauge indicates the quantity of oil in the crankcase.

    3.____

4. A lighter grade of oil should be used during cold weather driving.

    4.____

5. The purpose of the cooling fan is to help dissipate the heat from the cylinder block.

    5.____

6. The generator is a device which converts mechanical energy into electrical energy.

    6.____

7. A shunt generator without a voltage regulator will not tend to increase the voltage output with the increase in the engine speed.

    7.____

8. The output of a third brush generator is increased by moving the third brush away from the main brush.

    8.____

9. The cut-out relay prevents the battery from discharging through the generator when the engine is stopped.

    9.____

10. The coil in an ignition system is used to build up a high voltage in the primary circuit.

    10.____

11. To check the condition of a storage battery, it is only necessary to check the specific gravity of the acid in the storage battery.

    11.____

12. A specific gravity reading of 1.100 indicates a battery in full charge condition.

    12.____

13. When the battery acid reading varies between the cells of a storage battery, it is only necessary to add stronger acid to the weak cells.

    13.____

14. Distributor rotor shafts always rotate in a clockwise direction.

    14.____

15. A good spark at the spark plug depends entirely on the charge condition of the storage battery.

    15.____

16. The condenser helps to quench the spark at the breaker points.

    16.____

17. Breaker points will burn away rapidly if the cam angle is too great.

    17.____

18. If the lights dim considerably when the starting motor is operated, this indicates a faulty ground connection.

    18.____

19. Increasing temperatures cause oil to gain body and lose fluidity, while decreasing temperatures cause oil to lose body and gain fluidity.

    19.____

20. In a splash lubricating system, the oil is pumped under pressure to all working parts of the engine.

    20.____

21. An over-rich carburetor mixture is indicated by a white smoke emitted from the exhaust pipe. 21.____

22. When an engine stalls after a violent braking of the vehicle, it indicates that the carburetor idling mixture is too lean. 22.____

23. High speed fuel supply depends entirely on the idling jet in the carburetor. 23.____

24. The accelerator pump injects a supply of gasoline to the manifold when the throttle is opened suddenly. 24.____

25. To pressure flush a radiator, it is proper to exert a pressure at the top of the core to force the clogged material out of the bottom of the core. 25.____

26. An engine water thermostat is provided to restrict water circulation when the engine is cold. 26.____

27. Corrosion of the radiator and parts of the cooling system may be caused by exhaust gas leaking into the cooling system through a defective cylinder head gasket. 27.____

28. An L-head type of engine is one in which the intake valves are located on one side of the engine block and the exhaust valves are located on the other side of the engine block. 28.____

29. A worn valve guide will cause excessive oil consumption. 29.____

30. Counterweights on crankshafts are provided to compensate for the weight of the fly-wheel. 30.____

31. Worn main bearings will produce a typical crankshaft knock that is especially noticeable when the engine is under a hard pull. 31.____

32. An oil wiper ring on a piston is a device that insures proper lubrication to the cylinder walls. 32.____

33. The order in which the events of a four-stroke cycle occur is: 1 - compression, 2 - intake, 3 - power, 4 - exhaust. 33.____

34. Fuels for gasoline engines are rated according to octane number, those having the higher octane rating are those having the GREATEST tendency to knock. 34.____

35. An efficient combustible mixture for a gasoline engine is one part of gasoline to fifteen parts of air by volume. 35.____

36. A loose piston pin will indicate itself by a double knock MOSTLY noticeable during idling. 36.____

37. The operation of a clutch is based on the frictional contact between two smooth metallic surfaces and the facings riveted to the friction disk. 37.____

38. A slipping clutch may be caused by the lack of free clutch pedal action. 38.____

39. Hydraulic transmissions are operated by the vacuum produced in the engine intake manifold. 39.____

40. A chattering clutch may be caused by oil or gum on the pressure plate, friction disk, or flywheel facing.   40.____

41. A dragging clutch may be caused by a warped or distorted pressure plate.   41.____

42. Syncro mesh devices are designed to cause gears that are rotating and about to be meshed to rotate at the same speeds so that meshing can take place easily.   42.____

43. In constant mesh type transmissions, the gears are moved to become engaged or disengaged according to the need.   43.____

44. The vacuum or power gear shift uses intake manifold vacuum to provide the needed power to shift gears.   44.____

45. The overdrive unit reduces engine speed for high car speeds, providing more economical operation and less engine wear per car mile.   45.____

46. Hard gear shifting may be caused by sliding gears being tight on the splined shaft.   46.____

47. The propeller shaft universal joints are provided to allow for the difference in shaft positions when the wheels ride over a bump.   47.____

48. A differential is required to compensate for the difference in distances the rear wheels travel when the car rounds a turn.   48.____

49. In the semi-floating type of rear axle, the wheel end of the axle shaft is supported by a bearing in the axle housing.   49.____

50. A leaf spring has a slower rate of vibration than a coil spring, thereby giving a much easier ride.   50.____

—————

KEY (CORRECT ANSWERS)

1.	F	11.	F	21.	F	31.	T	41.	T
2.	T	12.	F	22.	T	32.	F	42.	T
3.	F	13.	F	23.	F	33.	F	43.	F
4.	T	14.	F	24.	T	34.	F	44.	T
5.	T	15.	F	25.	F	35.	F	45.	T
6.	T	16.	T	26.	T	36.	T	46.	T
7.	F	17.	T	27.	T	37.	T	47.	T
8.	F	18.	F	28.	F	38.	T	48.	T
9.	T	19.	F	29.	T	39.	F	49.	T
10.	F	20.	F	30.	F	40.	T	50.	F

TEST 3

DIRECTIONS: Each question consists of a statement. You are to indicate whether the statement is TRUE (T) or FALSE (F). *PRINT THE LETTER OF THE CORRECT ANSWER IN THE SPACE AT THE RIGHT.*

1. A weak front spring of the leaf type may cause a change in the caster effect. 1.____

2. Shock absorbers are provided to overcome the violent rebound action after a spring has been compressed. 2.____

3. The hydraulic type of shock absorber depends upon the difference of air pressure within the unit for its efficient operation. 3.____

4. Caster effect is put into a front axle by tilting the upper parts of the king pin towards the front of the car. 4.____

5. Excessive caster effect will cause the wheels to shimmy. 5.____

6. On modern vehicles, the camber effect is kept at a minimum due to the king pin inclination. 6.____

7. Excessive camber may cause tire wear at the outer edge of the tire. 7.____

8. Scuffing of the tire surface may be caused by a bent steering arm. 8.____

9. The pitman arm is the connecting link between the steering gear assembly and the drag link. 9.____

10. The reach rod connects the front wheels with the steering column. 10.____

11. Steering arms must be positioned to give proper toe-in when the car is on a turn. 11.____

12. If a car persistently pulls to one side, this may be caused by low or uneven tire pressures. 12.____

13. Steering gears are provided with adjustments to eliminate end play in the cross shaft and worm and wheel contact. 13.____

14. A properly adjusted steering gear will be indicated by a slight drag at the center position and free action at the extreme end positions. 14.____

15. When checking for caster, camber, or toe-in, it is necessary to have the car in a level position and the tires inflated to the proper pressures. 15.____

16. The effectiveness of hydraulic brakes is based upon the principle that hydraulic pressure is exerted equally in all directions in a liquid under pressure. 16.____

17. Noisy or squealing brakes may be caused by loose linings or rivets that touch the brake drum. 17.____

18. When all brakes drag on a car equipped with a hydraulic system, this condition may be caused by a clogged filler vent on the master cylinder. 18.____

19. Air in the hydraulic brake lines indicates the necessity for bleeding the entire brake system. 19.____

20. Piston displacement is the volume that the piston displaces as it moves from top dead center to bottom dead center position.   20.____

21. The stroke of an engine is the distance the piston travels from top dead center to bottom dead center.   21.____

22. Low pressure in a full force lubrication system may indicate loose bearings.   22.____

23. A cracked distributor cap may cause a miss in the engine.   23.____

24. The S.A.E. number of lubricating oils indicates the degree of viscosity of the oil.   24.____

25. Vapor lock will NOT affect the running of an engine.   25.____

26. Late spark timing will cause an engine to overheat.   26.____

27. Excessive pressure in air brake systems may be caused by sticking relief valves.   27.____

28. A magneto depends upon a battery for a current to operate the breaker system.   28.____

29. The intensity of a spark produced by a magneto depends upon the speed of the magneto armature.   29.____

30. The cam shaft of an engine rotates at one-half the speed of the crankshaft.   30.____

31. A battery that is badly sulphated may be corrected by placing the battery on a low charge for a long period of time.   31.____

32. A voltage regulator controls the voltage output of the battery.   32.____

33. Rebound clips on leaf springs are provided to prevent the spring from shifting on the spring saddle.   33.____

34. The fuel pump that delivers gasoline to the carburetor does so under pressure.   34.____

35. A high float level in the carburetor may cause an over-rich operating condition.   35.____

36. Crankcase ventilation is provided to help carry off the vapors of water and gasoline when the engine reaches operating temperature.   36.____

37. The pressure cap allows circulation of water in the cooling system at higher temperatures without boiling.   37.____

38. Excessive fuel consumption may be caused by underinflated tires.   38.____

39. Accelerator pump linkage control must be adjusted for winter and for summer driving.   39.____

40. Excessive oil consumption may be caused by a broken oil seal at the rear main bearing.   40.____

41. If a battery is allowed to stand for a long period of time, it will slowly self-discharge.   41.____

42. If the battery requires a considerable amount of water, it indicates that the charge rate is too low.   42.____

43. It is advisable to coat the battery terminals with petroleum jelly to prevent corrosion.   43.____

44. A low or unsteady output from a generator may be caused by a round, dirty, or worn commutator.   44.____

45. Valve tappet noise may be caused by excessive clearance between the valve stem and the valve guide.   45.____

46. A slipping clutch is caused by excessive pressure of the pressure springs.   46.____

47. The transmission interlocking device is provided to prevent the shifting of more than one gear at a time.   47.____

48. High speed driving will not wear tires more than slow speed driving.   48.____

49. High speed driving on hot pavements will cause a rise in pressure in the tire.   49.____

50. Spark plug gaps must be varied according to the compression ratio of the engine.   50.____

KEY (CORRECT ANSWERS)

1.	T	11.	F	21.	T	31.	T	41.	T
2.	T	12.	T	22.	T	32.	F	42.	F
3.	F	13.	T	23.	T	33.	F	43.	T
4.	F	14.	T	24.	T	34.	T	44.	T
5.	T	15.	T	25.	F	35.	T	45.	F
6.	T	16.	T	26.	T	36.	T	46.	F
7.	T	17.	T	27.	T	37.	T	47.	T
8.	T	18.	T	28.	F	38.	T	48.	F
9.	T	19.	T	29.	T	39.	T	49.	T
10.	F	20.	T	30.	T	40.	T	50.	F

EXAMINATION SECTION
TEST 1

DIRECTIONS: Each question or incomplete statement is followed by several suggested answers or completions. Select the one that BEST answers the question or completes the statement. *PRINT THE LETTER OF THE CORRECT ANSWER IN THE SPACE AT THE RIGHT.*

1. Of the following, the ACCEPTED method of reconditioning a connected rod big end bore is to

   A. use a press to return the rod cap's diameter to standard size
   B. hone the bore to the next standard bearing oversize
   C. remove an amount of stock equal to the oversize from the split on the cap and then hone to standard size
   D. remove equal amounts of stock from both the cap and the rod at the split and then hone to standard size

   1.____

2. After a cylinder that has a 3,000 inch bore has been honed, it is found to be tapered .003 inch. The removed aluminum piston is to be reused.
   The piston should be

   A. cleaned and reinstalled
   B. knurled to increase the diameter of the entire skirt by .003 inch
   C. knurled at the top of the skirt to 3.001 inches and at the bottom of the skirt to 3.000 inches
   D. knurled at the top of the skirt to 3.000 inches and at the bottom of the skirt to 3.001 inches

   2.____

3. Of the following, the PROPER sequence of operations in reconditioning valve seats for replacement valves that have oversize stems is to

   A. clean guide, ream guide, grind seat, and narrow seat
   B. clean guide, grind seat, ream guide, and narrow seat
   C. clean guide, narrow seat, grind seat, and ream guide
   D. grind seat, narrow seat, clean guide, and ream guide

   3.____

4. An engine cylinder measures 3.520 inches at the bottom of the bore and 3.529 inches near the top. The factory bore measured 3.500 inches.
   New pistons to be installed after boring should GENERALLY be _____ inch oversize.

   A. .010   B. .020   C. .030   D. .050

   4.____

5. An engine vacuum gauge used to measure intake-manifold pressure reads in

   A. pounds per square inch   B. inches of mercury
   C. pounds per square foot   D. ounces per inch

   5.____

6. A hydrometer is being used to determine the specific gravity of a lead-acid storage battery which is at a temperature of 120 degrees Fahrenheit. The hydrometer gives a reading of 1.230.
   The true specific gravity of the electrolyte at that temperature is MOST NEARLY

   A. 1.198   B. 1.205   C. 1.230   D. 1.246

   6.____

7.

The micrometer reading shown in the figure above is

A. .525"   B. .555"   C. .562"   D. .568"

8. In connection with the inspection and the turning or the grinding of brake drums on passenger cars, the BEST practice is to

A. weld a cracked brake drum
B. turn or grind the brake drum if it is out of round by more than .060 inches
C. turn or grind the drums in pairs so that both front drums are the same diameter and both back drums are the same diameter
D. increase the standard drum diameter to a maximum of 0.12 inches by turning or grinding

9. Of the following, the BEST tool to use to undercut mica on the commutator of a starting motor is a

A. round nose chisel   B. hacksaw blade
C. flat chisel   D. hand reamer

10. In a properly adjusted gasoline-powered automotive engine, the MAXIMUM percentage of the energy in the gasoline that can be transferred by the engine to the driving wheels of an automobile is MOST NEARLY

A. 20%   B. 40%   C. 60%   D. 80%

11. The lever length of a torque wrench is 24 inches. If a force of 50 pounds is properly applied at the handle when torquing a nut, the applied torque, in foot-pounds, is

A. 50   B. 100   C. 400   D. 1200

12. While a fuel pump discharge pressure test is being performed, it is found that the pressure drops rapidly when the engine is stopped.
This indicates a

A. leaking pump-outlet valve   B. leaking suction hose
C. leaking pump diaphragm   D. normal condition

13. Of the following, the size of copper conductor which has the GREATEST current-carrying capacity is _____ AWG.

A. 12   B. 8   C. 0   D. 000

14. Of the following, the statement pertaining to soldering which is MOST correct is:

A. 60/40 solder would best be used for automotive-body repair
B. Acid flux should not be used on copper parts such as radiators

C.   Main flux should be used on electrical connections
D.   The strength of the joint is not dependent on the joint thickness

15.   When a car axle ring gear and pinion is being adjusted, the ring gear is moved toward   15._____
      the pinion.
      This movement will change the tooth contact toward the _____ of the ring gear.

      A.   toe   B.   heel   C.   dedendum   D.   addendum

16.   An automotive hydraulic brake system has a 1 inch diameter master cylinder and a 1.2   16._____
      inch diameter wheel cylinder.
      The force applied by the wheel cylinder piston will be MOST NEARLY _____ the force
      applied to the master cylinder piston.

      A.   equal to   B.   1.44 times
      C.   1.20 times   D.   0.833 times

17.   Of the following, the statement regarding the rebuilding of a hydraulic brake master cylin- 17._____
      der which is MOST correct is that

      A.   a light coat of grease should be applied to the parts during assembly to prevent
           rusting
      B.   very light scratches in the bore can be polished out with emergy cloth
      C.   the parts must be cleaned in denatured alcohol
      D.   deep scratches and pitting can be removed by honing to permit cylinder reuse

18.   An automobile is standing still with the engine running and the clutch disengaged.   18._____
      Of the following, the part of the clutch assembly that is stationary is the

      A.   flywheel   B.   clutch cover
      C.   pressure plate   D.   clutch disk

19.   Of the following liquids, the BEST one to use for cleaning automotive cylinders after they 19._____
      have been honed is

      A.   hot, soapy water   B.   gasoline
      C.   turpentine   D.   kerosene

20.   In an in-line gasoline-powered automotive engine, the manifold heat-control valve is   20._____
      mounted to the

      A.   intake manifold   B.   cylinder head
      C.   exhaust manifold   D.   crankcase

———————

KEY (CORRECT ANSWERS)

1.	D	6.	D	11.	B	16.	B
2.	C	7.	C	12.	A	17.	C
3.	A	8.	C	13.	D	18.	D
4.	C	9.	B	14.	C	19.	A
5.	B	10.	A	15.	A	20.	C

———

TEST 2

DIRECTIONS: Each question or incomplete statement is followed by several suggested answers or completions. Select the one that BEST answers the question or completes the statement. *PRINT THE LETTER OF THE CORRECT ANSWER IN THE SPACE AT THE RIGHT.*

1. When a ring ridge is removed from a cylinder, the BEST practice is to   1.____

   A. pull the piston from the cylinder before removing the ridge
   B. cut slightly below the level of the ridge into the cylinder
   C. blend the ridge area into the cylinder proper after removing the ridge
   D. leave a slight undercut in the cylinder wall after removing the ridge

2. The cleaning of ball and roller bearings is MOST effectively and safely accomplished by   2.____
   first wiping off surplus grease and oil and then

   A. soaking them in kerosene
   B. soaking them in gasoline
   C. soaking them in carbon-tetrachloride
   D. spinning them by using air pressure

3. The overheating of an engine would NOT likely be caused by   3.____

   A. a stuck manifold heat-control valve
   B. advanced ignition timing
   C. a lean carburetor mixture
   D. a leaking cylinder-head gasket

4. The excitation of the field of an automotive alternator is provided by current from the   4.____

   A. stator   B. rotor   C. diode   D. battery

5. A clicking or tapping noise which persists after the engine has warmed up is USUALLY   5.____
   caused by

   A. loose fan belts
   B. loose main bearings
   C. defective valve lifters
   D. worn piston pins

6. Compression piston rings for gasoline-powered engines are MOST generally made from   6.____

   A. copper   B. high-quality cast iron
   C. aluminum   D. tempered steel

7. A vehicle has the coil spring mounted between the frame and the lower suspension arm.   7.____
   The front end ball joints on this vehicle may be checked by

   A. jacking up the lower suspension arm
   B. jacking up the frame
   C. blocking the upper suspension arm and jacking the frame
   D. jacking between the suspension arms

8. The capacity of a conventional automobile ignition system condenser is MOST NEARLY   8.____

    A. 0.02 microfarads   B. 0.2 microfarads
    C. 0.2 farads   D. 2.0 farads

9. Of the following, the BEST sequence of operations to follow when removing grease and   9.____
scale from carburetor and fuel pump parts would be

    A. degreasing soak, alkaline soak, water rinse, acid dip, hot water rinse
    B. acid dip, degreasing soak, alkaline rinse, water rinse
    C. acid dip, water rinse, alkaline dip, water rinse, degreasing soak, water rinse
    D. acid dip, water rinse, alkaline dip, degreasing soak, acid rinse, water rinse

10. A ballast-type resistor in the primary circuit of a conventional automotive ignition system   10.____
will

    A. deliver constant reduced voltage to the soil
    B. be bypassed at high engine speeds
    C. increase coil primary voltage at low engine speeds
    D. decrease in resistance value as its temperature increases

11. In order to minimize the coil load when installing a coil in an automobile in which the pos-   11.____
itive terminal of the battery is grounded, the coil should be wired with its

    A. *negative* terminal connected to the distributor
    B. *positive* terminal connected to the distributor
    C. *negative* terminal connected to the ground
    D. *positive* terminal connected to the positive battery terminal through the starter
        switch

12. Loose connecting-rod bearings are USUALLY indicated by a   12.____

    A. light rap or clatter when the engine is running with a light load at approximately 25
        mph
    B. metallic rattle when the engine is idling unevenly
    C. clicking noise when the engine is cold
    D. sharp metallic double knock when the engine is idling

13. An ignition system is not functioning properly. In order to check the system, the high ten-   13.____
sion wire from the coil is held close to a ground at the same time as the ignition points
are opened and closed.
If a good spark occurs from the high tension wire to the ground, it would indicate that
the problem is NOT with the

    A. motor   B. condenser
    C. spark plug wires   D. distributor cap

14. When an automotive generator regulator is adjusted, a 1/4 ohm resistor is inserted in the   14.____
line from the battery terminal of the regulator to the battery.
This permits adjustment to be made to the

    A. current regulator   B. circuit breaker
    C. voltage regulator   D. field relay

15. A tire showing excessive wear on one side of the tread indicates IMPROPER   15.____

    A. caster   B. camber
    C. toe-in   D. tire pressure

16. Front wheel roller bearings should be adjusted to   16.____

    A. .001 to .003 inch end play
    B. .010 inch end play
    C. a 20-foot-pound torque on nut
    D. a mild pressure

17. In automotive air conditioning systems, the MOST commonly used refrigerant is   17.____

    A. dichlorodifluoromethane (12)
    B. carbon dioxide (CO_2)
    C. ammonia (NH_3)
    D. sulfur dioxide (SO_2)

18. In an automotive air conditioning system, the opening of the expansion valve is con-   18.____
trolled PRIMARILY by the

    A. temperature within the vehicle
    B. evaporator temperature
    C. condenser temperature
    D. condenser pressure

19. When the front end of a vehicle with independent suspension is aligned, the front of the   19.____
upper suspension arm is moved away from the center line of the vehicle.
This adjustment will change

    A. the caster only, in the positive direction
    B. both the caster and the camber, in the positive direction
    C. both the caster and the camber, in the negative direction
    D. the caster in the positive direction and the camber in the negative direction

20. The vapor discharge valve in a diaphragm-type fuel pump normally   20.____

    A. controls pump discharge pressure
    B. is installed directly after the fuel outlet valve
    C. opens with rising fuel temperature
    D. is vented to the carburetor air cleaner to minimize pollution

KEY (CORRECT ANSWERS)

1.	C	6.	B	11.	B	16.	A
2.	A	7.	A	12.	A	17.	A
3.	B	8.	B	13.	B	18.	B
4.	D	9.	A	14.	C	19.	B
5.	C	10.	A	15.	B	20.	C

TEST 3

DIRECTIONS: Each question or incomplete statement is followed by several suggested answers or completions. Select the one that BEST answers the question or completes the statement. *PRINT THE LETTER OF THE CORRECT ANSWER IN THE SPACE AT THE RIGHT.*

1.   In an automotive ignition system, the distributor dwell   1.____

   A.   is governed by the ignition point gap
   B.   is equal to 360 degrees divided by the number of cylinders
   C.   is equal to the number of degrees of rotation that the points are open
   D.   will decrease with increasing centrifugal advance

2.   When an oscilloscope indicates too short a dwell in the ignition system, the MOST prob-   2.____
     able reason is that the

   A.   points are set too far apart
   B.   points are set too close together
   C.   *degrees of dwell* are too great
   D.   coil output is too high

3.   An automobile with a properly operating conventional differential assembly has one rear   3.____
     wheel jacked up. The engine is running in *drive* with 20 mph indicated on the speedome-
     ter.
     The MOST correct statement concerning this situation is that the

   A.   vehicle will move off the jack because it has been driven by the wheel on the
        ground
   B.   jacked rear wheel is turning at 20 mph road speed
   C.   jacked rear wheel is turning at 40 mph road speed
   D.   jacked rear wheel is turning at 10 mph road speed

4.   Of the following tubing materials and connections, the BEST one to use when replacing   4.____
     hydraulic brake lines is

   A.   steel tubing with compression fittings
   B.   steel tubing with double-lap flare
   C.   steel tubing with single-lap flare
   D.   half hard copper tubing with double-lap flare

5.   In a single-type brake master cylinder, a plugged compensating port would be suspected   5.____
     if

   A.   the brakes drag
   B.   the brake pedal is very low
   C.   the brakes fade
   D.   excessive pedal pressure is required

6.   The PRIMARY purpose of the diverter valve in an AIR (Thermactor) emission control   6.____
     system is to

   A.   prevent exhaust gases from reaching the pump
   B.   cut off the flow of air to the exhaust manifold when the manifold pressure
        decreases suddenly
   C.   provide maximum ignition advance when decelerating in order to prevent backfiring
   D.   provide advance timing during prolonged idling

7. An automotive clutch throw-out bearing   7.____

    A. is mounted on the transmission input shaft
    B. is mounted on the transmission bearing retainer
    C. rotates when the clutch is engaged
    D. must be in continuous contact with the clutch release levers

8. An advantage of using a clutch that utilizes a diaphragm spring instead of coil springs is   8.____
    that such a clutch eliminates the need for

    A. a throw-out bearing   B. a pivot ring
    C. a throw-out fork   D. clutch release levers

9. Of the following statements concerning disc brakes, the one which is INCORRECT is: 9.____

    A. All scoring of the disc must be ground out before the pads are replaced
    B. It is necessary to pump the brake pedal after changing the pads in order to make
        the brake function
    C. The piston seal automatically adjusts the pads to the disc clearance
    D. The run-out of the disc may not exceed .003"

10. Turning the carburetor idle air adjusting screw outward will   10.____

    A. enrich the idle air-fuel mixture
    B. lean the idle air-fuel mixture
    C. close down on the main throttle valve
    D. reduce the idle rpm

11. The function of an automatic choke vacuum break piston or diaphragm is to   11.____

    A. attempt to close the choke when the engine is accelerated
    B. apply an additional torque on the choke to assist the thermostatic spring in keeping
        the choke closed
    C. attempt to open the choke when the engine is accelerated
    D. act opposite to the incoming air pressure on the throat plate

12. A brake assembly has two single-ended cylinders, one on the top and one on the bottom.   12.____
    The opposite ends of the brake shoes are anchored to the backing plate.
    This type of brake would be considered as being

    A. a duo-servo   B. self-energizing
    C. self-centering   D. a uni-servo

13. An exhaust gas analyzer operating on the principle of thermal conductivity of the exhaust   13.____
    gas reads 12.0/1.0.
    This indicates that the

    A. mixture is lean
    B. mixture is rich
    C. carburetor setting conforms to Sec. 207 of the Federal Clean Air Act
    D. mixture has 12% excess air

14. When adjusting a recirculating ball, manual type, steering gear,   14.____

    A. the worm bearing preload adjustment should be made with the steering wheel in the *straight-ahead* position
    B. the pitman shaft preload adjustment should be made with the steering wheel in the *straight-ahead* position
    C. the pitman shaft preload should be made prior to worm bearing preload adjustments
    D. both worm bearing and pitman shaft preload adjustments should be made with the steering wheel one turn from the center

15. The device used in automatic transmissions to provide the force required to engage a band clutch is called a   15.____

    A. booster   B. shifter   C. spool   D. servo

16. The function of the governor valve in an automatic transmission NORMALLY is to   16.____

    A. maintain constant pressure in the control circuits
    B. provide proportionally increasing pressure to the shift valve as road speed increases
    C. provide pressure to the shift valve at a predetermined road speed
    D. increase band pressure during heavy acceleration

17. On many automatic transmissions, the function performed by the TV linkage is carried out by use of a   17.____

    A. vacuum modulator   B. servo
    C. dashpot   D. compensator valve

18. A centrifugal vacuum type of speed governor   18.____

    A. is mounted between the carburetor and intake manifold
    B. would not govern speed if the air lines were removed
    C. would close the throttle if the air lines were removed or tampered
    D. has a speed-control adjustment which is made at the carburetor

19. In an air brake system, a limiting quick release valve is NORMALLY found in   19.____

    A. the line to the front brake chamber
    B. the line to the rear brake chamber
    C. series with the trailer protection valve
    D. the governor control

20. Air-actuated brake shoes are adjusted by   20.____

    A. adjusting the length of the chamber piston rod
    B. shifting the brake chamber along the slotted holes in the mount
    C. moving the cam on the splined shaft
    D. rotating the cam shaft to move the shoe closer to the brake drum

KEY (CORRECT ANSWERS)

1.	A	6.	B	11.	A	16.	C
2.	A	7.	B	12.	B	17.	A
3.	C	8.	D	13.	A	18.	B
4.	B	9.	A	14.	B	19.	A
5.	A	10.	B	15.	D	20.	D

———

EXAMINATION SECTION
TEST 1

DIRECTIONS: Each question or incomplete statement is followed by several suggested answers or completions. Select the one that BEST answers the question or completes the statement. *PRINT THE LETTER OF THE CORRECT ANSWER IN THE SPACE AT THE RIGHT.*

1. If a carburetor drips continually, the MOST likely cause is a   1.____

    A. loose Venturi tube   B. needle valve not seating
    C. loose idle set screw   D. float set too low

2. The part used to control the ratio of air and gasoline in a truck engine is the   2.____

    A. bogie   B. filter   C. carburetor   D. pump

3. During cranking, all electrical energy is supplied by the   3.____

    A. alternator   B. battery
    C. generator   D. engine

4. A device for storing electric charges is known as a(n)   4.____

    A. commutator   B. condenser
    C. capacitance   D. exciter

5. Hydraulic brake fluid is a mixture of _____ and _____.   5.____

    A. kerosene; engine oil
    B. mineral oil; denatured alcohol
    C. castor oil; denatured alcohol
    D. ethelene glycol; mineral oil

6. When you are servicing the air brake chambers located at each wheel, the bolts and nuts holding the diaphragm plates should be tightened   6.____

    A. more tightly on the pressure plate than on the non-pressure plate
    B. more tightly on the non-pressure plate than on the pressure plate
    C. with only sufficient pressure to insure an air-tight seal
    D. with as much pressure as possible

7. The temperature gauge indicates the temperature of the   7.____

    A. air surrounding the engine
    B. water surrounding the cylinders
    C. oil in the crankcase
    D. pistons

8. Air drawn into the cooling system through the pump or hoses causes   8.____

    A. better cooling of the water
    B. the water to stop circulating
    C. a boost in the circulation
    D. rusting of the cylinder block

9. Diesel fuel filter elements on an International Harvester or Allis-Chalmers tractor are USUALLY serviced when too dirty for continued use by

9.____

   A. washing in kerosene
   B. steam cleaning
   C. washing in carbon tetrachloride
   D. oiling

10. To find out if a cylinder of a diesel engine is firing, it is necessary to

10.____

   A. remove the fuel pump
   B. disconnect the vent valve
   C. remove the vent valve
   D. prime the injection pump

11. In diesel engines, piston rings are held against the side of the cylinder PRIMARILY by

11.____

   A. gas pressure behind the ring
   B. thermal expansion of the ring
   C. an oil wedge behind the ring
   D. spring forces within the ring itself

12. In addition to lighter weight, the PRINCIPAL advantage of aluminum alloy pistons in diesel engines is that

12.____

   A. piston rings have less tendency to collect sludge and stick
   B. they have a much higher heat transfer rate than cast iron pistons
   C. they expand less under heat and thus reduce liner wear
   D. area for area, they are stronger than cast iron

13. All the refrigerant now used for automotive air conditioners is R

13.____

   A. 10   B. 12   C. 18   D. 22

14. When the right front wheel is turned 20° to the left, the left front wheel should turn APPROXIMATELY _____ degrees.

14.____

   A. 16   B. 18   C. 20   D. 24

15. In placing a new tire and a well-worn tire on dual wheels, it is BEST to place

15.____

   A. the new tire on the inside
   B. the worn tire on the inside
   C. either tire on the inside; it makes no difference
   D. the tires separately

16. The color of iron at welding heat is USUALLY a

16.____

   A. creamy white   B. dull yellow
   C. light yellow   D. light red

17. The _____ rating method measures the amount of current a battery can supply steadily for 20 hours, with no cell falling below 1.75 volts.

17.____

   A. cold-cranking   B. reserve-capacity
   C. watts   D. ampere-hour

18. In an automotive gasoline engine, the camshaft is used PRIMARILY to   18.____

    A. drive the transmission
    B. operate the valve lifters
    C. change the reciprocating motion of the pistons to rotary motion
    D. operate the choke mechanism

19. The PRIMARY function of the thermostat in the cooling system of an automobile engine   19.____
    is to

    A. control the operating temperature of the engine
    B. keep the operating temperature of the engine as low as possible
    C. provide the proper amount of heat for the heater
    D. retain engine heat when the engine gets hot

20. The PRIMARY purpose of the condenser in the ignition circuit of a gasoline engine is to   20.____

    A. boost the ignition voltage
    B. rectify the ignition voltage
    C. adjust the coil voltage
    D. reduce arcing at the distributor breaker points

21. The PRIMARY purpose of the differential in the rear drive train of an automotive vehicle   21.____
    is to allow each of the rear wheels to

    A. rotate at different speeds
    B. go in reverse
    C. rotate with maximum torque
    D. absorb road shocks

22. Of the following, the BEST tool to use for securely tightening a one-inch standard hexag-   22.____
    onal nut is a(n)

    A. monkey wrench
    B. open-end wrench
    C. Stillson wrench
    D. pair of heavy duty pliers

23. The purpose of the ignition coil in a gasoline engine is PRIMARILY to   23.____

    A. smooth the voltage   B. raise the voltage
    C. raise the current   D. smooth the current

24. Vapor lock in a vehicle with a gasoline engine is caused by excessive heat.   24.____
    To prevent vapor lock, it may be necessary to relocate

    A. the ignition system   B. the cooling system
    C. the starter motor   D. a part of the fuel line

25. It is important to use safety shoes PRIMARILY to guard the feet against   25.____

    A. tripping hazards   B. heavy falling objects
    C. shock hazards   D. mud and dirt

KEY (CORRECT ANSWERS)

1.	B	11.	D
2.	C	12.	C
3.	B	13.	B
4.	B	14.	D
5.	C	15.	D
6.	C	16.	A
7.	B	17.	B
8.	D	18.	B
9.	A	19.	A
10.	B	20.	D

21.	A
22.	B
23.	B
24.	D
25.	B

———

TEST 2

Each question or incomplete statement is followed by several suggested answers or completions. Select the one that BEST answers the question or completes the statement. *PRINT THE LETTER OF THE CORRECT ANSWER IN THE SPACE AT THE RIGHT.*

1. Which of the following is a PROBABLE result of a malfunctioning PCV valve?   1.____

   A. High fuel tank pressure   B. Improper idling
   C. Noisy engine valves   D. High fuel consumption

2. When a car goes into overdrive, the _____ gear is held stationary.   2.____

   A. pinion   B. ring   C. sun   D. planetary

3. A puller is NOT commonly used to remove or install   3.____

   A. valves   B. gears   C. pulleys   D. bearings

4. An engine turbocharger draws its energy from   4.____

   A. ignition spark   B. engine fan airflow
   C. cylinder combustion   D. hot exhaust gases

5. A four-gas automotive emissions analyzer will NOT measure the presence of   5.____

   A. HC   B. CO   C. CO_2 D. NO

6. An automotive cylinder head is attached to the   6.____

   A. bearing saddle   B. pan rail
   C. boss   D. block deck

7. Which of the following is a DISADVANTAGE associated with a magnetic reluctance crankshaft position sensor that is used in a microprocessor-based control/diagnostic system?   7.____

   A. Inability to directly measure crankshaft position
   B. Inability to exploit flywheel rotation
   C. Requires additional installation of a harmonic damper
   D. Inability to set engine timing statically

8. Which valve train component CANNOT be used on overhead cam engines?   8.____

   A. Finger follower   B. Bucket follower
   C. Tappet   D. Rocker arm

9. Which of the following would likely be indicated by uneven firing voltages that are displayed on an oscilloscope?   9.____

   A. Worn plug electrodes   B. Condenser failure
   C. Arcing contact points   D. Point contact failure

10. Power steering systems typically use each of the following types of pumps EXCEPT   10.____

    A. vane   B. diaphragm   C. roller   D. slipper

11. Most exhaust gas analyzers used in emission control maintenance indicate the percent- 11.____
    age of _____ in the exhaust.

    A. HC   B. CO   C. NO   D. CO_2

12. What is the term for the portion of a cam that has a constant diameter, and does not pro- 12.____
    duce lift as it rotates?

    A. Offset   B. Nose circle
    C. Flank circle   D. Radial circle

13. In a microprocessor-based control/diagnostic system, which type of sensor uses the   13.____
    compound zirconia oxide?

    A. MAP   B. Throttle angle
    C. EGO   D. Knock

14. Which measuring device is MAINLY used to find open circuits and excessive resistance   14.____
    by imposing a bypass on a portion of the existing circuit?

    A. Digital multimeter   B. Jumper wires
    C. Test light   D. Continuity tester

15. If a car engine is operating at 1500 rpm, at what speed (rpm) is the distributor running? 15.____
    A. 750   B. 1500   C. 3000   D. 4500

16. Throttle body fuel injection refers to   16.____

    A. the insertion of fuel below the throttle plate
    B. unregulated fuel flow
    C. a continuous flow fuel injection
    D. a form of fuel metering actuator used in micro-processor-based control/diagnostic
        systems

17. Which of the following conditions in the valve train is NOT consistent with the *open valve* 17.____
    position in engine operation?

    A. Upward oil flow
    B. Plunger extended
    C. Slight leakage between plunger and body
    D. Ball check valve closed

18. What is the term for projections on a plate or disc that interlock in hub or drum slots? 18.____
    A. Drive lugs   B. Toe cams
    C. Axial teeth   D. Plate threads

19. Which of the following conditions is a POSSIBLE result of evaporation control system   19.____
    failure?

    A. Collapsed fuel tank   B. High fuel tank pressure
    C. Improper idle   D. Vapor low from air cleaner

20. Each of the following is a problem commonly associated with improper casting angles EXCEPT   20.____

    A. pulling to one side   B. hard steering
    C. high speed instability   D. rapid tire wear

21. In a microprocessor-based control/diagnostic system, which type of crankshaft position sensor is located in the distributor?   21.____

    A. Optical   B. Ignition timing
    C. Hall-effect   D. Magnetic reluctance

22. When using a short finder to trace a short circuit, which of the following steps should be performed FIRST?   22.____

    A. Turn on all switches in a series with the circuit being tested
    B. Move the short finder meter along circuit wiring
    C. Remove the blown fuse while leaving the battery connected
    D. Connect the pulse unit of short finder across the fuse terminals

23. In a fuel injection system, which type of pump is used PRIMARILY as a transfer pump?   23.____

    A. Rotary   B. Diaphragm   C. Turbine   D. Roller

24. What type of electrical connectors are used to permanently join two stripped wire ends?   24.____

    A. Crimp   B. Flat blade
    C. Butt   D. Snap-splice

25. Discharges from the _____ appear as high voltage surges on an oscilloscope tester.   25.____

    A. distributor
    B. contact points
    C. coil high-tension terminal
    D. battery

KEY (CORRECT ANSWERS)

1.	B	11.	B
2.	C	12.	C
3.	A	13.	C
4.	D	14.	B
5.	D	15.	A
6.	D	16.	D
7.	D	17.	B
8.	C	18.	A
9.	A	19.	D
10.	B	20.	D

21.	C
22.	C
23.	B
24.	C
25.	C

EXAMINATION SECTION
TEST 1

DIRECTIONS: Each question or incomplete statement is followed by several suggested answers or completions. Select the one that BEST answers the question or completes the statement. *PRINT THE LETTER OF THE CORRECT ANSWER IN THE SPACE AT THE RIGHT.*

1. All of the following are probable causes of an engine's failure to start EXCEPT

    A. cylinders not wired in proper order
    B. poor coolant circulation
    C. resistance unit burned out
    D. defective condenser

1.____

2. In an *expert* system for offboard computer diagnosis, which stage of knowledge acquisition in developing problem-solving rules occurs FIRST?

    A. Implementation   B. Identification
    C. Formalization   D. Conceptualization

2.____

3. Some suspension units consist of tandem axles joined by a single cross support that also acts as a vertical pivot for the entire unit.
These units are known as

    A. axials   B. field frames
    C. bogies   D. helicals

3.____

4. In automotive electronics, the fractional duration that ignition points are closed is known as

    A. slip   B. gain   C. dwell   D. delay

4.____

5. A brake system's warning lights may be tested by

    A. testing the bulbs with an ohmmeter
    B. depressing the brake pedal and opening a wheel cylinder bleeder screw
    C. jumping the wires at the brake distributor switch assembly
    D. testing the system with an ammeter

5.____

6. Of the following procedures performed prior to grinding a valve seat, which should be performed FIRST?

    A. Reaming   B. Adjusting
    C. Cleaning   D. Replacement

6.____

7. What type of clutch is responsible for controlling a car's air conditioning compressor?

    A. Centrifugal   B. Free-wheeling
    C. Magnetic   D. Mechanical

7.____

8. Which of the following is a DISADVANTAGE associated with onboard computer diagnostic systems?

    A. Inability to incorporate self-diagnosis
    B. Limited number of systems available for diagnosis

8.____

C. Cannot be manually activated
D. Inability to detect intermittent failures

9. Which parts in a motor or generator contact the rotating armature commutator or rings?　9.____

A. Cams　　　B. Brushes　　　C. Rod caps　　　D. Bushings

10. What is the MAIN advantage associated with the use of offboard computer diagnostic systems?　10.____

A. Decreased task load
B. Continuous testing intervals
C. Can be manually activated by the driver
D. Capable of simultaneous multiple diagnoses

11. An EGO sensor used in a microprocessor-based control/diagnostic system　11.____

A. is perfectly linear
B. is unaffected by temperature
C. has two different output levels, depending on the fuel mixture
D. is unaffected by engine exhaust levels

12. To what drive train component is the ring gear in the differential bolted?　12.____

A. Drive pinion　　　　　　B. Axle shaft
C. Differential case　　　　D. Carrier

13. What is transmitted by the slip rings on an automotive alternator?　13.____

A. Alternating current to the field coils
B. Alternating current from the stator windings
C. Direct current from the field coils
D. Direct current to the alternator output terminals

14. Which of the following is a PROBABLE cause of an engine's missing at low speed?　14.____

A. Poor compression
B. Leaky head gasket
C. Carbon deposits in cylinders
D. Loose flywheel

15. In order for an onboard computer diagnostic system to detect a failure in the car's electronic system, the failure must be　15.____

A. associated with engine performance
B. intermittent
C. symptomatic
D. nonreversible

16. What is the term for the part of a shaft which rotates in a bearing?　16.____

A. Lunette　　　B. Journal　　　C. Jackshaft　　　D. Kingpin

17. What is the USUAL steering gear reduction for passenger vehicles?   17.____
    _____-to-1.

    A. 2   B. 4   C. 8   D. 12

18. What is indicated by a low reading from 5 to 10 on an engine vacuum test?   18.____

    A. Broken piston ring   B. Weak cylinders
    C. Late valve timing   D. Valve sticking

19. Which of the following is NOT a component of the automotive power train?   19.____

    A. Steering gear   B. Clutch
    C. Transmission   D. Differential

20. Which instrument is NORMALLY used to check the condition of a resistance spark plug?   20.____

    A. Voltmeter   B. Ohmmeter
    C. Ammeter   D. Potentiometer

21. Which device is used to measure the resistance of a circuit or electrical machine?   21.____

    A. Ohmmeter   B. Voltmeter   C. Resistor   D. Ammeter

22. What reading will appear on an infrared meter which indicates a failure of the catalytic   22.____
    converter?
    _____ HC/ _____ CO.

    A. Low; high   B. Low; low
    C. High; low   D. High; high

23. In automatic transmissions, the servo   23.____

    A. operates the shifter valves
    B. applies the clutch
    C. applies the bands
    D. controls the output from the variable vane pump

24. If an onboard diagnostic system's fault code indicates that the O_2 sensor is not ready, all   24.____
    of the following are possible causes EXCEPT

    A. O_2 sensor is not functioning correctly
    B. defective connections or leads
    C. lack of O_2 contacting sensor
    D. control unit is not processing O_2 signal

25. The mechanical compressor in a car's air conditioning system is driven by   25.____

    A. an electric motor   B. the axles
    C. the propeller shaft   D. the crankshaft

KEY (CORRECT ANSWERS)

1.	B	11.	C
2.	B	12.	C
3.	C	13.	C
4.	C	14.	A
5.	B	15.	D
6.	C	16.	B
7.	C	17.	B
8.	D	18.	C
9.	B	19.	A
10.	A	20.	B

21.	A
22.	C
23.	C
24.	C
25.	D

TEST 2

DIRECTIONS: Each question or incomplete statement is followed by several suggested, answers or completions. Select the one that BEST answers the question or completes the statement. *PRINT THE LETTER OF THE CORRECT ANSWER IN THE SPACE AT THE RIGHT.*

1. When installing disc brake linings, a hammer should be used to   1.____

    A. tighten the shoe retainer
    B. seat the pads in the calipers
    C. shape the pads
    D. remove the linings

2. What engine component is lubricated by the oil squirt hole in the connecting rod?   2.____

    A. Connecting rod bearing   B. Crankshaft
    C. Cylinder wall   D. Piston pin

3. Which of the following is a PROBABLE cause of backfiring through a carburetor?   3.____

    A. Short circuit in switch   B. Water in gasoline
    C. Overheating   D. Sticky thermostat

4. What is the GREATEST danger associated with hydraulic braking systems?   4.____

    A. Uneven braking
    B. Defective metering valve
    C. Loss of brake fluid
    D. Dirty or clogged wheel cylinder

5. Under what conditions must an engine be operated during a cylinder balance test?   5.____

    A. With the spark plugs firing, one at a time, at 1500 rpm
    B. With all plugs shorted but two which fire at non-simultaneous equal intervals, at 1500 rpm
    C. At idle speed, with all plugs shorted but two which fire at non-simultaneous equal intervals
    D. At idle speed, with the spark plugs shorted, one at a time

6. Which of the following is a requisite property of brake fluid?   6.____

    A. Has detergents for keeping hoses unobstructed
    B. High wetting characteristics
    C. High viscosity
    D. High boiling point and low freezing point

7. What is measured by the mass airflow sensor in a microprocessor-based control/diagnostic system?   7.____
The

    A. rate at which air is flowing into an engine
    B. composition of a given mass of air
    C. rate at which exhaust is flowing out of an engine
    D. density of atmospheric air

8. What is placed at the joint of a steel frame in order to strengthen the joint? 8.____

    A. Wobble plate
    C. Jackshaft
    B. Gusset plate
    D. Lint pin

9. What is indicated if a combustion meter reading is 10% higher with the air cleaner in place than when the air cleaner has been removed? 9.____

    A. Clogged injectors
    C. Clogged vent
    B. Dirty air cleaner
    D. Normal operation

10. Which of the following is a PROBABLE cause of an engine failing to stop? 10.____

    A. Lack of pressure on gasoline tank
    B. Disconnected magneto ground
    C. High altitude
    D. Spark plug gaps too wide

11. Automotive sensors used in computer-operated diagnostic or control systems typically see changes in each of the following EXCEPT 11.____

    A. electrical signals
    C. position
    B. temperature
    D. pressure

12. What type of feeler gauge should be used to set the gap on a new set of spark plugs? 12.____

    A. Flat   B. Ramp-type   C. Wire   D. Round

13. Intake and exhaust manifolds are built with their walls contacting each other in order to 13.____

    A. reduce atomization
    C. facilitate valve action
    B. pre-heat the fuel mixture
    D. conserve space

14. Fuel tank vapors stored in the charcoal canister 14.____

    A. are released to the atmosphere through a bleed valve
    B. are released to the atmosphere through a port in the canister
    C. are cycled back into the fuel tank
    D. become part of the fuel mixture when the engine is started

15. The information handled by a computerized engine control system flows from 15.____

    A. computer to sensor to display
    B. actuator to display to computer
    C. sensor to computer to actuator
    D. sensor to display to computer

16. In a car with manual transmission, spring pressure clamps the friction disc between the pressure plate and the _____ when the clutch is engaged. 16.____

    A. sun gear
    C. flywheel
    B. reaction plate
    D. differential

17. If the insulation material used with a crimp connector on electric wiring is coded red, what range of gauges is considered typical? 17.____

    A. 10-12   B. 12-18   C. 14-16   D. 18-22

18. An air conditioning system's expansion valve controls the   18.____

    A. pressure of refrigerant in the compressor
    B. temperature of refrigerant in the condenser
    C. amount of refrigerant in the evaporator
    D. temperature of air in the car's interior

19. Each of the following is a probable cause of engine overheating EXCEPT   19.____

    A. slipping fan belt
    B. frozen radiator
    C. improper valve timing
    D. short circuit in distributor rotor

20. When using a short finder to trace a short circuit, which of the following steps should be   20.____
performed LAST?

    A. Turn on all switches in a series with the circuit being tested
    B. Move the short finder meter along circuit wiring
    C. Remove the blown fuse while leaving the battery connected
    D. Connect the pulse unit of short finder across the fuse terminals

21. If a light load test is performed on a battery and the battery shows less than 1.95 volts in   21.____
all cells, then the battery

    A. is overly discharged   B. should be replaced
    C. needs charging   D. is in good condition

22. A *thermistor* is a   22.____

    A. newly-developed type of transistor
    B. device for regulating engine temperature
    C. temperature control system operated by a car passenger
    D. semiconductor temperature sensor

23. An *expert* system for offboard computer diagnosis differs from other computerized diag-   23.____
nostic systems because it is capable of

    A. carrying out several diagnostic operations at once
    B. recommending repair procedures
    C. determining the causes of problems without manual assistance
    D. sensing faults in a circuitry that is not related to engine performance

24. In which type of engine are all valves contained in the cylinder block?   24.____

    A. V-type   B. Two-stroke
    C. F-head   D. L-head

25. The function of a MAP sensor in a microprocessor-based control/diagnostic system is to   25.____

    A. sense anomalous changes in a vehicle's traveling direction
    B. measure changes in mean atmospheric pressure
    C. measure manifold absolute pressure
    D. measure fluctuations in manifold air flow

KEY (CORRECT ANSWERS)

1.	C		11.	A
2.	C		12.	C
3.	D		13.	B
4.	C		14.	D
5.	B		15.	C
6.	D		16.	C
7.	A		17.	D
8.	B		18.	C
9.	B		19.	C
10.	B		20.	B

21.	A
22.	D
23.	B
24.	D
25.	C

———

TEST 3

DIRECTIONS: Each question or incomplete statement is followed by several suggested answers or completions. Select the one that BEST answers the question or completes the statement. *PRINT THE LETTER OF THE CORRECT ANSWER IN THE SPACE AT THE RIGHT.*

1. What is indicated by a sudden periodic drop of 1 or 2 points during a vacuum test on a car's engine?

1.____

   A. Spark plug failure
   C. Coil failure
   B. Damaged distributor cap
   D. Low oil pressure

2. A stud axle is articulated to an axle-beam or steering head by means of a

2.____

   A. journal
   C. gusset plate
   B. kingpin
   D. poppet

3. Which of the following should be checked FIRST when examining a front suspension?

3.____

   A. Kingpins
   C. Bumper and frame level
   B. Steering connections
   D. Suspension arm pivots

4. Which of the following procedures involving a combustion efficiency tester will detect manifold leaks?

4.____

   A. Accelerating the engine to fast speed and checking for meter deflection
   B. Pumping the accelerator and checking for instant response in the combustion meter
   C. Applying a kerosene/oil mixture to the flange and manifold gaskets and checking for meter deflection
   D. Placing the engine on full choke and checking for meter deflection

5. If a car's battery is always fully charged, which of the following should be checked?

5.____

   A. Short circuiting in alternator
   B. Output amperage of the alternator
   C. Volt regulator output
   D. Volt regulator points

6. Which of the following are companion cylinders in a car's V-8 engine?

6.____

   A. 1 and 8   B. 2 and 8   C. 3 and 4   D. 2 and 7

7. Which of the following is a PROBABLE cause of firing in a car's muffler?

7.____

   A. Too rich a fuel mixture
   B. Carbon deposits in cylinder
   C. Improperly adjusted valve tappets
   D. Water in gasoline

8. What is the MAJOR benefit associated with the use of *expert* offboard computer diagnostic systems?

8.____

   A. High task load capability
   B. Continuous testing intervals
   C. Consistent application of problem-solving strategies
   D. Simultaneous multiple-system capability

9. Which type of valve is used to sense how fast a vehicle is traveling?   9.____

   A. Throttle   B. Governor   C. Manual   D. Modulator

10. A two-unit alternator is composed of a   10.____

   A. voltage limiter and current limiter
   B. current limiter and reverse current relay
   C. voltage limiter and field relay
   D. current limiter and field relay

11. Which type of gears are used for the forward speeds of fully synchronized standard transmissions?   11.____

   A. Helical   B. Double helical
   C. Hypoid   D. Spur

12. When checking a circuit for voltage drop, which of the following steps should be performed FIRST?   12.____

   A. Select the voltmeter range just above the battery circuit
   B. Connect the positive lead of the voltmeter to the end of the wire closest to the battery
   C. Connect the negative lead of the voltmeter to the end of the wire farthest from the battery
   D. Switch on the circuit

13. Each of the following is a probable cause of engine knocking EXCEPT   13.____

   A. compression too low   B. loose piston
   C. spark too far advanced   D. engine overheated

14. In what portion of an *expert* system for offboard computer diagnosis are logical operations performed?   14.____

   A. Domain   B. Inference engine
   C. Knowledge base   D. Interface

15. In the propeller shaft of an automotive transmission, a universal joint allows variation in the   15.____

   A. speed of rotation   B. angle of drive
   C. length of the shaft   D. direction of rotation

16. Which of the following is a POSSIBLE use for an engine analyzer?   16.____

   A. Setting the choke
   B. Measuring intake fuel flow rate
   C. Setting ignition points
   D. Measuring fuel mixture

17. What is the term for the smaller of two mating or meshing gears?   17.____

   A. Linch   B. Master   C. Pinion   D. Pilot

18. Conditioned air in an automotive air conditioning system is cooled as it passes through the   18.____

    A. condenser   B. evaporator
    C. compressor   D. receiver

19. In order to determine the correct valve timing of an engine, the opening and closing of the valves should be measured in reference to the   19.____

    A. cylinder compression ratio
    B. fuel mixing jets
    C. distributor setting
    D. piston position

20. In modern engines using computer-based control systems, diagnosis is performed   20.____

    A. with an engine analyzer
    B. with a timing light *only*
    C. with a timing light and voltmeter
    D. in the digital control system

21. What is the MOST probable cause of a car drifting from side to side on a level road?   21.____

    A. Bent steering arm
    B. Tight shock absorber
    C. Loose steering connections
    D. Bent axle

22. Which device, as part of a special type of pump, drives plungers back and forth as it rotates, producing the pumping action?   22.____

    A. Trunnion   B. Torus
    C. Camber link   D. Wobble plate

23. In a microprocessor-based control/diagnostic system, a typical engine crankshaft angular position sensor is MOST effectively located on the   23.____

    A. camshaft   B. crankshaft
    C. compressor pulley   D. flywheel

24. Which type of gauge will allow a mechanic to MOST accurately set the proper electrode gap on a spark plug?   24.____

    A. Flat feeler   B. Round wire feeler
    C. Square wire feeler   D. Dial

25. What type of logical rule bases are programmed into MOST expert diagnostic systems?   25.____

    A. Either/or   B. Set/subset
    C. If/then   D. Inductive

KEY (CORRECT ANSWERS)

1.	A		11.	A
2.	B		12.	B
3.	C		13.	A
4.	C		14.	B
5.	C		15.	B
6.	B		16.	C
7.	A		17.	C
8.	C		18.	B
9.	B		19.	D
10.	C		20.	D

21.	C
22.	D
23.	B
24.	B
25.	C

EXAMINATION SECTION
TEST 1

DIRECTIONS: Each question or incomplete statement is followed by several suggested answers or completions. Select the one that BEST answers the question or completes the statement. *PRINT THE LETTER OF THE CORRECT ANSWER IN THE SPACE AT THE RIGHT.*

1. A mechanic who discovers that the friction-disc facing of a dry clutch is saturated with oil should

    A. use a heavier oil
    B. wash the facing in solvent
    C. replace the facing
    D. increase clutch spring pressure

1.____

2. Which of the following steps, performed prior to the removal of a transmission oil cooler, should occur FIRST?

    A. Removal of transmission case
    B. Removal of valve body assembly
    C. Checking transmission fluid level
    D. Draining radiator

2.____

3. An alternator voltage regulator controls alternator output by

    A. grounding the negative diodes
    B. grounding the stator windings
    C. controlling the voltage output at the B terminal
    D. controlling the current feed to the rotor

3.____

4. Which clutch part is located between the engine flywheel and the pressure plate?

    A. Release lever   B. Fork
    C. Friction disc   D. Adjusting screw

4.____

5. In a digital microcomputer used for the control or diagnosis of an automotive engine, some device is needed to convert the computer's output data into a form readable by people.
The components which serve this function are known as

    A. data buses   B. microprocessors
    C. peripherals   D. accumulators

5.____

6. What is being adjusted when a mechanic pulls the entire control arm toward the frame?

    A. Caster   B. Camber
    C. Tracking   D. Kingpin inclination

6.____

7. Which of the following is a characteristic that could NOT typically be identified by an onboard computer diagnostic system?

    A. Faulty EGR circuits   B. The cause of a short circuit
    C. Low ECT input   D. Lean fuel mixture

7.____

8. In an automatic transmission, the oil filter is USUALLY secured by means of   8.___

    A. screws or a clip   B. the oil pan
    C. a bracket assembly   D. a spring

9. In a microprocessor-based control/diagnostic system, which type of actuator recirculates   9.___
exhaust gas to the intake charge?

    A. Fuel metering   B. Ignition
    C. EGR   D. EGO

10. Which of the following is a PROBABLE cause of an engine's missing at high speed?   10.___

    A. Carbon deposits in cylinder
    B. Scored cylinder
    C. Short circuit in distributor rotor
    D. Weak valve spring

11. Which of the following operations is performed by a sensor in a microprocessor-based   11.___
control/diagnostic system?

    A. Sending signals to the driver
    B. Selecting the transmission gear ratio
    C. Measuring variables in physical qualities
    D. Serving as an output device

12. When a hydraulic brake pedal is released quickly, the initial makeup fluid is supplied to   12.___
the master cylinder's pressure chamber through the

    A. piston bleeder holes   B. compensating port
    C. check valve   D. port holes

13. Which part of a transaxle drives the output shafts?   13.___

    A. Ring gear assembly   B. Pinion gears
    C. Side gears   D. Chain

14. Which of the following problems would be MOST difficult to solve with an onboard com-   14.___
puter diagnostic system?

    A. Air pump switching valve failure
    B. Imbalanced injectors
    C. Fuel pump circuit fault
    D. Defective electronic spark timing circuit

15. What is the MOST likely cause of a buzzing noise in the automatic transmission?   15.___

    A. Vacuum leakage   B. Malfunctioning front pump
    C. Bent pilot shaft   D. Worn clutch plates

16. What is the function of an actuator in a microprocessor-based control/diagnostic system?   16.___

    A. Indicates results of a measurement
    B. Creates a response to an electrical signal
    C. Serves as an input device
    D. Provides a mathematical model for an engine

17. The constant flow method of fuel injection places its burden on each of the following components EXCEPT
17._____

    A. an engine-driven injection pump equipped with plungers
    B. injector nozzles
    C. metering valve
    D. bypass unit

18. Which device is used specifically to regulate current by means of variable resistance?
18._____

    A. Capacitor   B. Rheostat
    C. Ohmmeter   D. Volute

19. Which type of spring is used in a spring-loaded disc clutch?
19._____

    A. Cantilever   B. Volute
    C. Helical   D. Diaphragm

20. When the engine is running, power steering fluid travels from
20._____

    A. control valve to reservoir to pump
    B. pump to control valve to reservoir
    C. reservoir to pump to control valve
    D. reservoir to control valve to pump

21. *Piezoresistivity* is
21._____

    A. a resistance property of insulators
    B. a property of certain semiconductors in which resistivity varies with strain
    C. the ratio of resistivity in a semiconductor to the property being measured by a sensor
    D. a type of metal bonding pad

22. Which of the following would be a PROBABLE cause of engine stoppage?
22._____

    A. Fuel pump breakdown
    B. Disconnected magneto ground
    C. High altitude
    D. Blown cylinder-head gasket

23. If the insulation material used with a crimp connector on electric wiring is coded yellow, what range of gauges is considered typical?
23._____

    A. 10-12   B. 12-18   C. 14-16   D. 18-22

24. What is the MOST common firing order of an in-line 6-cylinder engine?
24._____

    A. 1-6-2-5-3-4   B. 1-3-6-4-2-5
    C. 1-2-5-6-3-4   D. 1-5-3-6-2-4

25. The pressure sensor of most fuel injection systems is located
25._____

    A. in the injection chamber
    B. at the nozzle port
    C. within the pump housing
    D. beneath the floor, at the side of the engine compartment

KEY (CORRECT ANSWERS)

1.	C		11.	C
2.	D		12.	D
3.	C		13.	C
4.	C		14.	A
5.	C		15.	B
6.	B		16.	B
7.	B		17.	A
8.	A		18.	B
9.	C		19.	A
10.	D		20.	B

21. C
22. A
23. A
24. D
25. D

TEST 2

DIRECTIONS: Each question or incomplete statement is followed by several suggested answers or completions. Select the one that BEST answers the question or completes the statement. *PRINT THE LETTER OF THE CORRECT ANSWER IN THE SPACE AT THE RIGHT.*

1. What is the term for a spring-loaded ball that engages a notch?   1.____

   A. Roller bearing   B. Poppet
   C. Venturi   D. Lunette

2. What changes alternating current to direct current in the alternator?   2.____

   A. Field relay   B. Stator windings
   C. Rotor slip rings   D. Diodes

3. If a mechanic is using an expert diagnostic system and encounters no rules in the con-   3.____
   flict set, what should be done?

   A. Use highest-priority rules for predicted condition
   B. Stop the procedure
   C. Use the rule that most commonly appears under similar conditions
   D. Switch to a different database

4. With which drive train component does a transmission's reverse idler gear ALWAYS   4.____
   mesh?

   A. Clutch plate
   B. Second gear
   C. Countershaft reverse gear
   D. Main shaft reverse gear

5. Which of the following is the MOST probable cause for a noise that is present in the rear   5.____
   end only when a car goes around curves?

   A. Loose universal joint
   B. Trouble in the differential case assembly
   C. Trouble in the drive-pinion assembly
   D. Dry wheel bearing

6. In a microprocessor-based control/diagnostic system, which type of sensor is basically a   6.____
   resistor with a movable contact?

   A. Crankshaft position   B. Throttle angle
   C. EGO   D. Knock

7. What is being indicated by bubbles in an air conditioning sight gauge if the unit has been   7.____
   running for several minutes?

   A. Low refrigerant   B. Low compressor pressure
   C. System leakage   D. Normal operation

8. When checking connecting rods for alignment, the angle the rod aligner mandrel makes   8.____
   with the face plate should be _____ degrees, depending on the type of jig used.

   A. 10 or 20   B. 45 or 90
   C. 90 or 180   D. 180 or 320

9. Which type of fuel injection system typically sprays fuel into each intake port on the manifold side of the intake valve?   9._____

    A. Direct   B. Port
    C. Sequential   D. Single-point

10. The purpose of a suction throttling valve used in an automotive air conditioning system is to   10._____

    A. prevent freezing in the evaporator
    B. control compressor cycles
    C. control the metering of the expansion valve
    D. maintain low condenser pressure

11. In a microprocessor-based electronic control/diagnostic system, which type of actuator consists of a spray nozzle and a solenoid-operated plunger?   11._____

    A. Thermostat   B. Ignition
    C. EGO   D. Fuel injector

12. Which component of a band and servo assembly is DIRECTLY affected by hydraulic pressure?   12._____

    A. Anchor   B. Band
    C. Servo piston   D. Stem

13. If an ammeter shows a small fluctuating reading and a spark test reveals no spark, what is the MOST likely source of the trouble?   13._____

    A. Primary circuit   B. Secondary circuit
    C. Battery   D. Ignition switch

14. All of the following are characteristics of a top-feed fuel injector as opposed to a bottom-feed EXCEPT   14._____

    A. uses incoming air for cooling purposes
    B. higher cost
    C. greater pressure requirements
    D. heavier mass

15. All of the following are probable causes of an engine's lacking power EXCEPT   15._____

    A. too rich a fuel mixture   B. lack of coolant
    C. high altitude   D. leaky manifold gaskets

16. Which device should be used to check for runout or wobble on a disc brake that has been lathe-mounted?   16._____

    A. Timing light   B. Electric meter
    C. Dial indicator   D. Torque wrench

17. A(n) _____ is the term for a wire or wires that form a common path to and from the various components a microcomputer uses for the diagnosis or control of an automotive engine.   17._____

    A. analog   B. runner
    C. bus   D. port

18. The notch on the head of a piston should be facing the _____ during the installation of a piston assembly.

    A. minor thrust side   B. major thrust side
    C. rear of the engine   D. front of the engine

18.____

19. The requisite knowledge and expertise used in an expert diagnostic system's programming is acquired from a person known as the

    A. domain expert   B. user
    C. inference engine   D. knowledge engineer

19.____

20. All of the following are probable causes of an engine's missing at all speeds EXCEPT

    A. valve tappets adjusted too closely
    B. dirty plug
    C. loose piston
    D. leak in intake manifold

20.____

21. The function of a MAP sensor in a microprocessor-based control/diagnostic system is to measure

    A. anomalous changes in a vehicle's traveling direction
    B. changes in mean atmospheric pressure
    C. manifold absolute pressure
    D. fluctuations in manifold air flow

21.____

22. What procedure is recommended upon discovering that brake fluid is contaminated?

    A. Bleed the hydraulic system
    B. Flush the system with alcohol, and then adding clean fluid
    C. Add a detergent oil to the system
    D. Replace the fluid, along with all hydraulic rubber cups and seals

22.____

23. Which of the following could be indicated by a vibrating reading on a vacuum gauge that appears only at high engine speeds?

    A. Pitted distributor points
    B. Incorrect ignition timing
    C. Blow-by
    D. Weak valve springs

23.____

24. In a microprocessor-based control/diagnostic system, which type of sensor uses magnetostrictive techniques?

    A. Knock   B. Throttle angle
    C. EGO   D. MAP

24.____

25. The amount that the steering knuckle pivots are angled away from a true vertical is known as

    A. camber   B. phase   C. tilt   D. caster

25.____

KEY (CORRECT ANSWERS)

1.	B	11.	D
2.	D	12.	C
3.	B	13.	B
4.	C	14.	A
5.	C	15.	D
6.	B	16.	C
7.	A	17.	C
8.	C	18.	D
9.	B	19.	D
10.	A	20.	C

21.	C
22.	D
23.	D
24.	A
25.	D

TEST 3

DIRECTIONS: Each question or incomplete statement is followed by several suggested answers or completions. Select the one that BEST answers the question or completes the statement. *PRINT THE LETTER OF THE CORRECT ANSWER IN THE SPACE AT THE RIGHT.*

1. All of the following are components of a positive crankcase ventilating system EXCEPT the

    A. manifold suction tube
    C. road draft tube
    B. metering valve
    D. intake breather

    1.____

2. The MAXIMUM voltage for sensor and actuator circuits used in onboard diagnostic systems is

    A. 3
    B. 5
    C. 10
    D. 15

    2.____

3. Which of the following is a PROBABLE result of adjusting valves with too little clearance?

    A. Delayed timing
    C. Lower fuel economy
    B. Burning oil
    D. Overheated valves

    3.____

4. In a fuel metering actuator that is used in a microprocessor-based control/diagnostic system, *duty cycle* refers to the ratio of fuel

    A. *off* time to fuel *on* time
    B. *on* time to fuel *off* time
    C. *on* time to fuel *on* time plus fuel *off* time
    D. *off* time to fuel *off* time plus fuel *on* time

    4.____

5. In a synchromesh transmission, gears are engaged by a _____ in order to prevent gear clashing.

    A. slip joint or spline
    C. planetary unit
    B. friction and dog clutch
    D. dog clutch

    5.____

6. An EGO sensor is a

    A. device for measuring the oxygen concentration in automotive engine exhaust
    B. spark plug advance mechanism
    C. device for measuring crankshaft acceleration
    D. device for measuring the concentrations of various exhaust gases

    6.____

7. What type of expander must be used under an oil ring?

    A. Step joint
    C. Rigid
    B. Diagonal joint
    D. Vented

    7.____

8. Which of the following procedures is included in the performance of a compression test on a car engine?

    A. Perform entire test while engine is cold
    B. Test one cylinder at a time, with the corresponding plug temporarily removed
    C. Crank for no more than two compression strokes
    D. Block open throttle and choke

    8.____

9. Air enters most Bosch electronic fuel injection systems through the   9.____

    A. oil bath cleaner   B. injector choke
    C. compressor line   D. injector manifold

10. The idler arm is attached to the _____ in a typical steering mechanism linkage.   10.____

    A. center link   B. tie rod
    C. pitman arm   D. spindle

11. In a microprocessor-based control/diagnostic system, which type of crankshaft position   11.____
sensor uses a disk having several holes?

    A. Optical   B. Ignition timing
    C. Hall-effect   D. Magnetic reluctance

12. In a mechanical fuel pump, pressure is maintained by means of   12.____

    A. a spring under the diaphragm
    B. a motor
    C. a needle valve
    D. rotating vanes

13. If a third pump is used in a fuel injection system, it is mounted   13.____

    A. on the fuel tank pump pickup tube
    B. in the line between the pickup tube and the pressure pump
    C. in the line between the pressure pump and fuel metering assembly
    D. at the fuel metering assembly

14. Which part of a cooling system thermostat opens and closes system valves?   14.____

    A. Pressure valve   B. Vacuum valve
    C. Bellows   D. Seater

15. What is the term for the front portion of a vehicle body or cab which partially encloses the   15.____
dash panel and forms the windshield frame?

    A. Cowl   B. Hull   C. Head   D. Mask

16. How many digits make up a fault code used in a typical onboard computer diagnostic   16.____
system?

    A. 1   B. 2   C. 3   D. 4

17. Which of the following should be checked FIRST when all brakes are dragging?   17.____

    A. Brake fluid level
    B. Master cylinder compensating port
    C. Wheel cylinders
    D. Brake pedal free travel

18. Which type of sensor measure is NOT capable of measuring the amount of air flowing   18.____
through a fuel injection system?

    A. Speed-density   B. Plate
    C. Differential   D. Mass airflow

19. Which type of engine contains valves both in the head and the cylinder block?   19.____

    A. V-type   B. Two-stroke   C. F-head   D. L-head

20. Toe-in adjustments made by turning the adjusting sleeves on the tie rods in equal   20.____
    amounts in opposite directions are done to

    A. keep the wheels in balance
    B. keep the steering wheel centered
    C. avoid over-adjustment
    D. prevent excessive steering wheel play

21. Which of the following is NOT a possible cause of an overly lean fuel mixture that   21.____
    appears during a no-load carburetor mixture test?

    A. Plugged metering jets
    B. Stuck float
    C. Bad metering rod adjustment
    D. Manifold air leak

22. Which of the following is NOT a component of a pressure regulator used in fuel injection   22.____
    systems?

    A. Spring   B. Manifold   C. Diaphragm   D. Valve

23. During installation of the transmission, _____ can be used to turn the drive plate in   23.____
    order to connect it with the converter.

    A. the transmission unit   B. the cranking motor
    C. the output shaft   D. a wrench

24. Which type of bearing is NOT used on automotive drive axles?   24.____

    A. Sleeve   B. Roller   C. Taper   D. Ball

25. What is the term for the action or process of producing voltage by the relative motion of a   25.____
    magnetic field and a conductor?

    A. Induction   B. Resistance
    C. Condensation   D. Conduction

KEY (CORRECT ANSWERS)

1.	C		11.	A
2.	B		12.	A
3.	D		13.	D
4.	C		14.	C
5.	B		15.	A
6.	A		16.	B
7.	B		17.	D
8.	D		18.	C
9.	A		19.	C
10.	A		20.	B

21.	C
22.	B
23.	B
24.	A
25.	A

EXAMINATION SECTION
TEST 1

DIRECTIONS: Each question or incomplete statement is followed by several suggested answers or completions. Select the one that BEST answers the question or completes the statement. *PRINT THE LETTER OF THE CORRECT ANSWER IN THE SPACE AT THE RIGHT.*

1. All of the following are probable sources of drivability problems EXCEPT the
   1.____

   A. battery system
   C. ignition system
   B. engine condition
   D. fuel delivery system

2. Bending the _____ is the BEST way to adjust the ignition point contact.
   2.____

   A. movable point arm
   B. breaker plate
   C. stationary point bracket
   D. pivot post

3. If an ignition system's breaker points are pitted, what should a mechanic check FIRST?
   3.____

   A. Distributor condenser
   C. Circuit breaker
   B. Distributor cap
   D. Coil

4. Which cooling system component should be checked if a car's air conditioning blower operates properly but system output is still inadequate?
   4.____

   A. Receiver-drier
   C. Temperature control
   B. Evaporator core
   D. Condenser

5. Excessive wear of brake linings will MOST likely cause
   5.____

   A. stiff pedal
   C. sticky wheel
   B. drum scoring
   D. drag on brakes

6. The PCV valve is connected between the
   6.____

   A. transmission and clutch
   B. injector and fuel pump
   C. exhaust pipe and intake manifold
   D. crankcase and intake manifold

7. What device is MOST effective for checking fuel pump performance?
   7.____

   A. Vacuum switch
   C. Voltmeter
   B. Micrometer
   D. Stethoscope prod

8. For what purpose are the points of a conventional ignition system adjusted to increase the point gap?
   To
   8.____

   A. advance the ignition timing
   B. increase the dwell angle
   C. decrease the dwell angle with no change in timing
   D. slow the ignition timing

9. Which of the following is NOT a type of temperature sensor used in microprocessor-based control/diagnostic systems?

    A. Wire-wound resistor
    B. Potentiometer
    C. Semiconductor resistor
    D. Thermistor

9.____

10. The various relationships and fundamental data associated with the use of an expert diagnostic system are known as the

    A. domain
    B. inference engine
    C. knowledge base
    D. interface

10.____

11. Which type of electric starting motor is often used because of its high starting torque?

    A. Compound-wound
    B. Shunt-wound
    C. Series-wound
    D. Capacitor

11.____

12. The auto system that is LEAST likely to cause engine operating problems is the _____ system.

    A. starting
    B. charging
    C. ignition
    D. fuel injection

12.____

13. Which device is capable of measuring volts, ohms, and amperes in solid-state electronic equipment?

    A. Digital multimeter
    B. Analog multimeter
    C. Jumper wires
    D. Continuity tester

13.____

14. Which of the following is a PROBABLE cause of backfiring in an intake manifold?

    A. Broken connecting rod
    B. Incorrect valve timing
    C. Sticky choke valve
    D. A lean cold-engine fuel mixture

14.____

15. An EGO sensor that is used in a microprocessor-based control/diagnostic system should NOT be used for control at a temperature less than _____ °C.

    A. 0
    B. 100
    C. 200
    D. 300

15.____

16. What is the PROBABLE result of setting a spark plug gap more closely than normal?

    A. Smoother idling
    B. Hard starting
    C. Easier starting
    D. Rougher idling

16.____

17. Adjusting the _____ will help the steering of a car return to a straight position after cornering.

    A. toe-in
    B. toe-out
    C. caster
    D. camber

17.____

18. What is the basic work register in microcomputers that is used for automotive engine control and diagnostics?

    A. Status register
    B. Condition code register
    C. Brancher
    D. Accumulator

18.____

19. A car lacks power and a popping sound can be heard.   19._____
What is the MOST likely cause?

    A. Shorted spark plug   B. Uneven fuel supply
    C. Pitted breaker points   D. Bad distributor timing

20. What is the term for the reinforcing ridge around a tire opening where it fits the wheel   20._____
rim?

    A. Piping   B. Binder   C. Ram   D. Bead

21. When checking a circuit for voltage drop, which of the following steps should be per-   21._____
formed LAST?

    A. Select the voltmeter range just above the battery circuit
    B. Connect the positive lead of the voltmeter to the end of the wire closest to the bat-
tery
    C. Connect the negative lead of the voltmeter to the end of the wire farthest from the
battery
    D. Switch on the circuit

22. If a battery frequently needs recharging, all of the following are probable causes   22._____
EXCEPT

    A. poorly sized alternator drive pulley
    B. cell leakage
    C. poorly grounded voltage regulator
    D. sulfated battery

23. The diagnosis of intermittent failures in computer-based engine control systems is   23._____

    A. readily found using standard service bay equipment
    B. accomplished by displaying fault codes to the driver at the time of the failure
    C. sometimes accomplished by means of warning lamps on the dash display
    D. routinely accomplished with the onboard diagnostic capability of the control system

24. Before disassembling an air-release parking brake, it is necessary to FIRST   24._____

    A. remove the diaphragm clamp
    B. remove the quick release valve
    C. compress the apply spring
    D. fill the air reservoir

25. What is the MOST probable result of incorrect camber on car wheels?   25._____

    A. Abnormal tire wear along one side of the tread
    B. Damaged shocks
    C. Front-end shimmy
    D. Pulling to the side while braking

_____

KEY (CORRECT ANSWERS)

1.	A		11.	C
2.	C		12.	D
3.	A		13.	A
4.	C		14.	D
5.	B		15.	D
6.	D		16.	D
7.	D		17.	B
8.	A		18.	D
9.	B		19.	B
10.	C		20.	D

21.	D
22.	B
23.	C
24.	C
25.	A

TEST 2

DIRECTIONS: Each question or incomplete statement is followed by several suggested answers or completions. Select the one that BEST answers the question or completes the statement. *PRINT THE LETTER OF THE CORRECT ANSWER IN THE SPACE AT THE RIGHT.*

1. The fuel pump in MOST fuel injection systems operates when the engine has oil pressure, and when the cranking speed is above _____ rpm.

    A. 50-75   B. 150-200   C. 500-1000   D. 1000-2000

    1.____

2. What is indicated by an occasional 3-4 inch drop in a vacuum gauge test?

    A. Slowed timing   B. Carburetor failure
    C. Valve sticking   D. Incorrectly gapped plugs

    2.____

3. All of the following are types of compressors used in automotive air conditioning systems EXCEPT

    A. 90-degree *V*   B. 2-cylinder in-line
    C. axial   D. hermetically sealed

    3.____

4. How much free action does a mechanic typically allow in the brake pedal?

    A. None   B. 1/8 inch   C. 1/4 inch   D. 1/2 inch

    4.____

5. Tire wear that is concentrated on both sides of the tread is USUALLY the result of

    A. toe-out   B. improper balance
    C. over-inflation   D. under-inflation

    5.____

6. Temperature sensors that are a part of microprocessor-based electronic control/diagnostic systems use a type of semiconductor to measure temperature.
   The resistance of this semiconductor

    A. is always 100,000 ohms
    B. varies in direct proportion to temperature
    C. varies in inverse proportion to temperature
    D. varies in direct proportion to engine speed

    6.____

7. Using a test lamp across the breaker points, and with the ignition switch on, a mechanic will rotate the _____ to obtain the correct timing.

    A. distributor housing until the light goes out
    B. distributor housing until the light goes on
    C. engine until the light goes out
    D. engine until the light goes on

    7.____

8. In constant-flow fuel injection systems, pressure and circulation are provided by a(n)

    A. injection pump
    B. hydraulic line
    C. engine-driven rotary pump
    D. bellows

    8.____

9. Which of the following could NOT be determined by using an armature growler to test a starting motor armature? 9.____

    A. Insulation condition   B. Location of short circuits
    C. Amount of resistance   D. Commutator condition

10. What is measured by the crankshaft angular position sensor in a microprocessor-based control/diagnostic system? 10.____
The

    A. oil pressure angle
    B. angle between a line drawn through a crankshaft axis, a mark on the flywheel, and a reference line
    C. angle between the connecting rods and the crankshaft
    D. pitch angle of the crankshaft

11. If the insulation material used with a crimp connector on electric wiring is coded blue, what range of gauges is considered typical? 11.____

    A. 10-12   B. 12-18   C. 14-16   D. 18-22

12. Which type of pump is used ONLY as a supply pump in some fuel injection systems? 12.____

    A. Rotary   B. Diaphragm   C. Turbine   D. Roller

13. In what part of a car's air conditioning system does the refrigerant lose heat? 13.____

    A. Receiver   B. Compressor
    C. Condenser   D. Evaporator

14. When disc brake pads are retracted so as not to make contact with the rotor surface, the amount of retraction 14.____

    A. is limited by the metering valve
    B. must be a minimum of 1/16 inch
    C. is affected by the piston return springs
    D. is affected by the piston seals

15. What is the term for the high curved portion of a cam that produces maximum valve lift? 15.____

    A. Peak   B. Nose circle
    C. Flank circle   D. Radial circle

16. The current from a battery generally flows to the alternator _____ when a vehicle is started. 16.____

    A. rectifier   B. rotor windings
    C. stator windings   D. commutator

17. If the cam dwell angle of a distributor is less than the specified minimum, it is LIKELY that the 17.____

    A. rubbing block will wear down
    B. distributor contact points will become pitted
    C. ignition coil output will increase at high engine speeds
    D. ignition timing will be off

18. The ignition quality of diesel fuel is measured against an index known as the   18.____

    A. lean parameter   B. cetane rating
    C. atomization ratio   D. vortex flow chart

19. During timing operations on a six-cylinder engine, a timing light should be connected to   19.____
spark plug number

    A. 6   B. 4   C. 2   D. 1

20. In a microprocessor-based control/diagnostic system, which type of actuator serves to   20.____
lower NO emissions?

    A. Ignition   B. Fuel metering
    C. EGR   D. EGO

21. What is indicated by a faintly vibrating needle during an engine vacuum test?   21.____

    A. Weak cylinders
    B. Leaking valves
    C. Obstruction in the exhaust system
    D. A broken piston ring

22. Which of the following components is NOT carried by a car's wheel knuckle assembly?   22.____

    A. Disc brake caliper mounting
    B. Rotor
    C. Steering arm
    D. Drum backing plate

23. If a mechanic hears a squealing noise during operation after the installation of an auto-   23.____
matic transmission, what is the MOST likely source of the trouble?

    A. Rear bearing
    B. Regulator body mating surfaces
    C. Speedometer pinion
    D. Front pump drive sleeve or pump pinion

24. How should a mechanic decrease ignition point dwell?   24.____

    A. Rotate distributor body in the direction opposite the distributor shaft rotation
    B. Install weaker springs in the advance unit
    C. Increase the point gap
    D. Decrease the point gap

25. Before charging a battery, the battery ground cable should be disconnected at the bat-   25.____
tery.
This is done in order to protect the

    A. alternator regulator   B. alternator diodes
    C. ignition coil   D. ignition module

KEY (CORRECT ANSWERS)

1.	B		11.	C
2.	C		12.	C
3.	D		13.	C
4.	C		14.	D
5.	D		15.	B
6.	C		16.	B
7.	B		17.	D
8.	C		18.	B
9.	C		19.	D
10.	B		20.	C

21. A
22. B
23. D
24. A
25. B

———

TEST 3

DIRECTIONS: Each question or incomplete statement is followed by several suggested answers or completions. Select the one that BEST answers the question or completes the statement. *PRINT THE LETTER OF THE CORRECT ANSWER IN THE SPACE AT THE RIGHT.*

1. Against what part of a bearing do rollers or balls move?   1.____

   A. Sleeve   B. Spread   C. Knuckle   D. Race

2. All of the following are desirable characteristics of an EGO sensor used in a micropro-   2.____
   cessor-based electronic control/diagnostic system EXCEPT

   A. variable voltages with respect to exhaust temperature
   B. rapid switching of output voltage in response to exhaust gas oxygen changes
   C. abrupt change in voltage at the optimal combustion ratio
   D. large difference in sensor output voltage between rich and lean mixture conditions

3. A _____ joint is used to allow changes in the length of a propeller shaft.   3.____

   A. slip   B. shaft   C. universal   D. idler

4. Which of the following should be adjusted LAST in performing a tune-up on a car with a   4.____
   carburetor?

   A. Drive belts
   B. Manifold heat control valve
   C. Carburetor
   D. EGR valve

5. What device operates the plungers in a fuel injection pump?   5.____

   A. Pump camshaft   B. Belt
   C. Engine camshaft   D. Drive chain

6. Ignition of the combustion charge before the spark has formed across the plug elec-   6.____
   trodes is known as

   A. cold firing   B. knocking
   C. backfiring   D. preignition

7. Gear-train end play can be adjusted by   7.____

   A. changing the snap ring
   B. removing the clutch plates and installing retainer rings
   C. changing the selective thrust washer
   D. installing different pinion carriers

8. Unlike a conventional spark plug, a resistor plug will   8.____

   A. require higher voltage to function
   B. lengthen the capacitive part of the spark
   C. shrink the inductive part of the spark
   D. have an auxiliary air gap

9. Which measuring device is used MAINLY to check for voltage in a circuit while power is connected to the circuit?

    A. Digital multimeter   B. Jumper wires
    C. Test lights   D. Short finder

9.____

10. The flexible link that allows a suspension spring's length to change as it flexes is the

    A. shackle   B. strut
    C. flange   D. trailing arm

10.____

11. What type of electrical connectors are generally used with components that are occasionally disconnected?

    A. Crimp   B. Bullet
    C. Butt   D. Snap-splice

11.____

12. Which of the following devices is NOT appropriate for checking the distributor automatic advance operations?

    A. Tachometer   B. Voltmeter
    C. Vacuum pump   D. Timing light

12.____

13. Engine bearings are commonly made from each of the following materials EXCEPT

    A. babbit   B. case-hardened steel
    C. aluminum   D. copper-lead mix

13.____

14. What should be used with bolts or screws on bearing surfaces designed to retain end thrust?

    A. Toggles   B. Plain washers
    C. Thrust washers   D. Lock washers

14.____

15. An automotive technician's basic measurement tool is the

    A. dial gauge   B. feeler gauge
    C. telescopic gauge   D. micrometer

15.____

16. What is used to attach a thrust plate to an engine block?

    A. Sheet metal screws   B. Cap screws
    C. Wire spring clips   D. Stamped metal clips

16.____

17. In an *expert* system for offboard computer diagnosis, which stage of knowledge acquisition in developing problem-solving rules occurs LAST?

    A. Implementation   B. Identification
    C. Formalization   D. Conceptualization

17.____

18. All of the following are possible causes of incorrect steering axis inclination and toe-out figures EXCEPT

    A. worn tires   B. bent suspension
    C. worn ball joint   D. worn steering parts

18.____

19. In a magnetic circuit, reluctance is a quality that is analogous to the _____ of an electrical circuit.   19.____

    A. capacitance   B. voltage
    C. amperage   D. resistance

20. Which device is used MAINLY to check for both open and short circuits?   20.____

    A. Short finder   B. Jumper wires
    C. Test light   D. Continuity tester

21. Which type of spring is MOST commonly used in automotive suspension systems?   21.____

    A. Torsion bar   B. Coil spring
    C. Multiple-leaf spring   D. Monoleaf spring

22. At the most basic level, the special type of language used to form microcomputer instructions, such as the ones used in automotive controls and diagnostics, is known as   22.____

    A. digital coding   B. assembly language
    C. branch language   D. fault coding

23. Most automotive camshafts are made from   23.____

    A. hardenable alloy cast-iron
    B. steel
    C. sintered iron
    D. tempered aluminum alloy

24. What progressively increasing quality should be indicated by a combustion tester as an engine accelerates from idle to cruising speeds?   24.____

    A. Higher rate of combustion
    B. Higher fuel-air ratio
    C. Lower thermal efficiency
    D. Leaner fuel mixture

25. What sizing process conforms metal to size by applying pressure?   25.____

    A. Stamping   B. Burnishing
    C. Canting   D. Beading

———

KEY (CORRECT ANSWERS)

1.	D		11.	B
2.	A		12.	B
3.	A		13.	B
4.	C		14.	C
5.	A		15.	D
6.	D		16.	B
7.	C		17.	A
8.	C		18.	A
9.	C		19.	D
10.	A		20.	D

21.	B
22.	B
23.	A
24.	D
25.	B

———————

EXAMINATION SECTION
TEST 1

DIRECTIONS: Each question or incomplete statement is followed by several suggested answers or completions. Select the one that BEST answers the question or completes the statement. *PRINT THE LETTER OF THE CORRECT ANSWER IN THE SPACE AT THE RIGHT.*

1. A supervisor was given a booklet that showed a new work method that could save time. He didn't tell his men because he thought that they would get the booklet anyway.
   For the supervisor to have acted like this is a

   A. *good* idea because he saves the time and bother of talking to the men
   B. *bad* idea because he should make sure his men know about better work methods
   C. *good* idea because the men would rather read about it themselves
   D. *bad* idea because a supervisor should always show his men every memo he gets from higher authority

1.____

2. A supervisor found it necessary to discipline two subordinates. One man had been operating his equipment in a wrong way, while the other man came to work late for three days in a row. The supervisor decided to talk to both men together.
   For the supervisor to deal with the problems in this way is a

   A. *good* idea because each man will learn about the difficulties of the other person and how to solve such difficulties
   B. *bad* idea because the supervisor should wait until he can bring a larger group together and save time in discussing such questions
   C. *good* idea because he will be able to get the men to see that their problems are related
   D. *bad* idea because he should meet with each man separately and give him his full attention

2.____

3. A supervisor should try to make his men feel their jobs are important in order to

   A. get the men to say good things about their supervisor to his own superior
   B. get the men to think in terms of advancing to better jobs
   C. let higher management in the agency know that the supervisor is efficient
   D. help the men to be able to work more efficiently and enthusiastically

3.____

4. A supervisor should know approximately how long it takes to do a particular kind of job CHIEFLY because he

   A. will know how much time to take if he has to do it himself
   B. will be able to tell his men to do it even faster
   C. can judge the performance of the person doing the job
   D. can retrain experienced employees in better work habits

4.____

5. Supervisors often get their employees' opinions about better work methods because

   A. the men will know that they are respected
   B. the men would otherwise lose all their confidence in the supervisor
   C. the supervisor might find in this way a good suggestion he could use
   D. this is the best method for improvement of work methods

5.____

6. Right after you have trained your subordinates in doing a new job, you find that they seem to be doing all right, but that it will take them several days to finish. You also have several groups of men working at other locations. The MOST efficient way for you to make sure that the men continue doing the new job properly is to

    6.____

    A. stay on that job with the men until it is finished just in case trouble develops
    B. visit the men every half hour until the job is done
    C. stay away from their job that day and visit the men the next day to ask them if they had any problems
    D. visit the men a few times each day until they finish the new job

7. Assume that one of your new employees is older than you are. You also think that he may be hard to get along with because he is older than you. The BEST way for you to avoid any problems with the older worker is for you to

    7.____

    A. lay down the law immediately and tell the man he better not cause you any trouble
    B. treat the man just the way you would any other worker
    C. always ask the older worker for advice in the presence of all the men
    D. ignore the man entirely until he realizes that you are the boss

8. Assume that you have tried a new method suggested by one of your employees and find that it is easier and cheaper than the method you had been using.
The proper thing for you to do NEXT is to

    8.____

    A. say nothing to anyone but train your men to use the new method
    B. train your men to use the new method and tell your crew that you got the idea from one of the men
    C. continue using the old method because a supervisor should not use suggestions of his men
    D. have your crew learn the new method and take credit for the idea since you are the boss

9. Suppose you are a supervisor and your superior tells you that the way your men are doing a certain procedure is wrong and that you should re-train your men as soon as possible.
When you begin to re-train the men, the FIRST thing you should do is

    9.____

    A. tell your men that a wrong procedure had been used and that a new method must be learned as a result
    B. train your employees in the new method with no explanation since you are the boss
    C. tell the crew that your superior has just decided that everyone should learn a new method
    D. tell the crew that your superior says your method is wrong but that you don't agree with this

10. It is BAD practice to criticize a man in front of the other men because

    10.____

    A. people will think you are too strict
    B. it is annoying to anyone who walks by
    C. it is embarrassing to the man concerned
    D. it will antagonize the other men

11. A supervisor decides not to put his two best men on a work detail because he knows that 11.____
they won't like it.
For the supervisor to make the work assignment this way is a

    A. *good* idea because it is only fair to give your best men a break once in a while
    B. *bad* idea because you should treat all of your men fairly and not show favoritism
    C. *good* idea because you save the strength of these men for another job
    D. *bad* idea because more of the men should be exempted from the assignment

12. Suppose you are a supervisor and you find it inconvenient to obey an established proce- 12.____
dure set by your agency. You think another procedure would be better.
The BEST thing to do first about this procedure that you don't like is for you to

    A. obey the procedure even if you don't want to and suggest your idea to your own
       supervisor
    B. disregard the procedure because a supervisor is supposed to have some privi-
       leges
    C. follow the procedure some of the time but ignore it when the men are not watching
    D. organize a group of other supervisors to get the procedure changed

13. A supervisor estimated that it would take his crew one workday per week to do a certain 13.____
job each week. However, after a month he noticed that the job averaged two and a half
days a week and this delayed other jobs that had to be done.
The FIRST thing that the supervisor should do in this case is to

    A. call his men together and warn them that they will get a poor work evaluation if they
       do not work harder
    B. talk to each man personally, asking him to work harder on the job
    C. go back and study the maintenance job by himself to see if more men should be
       assigned to the job
    D. write his boss a report describing in detail how much time it is taking the men to do
       the job

14. An employee complains to you that some of his work assignments are too difficult to do 14.____
alone.
Which of the following is the BEST way for you to handle this complaint?

    A. Go with him to see exactly what he does and why he finds it so difficult.
    B. Politely tell the man that he has to do the job or be brought up on charges.
    C. Tell the man to send his complaint to the head of your agency.
    D. Sympathize with the man and give him easier jobs.

15. The BEST way for a supervisor to keep control of his work assignments is to 15.____

    A. ask the men to report to him immediately when their jobs are finished
    B. walk around the buildings once a week and get a firsthand view of what is being
       done
    C. keep his ears open for problems and complaints, but leave the men alone to do the
       work
    D. write up a work schedule and check it periodically against the actual work done

16. A supervisor made a work schedule for his men. At the bottom of it, he wrote, *No changes or exceptions will be made in this schedule for any reason.*
For the supervisor to have made this statement is

    A. *good* because the men will respect the supervisor for his attitude
    B. *bad because* there are emergencies and special situations that occur
    C. *good* because each man will know exactly what is expected of him
    D. *bad* because the men should expect that no changes will ever be made in the work schedule without written permission

16.____

17. Which one of the following would NOT be a result of a well-planned work schedule?
The schedule

    A. makes efficient use of the time of the staff
    B. acts as a check list for an important job that might be left out
    C. will give an idea of the work to a substitute supervisor
    D. shows at a glance who the best men are

17.____

18. A new piece of equipment you have ordered is delivered. You are familiar with it, but the men under you who will use it do not know the equipment. Of the following methods, which is the BEST to take in explaining to them how to operate this equipment?

    A. Ask the men to watch other crews using the equipment.
    B. Show one reliable man how to operate the equipment and ask him to teach the other men.
    C. Ask the men to read the instructions in the manual for the equipment.
    D. Call the men together and show them how to operate the equipment.

18.____

19. One supervisor assigns work to his men by calling his crew together each week and describing what has to be done that week. He then tells them to arrange individual assignments among themselves and to work as a team during the week.
This method of scheduling work is a

    A. *good* idea because this guarantees that the men will work together
    B. *bad* idea because responsibility for doing the job is poorly fixed
    C. *good idea because the men will finish the job in less time, working together*
    D. *bad* idea because the supervisor should always stay with his men

19.____

20. Suppose that an employee came to his supervisor with a problem concerning his assignment.
For the supervisor to listen to this problem is a

    A. *good* idea because a supervisor should always take time off to talk when one of his men wants to talk
    B. *bad* idea because the supervisor should not be bothered during the work day
    C. *good* idea because it is the job of the supervisor to deal with problems of job assignment
    D. *bad* idea because the employee could start annoying the supervisor with all sorts of problems

20.____

21. Suppose that on the previous afternoon you were looking for an experienced employee in order to give him an emergency job and he was missing from his job location. The next morning, he tells you that he got sick suddenly and had to go home, but could not tell you since you were not around. He has never done this before.
What should you do?

    A. Tell the man he is excused and that in such circumstances he did the wisest thing.
    B. Bring the man up on charges because whatever he says he could still have notified you.
    C. Have the man examined by a doctor to see if he really was sick the day before.
    D. Explain to the man that he should make every effort to tell you or to get a message to you if he must leave.

21.____

22. An employee had a grievance and went to his supervisor about it. The employee was not satisfied with the way the supervisor tried to help him and told him so. Yet, the supervisor had done everything he could under the circumstances.
The PROPER action for the supervisor to take at this time is to

    A. politely tell the employee that there is nothing more for the supervisor to do about the problem
    B. let the employee know how he can bring his complaint to a higher authority
    C. tell the employee that he must solve the problem on his own since he did not want to follow the supervisor's advice
    D. suggest to the employee that he ask another supervisor for assistance

22.____

23. In which of the following situations is it BEST to give your men spoken rather than written orders?

    A. You want your men to have a record of the instructions.
    B. Spoken instructions are less likely to be forgotten.
    C. An emergency situation has arisen in which there is no time to write up instructions.
    D. There are instructions on time and leave regulations which are complicated.

23.____

24. One of your employees tells you that a week ago he had a small accident on the job but he did not bother telling you because he was able to continue working.
For the employee not to have told his supervisor about the accident was

    A. *good* because the accident was a small one
    B. *bad* because all accidents should be reported, no matter how small
    C. *good* because the supervisor should be bothered only for important matters
    D. *bad* because having an accident is one way to get excused for the day

24.____

25. For a supervisor to deal with each of his subordinates in exactly the same manner is

    A. *poor* because each man presents a different problem and there is no one way of handling all problems
    B. *good* because once a problem is handled with one man, he can handle another man with the same problem
    C. *poor* because the men will resent it if they are not handled each in a better way than others
    D. *good* because this assures fair and impartial treatment of each subordinate

25.____

KEY (CORRECT ANSWERS)

1.	B		11.	B
2.	D		12.	A
3.	D		13.	C
4.	C		14.	A
5.	C		15.	D
6.	D		16.	B
7.	B		17.	D
8.	B		18.	D
9.	A		19.	B
10.	C		20.	C

21.	D
22.	B
23.	C
24.	B
25.	A

TEST 2

DIRECTIONS: Each question or incomplete statement is followed by several suggested answers or completions. Select the one that BEST answers the question or completes the statement. *PRINT THE LETTER OF THE CORRECT ANSWER IN THE SPACE AT THE RIGHT.*

1. Jim Johnson has been on your staff for over four years. He has always been a conscientious and productive worker. About a month ago, his wife died; and since that time, his work performance has been very poor.
   As his supervisor, which one of the following is the BEST way for you to deal with this situation?

   A. Allow Jim as much time as he needs to overcome his grief and hope that his work performance improves.
   B. Meet with Jim to discuss ways to improve his performance.
   C. Tell Jim directly that you are more concerned with his work performance than with his personal problem.
   D. Prepare disciplinary action on Jim as soon as possible.

   1.____

2. You are responsible for the overall operation of a storehouse which is divided into two sections. Each section has its own supervisor. You have decided to make several complex changes in the storekeeping procedures which will affect both sections.
   Of the following, the BEST way to make sure that these changes are understood by the two supervisors is for you to

   A. meet with both supervisors to discuss the changes
   B. issue a memorandum to each supervisor explaining the changes
   C. post the changes where the supervisors are sure to see them
   D. instruct one supervisor to explain the changes to the other supervisor

   2.____

3. You have called a meeting of all your subordinates to tell them what has to be done on a new project in which they will all be involved. Several times during the meeting, you ask if there are any questions about what you have told them.
   Of the following, to ask the subordinates whether there are any questions during the meeting can BEST be described as

   A. *inadvisable* because it interferes with their learning about the new project
   B. *advisable* because you will find out what they don't understand and have a chance to clear up any problems they may have
   C. *inadvisable* because it makes the meeting too long and causes the subordinates to lose interest in the new project
   D. *advisable* because it gives you a chance to learn which of your subordinates are paying attention to what you say

   3.____

4. As a supervisor, you are responsible for seeing to it that absenteeism does not become a problem among your subordinates.
   Which one of the following is NOT an acceptable way of controlling the problem of excessive absences?

   A. Distribute a written statement to your staff on the policies regarding absenteeism in your organization.
   B. Arrange for workers who have the fewest absences to talk to those workers who have the most absences.
   C. Let your subordinates know that a record is being kept of all absences.
   D. Arrange for counseling of those employees who are frequently absent.

   4.____

5. One of your supervisors has been an excellent worker for the past two years. There are 5.___
no promotion opportunities for this worker in the foreseeable future. Due to the city's
present budget crisis, a salary increase is not possible.
Under the circumstances, which one of the following actions on your part would be
MOST likely to continue to motivate this worker?

    A. Tell the worker that times are bad all over and jobs are hard to find.
    B. Give the worker less work and easier assignments.
    C. Tell the worker to try to look for a better paying job elsewhere.
    D. Seek the worker's advice often and show that the suggestions provided are appreciated.

6. As a supervisor in a warehouse, it is important that you use your available work force to 6.___
its fullest potential. Which one of the following actions on your part is MOST likely to
increase the effectiveness of your work force?

    A. Assigning more workers to a job than the number actually needed.
    B. Eliminating all job training to allow more time for work output.
    C. Using your best workers on jobs that average workers can do.
    D. Making sure that all materials and equipment used are maintained in good working
order.

7. You learn that your storage area will soon be undergoing changes which will affect the 7.___
work of your subordinates. You decide not to tell your subordinates about what is to happen.
Of the following, your action can BEST be described as

    A. wise because your subordinates will learn of the changes for themselves
    B. unwise because your subordinates should be advised about what is to happen
    C. wise because it is better for your subordinates to continue working without being
disturbed by such news
    D. unwise because the work of your subordinates will gradually slow down

8. In making plans for the operation of your unit, you are MOST likely to see these plans 8.___
carried out successfully if you

    A. allow your staff to participate in developing these plans
    B. do not spend any time on the minor details of these plans
    C. base these plans on the past experiences of others
    D. allow these plans to interact with outside activities in other units

9. As a supervisor in charge of the total operation of a food supply warehouse, you find 9.___
vandalism to be a potentially serious problem. On occasion, trespassers have gained
entrance into the facility by climbing over an unprotected 8-foot fence surrounding the
warehouse whose dimensions measure 100 feet by 100 feet.
Assuming that all of the following would be equally effective ways in preventing these
breaches in security in the situation described above, which one would be LEAST
costly?

    A. Using two trained guard dogs to roam freely throughout the facility at night.
    B. Hiring a security guard to patrol the facility after working hours.
    C. Installing tape razor wire on top of the fence surrounding the facility.
    D. Installing an electronic burglar alarm system requiring the installation of a new
fence.

10. The area for which you have program responsibility has undergone recent changes. Your 10.____
staff is now required to perform many new tasks, and morale is low.
The LEAST effective way for you to improve long-term staff morale would be to

    A. develop support groups to discuss problems
    B. involve staff in job development
    C. maintain a comfortable social environment within the group
    D. adequately plan and give assignments in a timely manner

11. As a supervisor in a large office, one of your subordinate supervisors stops you in the 11.____
middle of the office and complains loudly that he is being treated unfairly. The rest of the
staff ceases work and listens to the complaint. The MOST appropriate action for you to
take in this situation is to

    A. ignore this unprofessional behavior and continue on your way
    B. tell the supervisor that his behavior is unprofessional and he should learn how to
conduct himself
    C. explain to the supervisor why you believe he is not being treated unfairly
    D. ask the supervisor to come to your office at a specific time to discuss the matter

12. You are told that one of your subordinates is distributing literature which attempts to 12.____
recruit individuals to join a particular organization. Several workers complain that their
rights are being violated. Of the following, the BEST action for you to take FIRST is to

    A. ignore the situation because no harm is being done
    B. discuss the matter further with your supervisor
    C. ask the worker to stop distributing the literature
    D. tell the workers that they do not have to read the material

13. You have been assigned to develop a short training course for a recently issued proce- 13.____
dure.
In designing this course, which of the following statements is the LEAST important for
you to consider?

    A. The learning experience must be interesting and meaningful in terms of the staff
member's job.
    B. The method of teaching must be strictly followed in order to develop successful
learning experiences.
    C. The course content should incorporate the rules and regulations of the agency.
    D. The procedure should be consistent with the agency's objectives.

14. As a supervisor, there are several newly-promoted employees under your supervision. 14.____
Each of these employees is subject to a probationary period PRIMARILY to

    A. assess the employee's performance to see if the employee should be retained or
removed from the position
    B. give the employee the option to return to his former employment if the employee is
unhappy in the new position
    C. give the employee an opportunity to learn the duties and responsibilities of the
position
    D. judge the employee's potential for upward mobility in the future

15. An employee under your supervision rushes into your office to tell you he has just received a telephone bomb threat.
As the administrative supervisor, the FIRST thing you should do is

    A. evacuate staff from the floor
    B. call the police and building security
    C. advise your administrator
    D. do a preliminary search

15.____

16. After reviewing the Absence Control form for a unit under your supervision, you find that one of your staff members has a fifth undocumented sick leave within a six-month period.
In this situation, the FIRST action you should take is to

    A. discuss the seriousness of the matter with the staff member when he returns to work and fully document the details of the discussion
    B. review the case with the location director and warn the staff member that future use of sick leave will be punished
    C. submit the proper disciplinary forms to ensure that the staff member is penalized for excessive absences
    D. request that the timekeeper put the staff member on doctor's note restriction

16.____

17. A subordinate supervisor recently assigned to your office begins his first conference with you by saying that he has learned something that another supervisor is doing that you should know about.
After hearing this statement, of the following, the BEST approach for you to take is to

    A. explain to the supervisor that the conference is to discuss his work and not that of his co-workers
    B. tell the supervisor that you do not encourage a spy *system* among the staff you supervise
    C. tell the supervisor that you will listen to his report only if the other supervisor is present
    D. allow the supervisor to continue talking until you have enough information to make a decision on how best to respond

17.____

18. Assume that you are a supervisor recently assigned to a new unit. You notice that, for the past few days, one of the employees in your unit whose work is about average has been stopping work at about four o'clock and has been spending the rest of the afternoon relaxing at his desk.
The BEST of the following actions for you to take in this situation is to

    A. assign more work to this employee since it is apparent that he does not have enough work to keep him busy
    B. observe the employee's conduct more closely for about ten days before taking any more positive action
    C. discuss the matter with the employee, pointing out to him how he can use the extra hour daily to raise the level of his job performance
    D. question the previous supervisor in charge of the unit in order to determine whether he had sanctioned such conduct when he supervised that unit

18.____

19. A new supervisor was assigned to your program four months ago. Although he tries   19.____
hard, he has been unable to meet certain standards because he still has a lot to learn. As
his supervisor, you are required to submit performance evaluations within a few days.
How would you rate this employee on the tasks where he fails to meet standards
because of lack of experience?

    A.   Satisfactory   B.   Conditional
    C.   Unsatisfactory   D.   Unratable

20. You find that there is an important procedural error in a memo which you distributed to   20.____
your staff several days ago. The BEST approach for you to take at this time is to

    A.   send a corrected memo to the staff, indicating what prior error was made
    B.   send a corrected memo to the staff without mentioning the prior error
    C.   tell the staff about the error at the next monthly staff meeting
    D.   place the corrected memo on the office bulletin board

21. Your superior asks you, a supervisor, about the status of the response to a letter from a   21.____
public official concerning a client's case. When you ask the subordinate who was
assigned to prepare the response to give you the letter, the subordinate denies that it
was given to him. You are certain that the subordinate has the letter, but is withholding it
because the response has not yet been prepared.
Of the following, in order to secure the letter from the subordinate, you should FIRST

    A.   accuse the subordinate of lying and demand that the letter be given to you immedi-
ately
    B.   say that you would consider it a personal favor if the subordinate would find the let-
ter
    C.   continue to question the subordinate until he admits to having been given the letter
    D.   offer a face-saving solution, such as asking the subordinate to look again for the
letter

22. As a supervisor, you have been assigned to write a few paragraphs to be included in the   22.____
agency's annual report, describing a public service agency department this year as compared to last year.
Which of the following elements basic to the agency is LEAST likely to have changed
since last year?

    A.   Mission   B.   Structure
    C.   Technology   D.   Personnel

23. As a supervisor, you have been informed that a grievance has been filed against you,   23.____
accusing you of assigning a subordinate to out-of-title tasks. Of the following, the BEST
approach for you to take is to

    A.   waive the grievance so that it will proceed to a Step II hearing
    B.   immediately change the subordinate's assignment to avoid future problems
    C.   respond to the grievance, giving appropriate reasons for the assignment
    D.   review the job description to ensure that the subordinate's tasks are not out-of-title

24. Which of the following is NOT a correct statement about agency group training programs in a public service agency?   24.____

    A. Training sessions continue for an indefinite period of time.
    B. Group training sessions are planned for designated personnel.
    C. Training groups are organized formally through administrative planning.
    D. Group training is task-centered and aimed toward accomplishing specific educational goals.

25. As a supervisor, you have submitted a memo to your superior requesting a conference to discuss the performance of a manager under your supervision. The memo states that the manager has a good working relationship with her staff; however, she tends to interpret agency policy too liberally and shows poor administrative skills by missing some deadlines and not keeping proper controls.   25.____
Which of the following steps should NOT be taken in order to prepare for this conference with your superior?

    A. Collect and review all your notes regarding the manager's prior performance.
    B. Outline your agenda so that you will have sufficient time to discuss the situation.
    C. Tell the manager that you will be discussing her performance with your superior.
    D. Clearly define objectives which will focus on improving the manager's performance.

KEY (CORRECT ANSWERS)

1.	B		11.	D
2.	A		12.	C
3.	B		13.	B
4.	B		14.	A
5.	D		15.	B
6.	D		16.	A
7.	B		17.	D
8.	A		18.	C
9.	C		19.	B
10.	C		20.	A

21.	D
22.	A
23.	C
24.	A
25.	C

READING COMPREHENSION
UNDERSTANDING AND INTERPRETING WRITTEN MATERIAL
EXAMINATION SECTION
TEST 1

Questions 1-22.

DIRECTIONS: Each question or incomplete statement is followed by several suggested answers or completions. Select the one that BEST answers the question or completes the statement. *PRINT THE LETTER OF THE CORRECT ANSWER IN THE SPACE AT THE RIGHT.*

Questions 1-2.

DIRECTIONS: Questions 1 and 2 are to be answered in accordance with the following paragraph.

Steam cleaners get their name from the fact that steam is used to generate pressure and is also a by-product of heating the cleaning solution. Steam itself has little cleaning power. It will melt some soils, but it does not dissolve them, break them up, or destroy their clinging power. Rather surprisingly, good machines generate as little steam as possible. Modern surface chemistry depends on a chemical solution to dissolve dirt, destroy its clinging power, and hold it in suspension. Steam actually hinders such a solution, but heat helps its physical and chemical action. Cleaning is most efficient when a hot solution reaches the work in heavy volume.

1. In accordance with the above paragraph, for MOST efficient cleaning,   1.____

   A. a heavy volume of steam is needed
   B. hot steam is needed to break up the soils
   C. steam is used to dissolve the surface dirt
   D. a hot chemical solution should always be used

2. With reference to the above paragraph, the steam in a steam cleaner is used to   2.____

   A. generate pressure
   B. create by-product chemicals
   C. slow down the chemical action of the cleaning solution
   D. dissolve accumulations of dirt

Questions 3-5.

DIRECTIONS: Questions 3 through 5 are based upon the information given in the following paragraphs. Use ONLY the information given in these paragraphs in answering these questions.

METHOD A - Move voltmeter lead from *BAT* to *GEN* terminal of regulator. Retard generator speed until generator voltage is reduced to 2 volts on a 6-volt system or 4 volts on a 12-volt system. Move voltmeter lead back to *BAT* terminal of regulator. Bring generator back to specified speed and note voltage setting.

METHOD B - Connect a variable resistance into the field circuit. Turn out all resistance. Operate generator at specified speed. Slowly increase (turn in) resistance until generator voltage is reduced to 2 volts on a 6-volt system or 4 volts on a 12-volt system. Turn out all resistance again, and note voltage setting. Regulator cover must be in place. To adjust voltage setting, turn adjusting screw. Turn clockwise to increase setting and counterclockwise to decrease voltage setting.

3.   According to the instructions given in the paragraphs, when taking readings,   3.____

    A.   a variable resistance is to be connected into the generator armature circuit
    B.   the generator voltage on a 12-volt system is reduced to 2 volts
    C.   the cover is to be in place
    D.   the voltmeter lead should be continuously connected to the *BAT* terminal

4.   In following the instructions given in the paragraphs, the one of the following statements   4.____
    that is MOST nearly correct is:

    A.   The adjusting screw must be turned clockwise to increase the voltage setting
    B.   Method B makes use of a fixed resistor
    C.   Method A makes use of a variable resistor
    D.   The generator voltage is reduced by decreasing the resistance

5.   The above instructions pertain MOST likely to a(n)   5.____

    A.   voltage regulator   B.   starting regulator
    C.   amperage regulator   D.   circuit breaker

Questions 6-7.

DIRECTIONS: Questions 6 and 7 are based upon the following paragraph. Use ONLY the information contained in this paragraph in answering these questions.

    With the engine running at normal idling speed and the engine hood open, attach the vacuum gauge to the intake manifold. The vacuum gauge should read about 18 to 21 inches, and the pointer should be steady. A needle fluctuating between 10 and 15 inches may indicate a defective cylinder-head, gasket, or valve. An extremely low reading indicates a leak in the intake manifold or gaskets. Accelerate the engine with full throttle momentarily. Notice if the gauge indicator fails to drop to approximately 2 inches as the throttle is opened, and recoil to at least 24 inches as the throttle is closed. If so, this may be an indication of diluted oil, poor piston-ring sealing, or an abnormal restriction in the exhaust, carburetor, or air cleaner. The above readings apply to sea level. There will be approximately a 1-inch drop for each 1,000 feet of altitude.

6.   If a vacuum test is made on a properly operating engine at an altitude of 3,000 feet, the   6.____
    vacuum gauge should read MOST NEARLY

    A.   12"   B.   15"   C.   13"   D.   24"

7.   If a vacuum test is made on an engine which has an abnormal restriction in the exhaust,   7.____
    this will be evidenced by

    A.   a leak in the intake manifold
    B.   the gauge indicator failing to drop to approximately 3 inches on opening the throttle

C. the gauge fluctuating around 12 inches
D. a steady high gauge reading

Questions 8-10.

DIRECTIONS: Questions 8 through 10 are to be answered in accordance with the information in the following paragraph.

The following is a set of instructions on engine shut-down procedure: When an engine equipped with an electric shut-down valve is used, the engine can be shut down completely by turning off the switch key on installations equipped with an electric shut-down valve, or by turning the manual shut-down valve lever. Turning off the switch key which controls the electric shut-down valve always stops the engine unless the override button on the shutdown valve has been locked in the open position. If the manual override on the electric shut-down valve is being used, turn the button full counterclockwise to stop the engine.

CAUTION: Never leave the switch key or the override button in the valve open or run position when the engine is not running. With overhead tanks, this would allow fuel to drain into the cylinders, causing hydraulic lock.

8. According to the above paragraph, it becomes apparent that if an engine does not stop when the electric shut-down valve switch key is shut off,   8._____

    A. an open manual switch is present
    B. the override button is locked in the closed position
    C. a closed manual switch is functioning
    D. the override button is locked in the open position

9. When using an engine equipped with an electric shut-down valve,   9._____

    A. no alternate method is available
    B. a manual method is not present
    C. a manual override can shut the engine down
    D. a manual override will not work

10. As a matter of caution, the switch key in the closed position or the override button in the   10._____
    stop position will

    A. assist in keeping fuel in the cylinders
    B. prevent fuel from flooding the cylinder cavities
    C. assist in producing hydraulic lock
    D. aid fuel dilution

Questions 11-12.

DIRECTIONS: Questions 11 and 12 are to be answered according to the information given in the following paragraph.

You have been instructed to expedite the fabrication of four special salt spreader trucks using chassis that are available in the shop. All four trucks must be delivered before the opening of business on December 1. Based on workload and available hours, the foreman of the body shop indicates that he could manufacture one complete salt spreader body in five weeks, with one additional week required for mounting and securing each body to the available chassis. No work could begin on the body until the engines and hydraulic components, which would have to be purchased, were available for use. The Purchasing Department has promised delivery of engines and hydraulic components three months after the order is placed. (Assume that all months have four weeks, and the same crew is doing the assembling and manufacturing.)

11. With reference to the above paragraph, assuming that the Purchasing Department placed the order at the beginning of the first week in February and ultimate delivery of the engines and components was delayed by six weeks, the date of completion of the first salt spreader truck would be CLOSEST to the end of the _____ week in _____.

    A. fourth; July
    C. fourth; August
    B. second; August
    D. first; September

11.___

12. With reference to the above paragraph, the LATEST date that the engines and associated hydraulic components could be requisitioned in order to meet the specified deadline would be CLOSEST to the beginning of the _____ week in _____.

    A. first; February
    C. third; March
    B. first; March
    D. first; April

12.___

Questions 13-20.

DIRECTIONS: Questions 13 through 20 are based on the paragraph on JACKS shown below. When answering these questions, refer to this paragraph.

JACKS

When using a jack, a workman should check the capacity plate or other markings on the jack to make sure the device is heavy enough to support the load. Where there is no plate, capacity should be determined and painted on the side of the jack. The workman should see that jacks are well lubricated, but only at points where lubrication is specified, and should inspect them for broken teeth or faulty holding fixtures. A jack should never be thrown or dropped upon the floor; such treatment may crack or distort the metal, thus causing the jack to break when a load is lifted. It is important that the floor or ground surface upon which the jack is placed be level and clean, and the safe limit of floor loading is not exceeded. If the surface is earth, the jack base should be set on heavy wood blocking, preferably hardwood, of sufficient size that the blocking will not turn over, shift, or sink. If the surface is not perfectly level, the jack may be set on blocking, which should be leveled by wedges securely placed so that they cannot be brushed or forced out of place. *Extenders* of wood or metal, intended to provide a higher rise where a jack cannot reach up to load or lift it high enough, should never be used. Instead, a larger jack should be obtained or higher blocking which is correspondingly wider and longer – should be placed under the jack. All lifts should be vertical with the jack correctly centered for the lift. The base of the jack should be on a perfectly level surface, and the jack head, with its hardwood shim, should bear against a perfectly level meeting surface.

13. To make sure the jack is heavy enough to support a certain load, the workman should

    A. lubricate the jack
    C. check the capacity plate
    B. shim the jack
    D. use a long handle

13.___

14. A jack should be lubricated

    A. after using   B. before painting
    C. only at specified points   D. to prevent slipping

14.____

15. The workman should inspect a jack for

    A. manufacturer's name   B. broken teeth
    C. paint peeling   D. broken wedges

15.____

16. Metal parts on a jack may crack if

    A. the jack is thrown on the floor
    B. the load is leveled
    C. blocking is used
    D. the handle is too short

16.____

17. It would NOT be a safe practice for a workman to

    A. center the jack under the load
    B. set the jack on a level surface
    C. use hardwood for blocking
    D. use *extenders* to reach up to the load

17.____

18. Wedges may safely be used to

    A. replace a broken tooth
    B. prevent the overloading of a jack
    C. level the blocking under a jack
    D. straighten distorted metal

18.____

19. Blocking should be

    A. made of a soft wood
    B. placed between the jack base and the earth surface
    C. well lubricated
    D. used to repair a broken tooth

19.____

20. A hardwood shim should be used

    A. between the head and its meeting surface
    B. under the jack
    C. as a filler
    D. to level a surface

20.____

Questions 21-22.

DIRECTIONS: Questions 21 and 22 are to be answered ONLY on the basis of the information contained in the following paragraph.

    Many experiments have been made on the effects of alcoholic beverages. These studies show that alcohol decreases alertness and efficiency. It decreases self-consciousness and, at the same time, increases confidence and feelings of ease and relaxation. It impairs attention and judgment. It destroys fear of consequences. Usual cautions are thrown to the winds. Habit systems become disorganized. The driver who uses alcohol tends to disregard his usual safety practices. He may not even be aware that he is disregarding them. His reaction time slows down; normally quick reactions are not possible for him. To make matters worse, he may not realize he is slower. His eye muscles may be so affected that his vision is not normal. He cannot correctly judge the speed of his car or of any other car. He cannot correctly estimate distances being covered by each. He becomes a highway menace.

21. The paragraph states that the drinking of alcohol makes a driver   21.____

    A. *more* alert   B. *less* confident
    C. *more* efficient   D. *less* attentive

22. From the above paragraph, it is reasonable to assume that a driver may overcome the   22.____
    bad effects of drinking alcohol by

    A. being more cautious
    B. relying on his good driving habits to a greater extent than normally
    C. watching the road more carefully
    D. waiting for the alcohol to wear off before drinking

Questions 23-25.

DIRECTIONS: Each question consists of a statement. You are to indicate whether the statement is TRUE(T) or FALSE (F). *PRINT THE LETTER OF THE CORRECT ANSWER IN THE SPACE AT THE RIGHT.*

    When in use, the storage battery becomes hot, and water evaporates from the cells of the battery, so clean water, preferably distilled, must be added at frequent intervals. This action keeps the level of the battery liquid above the top of the battery plates.

23. All water loss from a storage battery occurs when the battery is in use.   23.____

24. The water added to a storage battery does not have to be distilled.   24.____

25. Water in the storage battery must be kept level with the top of the battery plates.   25.____

KEY (CORRECT ANSWERS)

1.	D		11.	A
2.	A		12.	B
3.	C		13.	C
4.	A		14.	C
5.	A		15.	B
6.	B		16.	A
7.	B		17.	D
8.	D		18.	C
9.	C		19.	B
10.	B		20.	A

21.	D
22.	F
23.	F
24.	T
25.	F

TEST 2

DIRECTIONS: Each question or incomplete statement is followed by several suggested answers or completions. Select the one that BEST answers the question or completes the statement. *PRINT THE LETTER OF THE CORRECT ANSWER IN THE SPACE AT THE RIGHT.*

Questions 1-2.

DIRECTIONS: Questions 1 and 2 are based on the following paragraph.

Because electric drills run at high speed, the cutting edges of a twist drill are heated quickly. If the metal is thick, the drill point must be withdrawn from the hole frequently to cool it and clear out chips. Forcing the drill continuously into a deep hole will heat it, thereby spoiling its temper and cutting edges. A portable electric drill has the advantage that it can be taken to the work and used to drill holes in material too large to handle in a drill press.

1. According to the above paragraph, overheating of a twist drill will   1._____

    A.   slow down the work
    B.   cause excessive drill breakage
    C.   dull the drill
    D.   spoil the accuracy of the work

2. According to the above paragraph, one method of preventing overheating of a twist drill is to   2._____

    A.   use cooling oil
    B.   drill a smaller pilot hole first
    C.   use a drill press
    D.   remove the drill from the work frequently

Questions 3-5.

DIRECTIONS: Questions 3 through 5, inclusive, are to be answered in accordance with the paragraph below.

A steam heating system with steam having a pressure of less than 10 pounds is called a low-pressure system. The majority of steam-heating systems are of this type. The steam may be provided by low-pressure boilers installed *expressly* for the purpose, or it may be generated in boilers at a higher pressure and reduced in pressure before admitted to the heating mains. In other instances, it may be possible to use exhaust steam which has been made to run engines and other machines and which still contains enough heat to be utilized in the heating system. The first case represents the system of heating used in the ordinary residence or other small building; the other two represent the systems of heating employed in industrial buildings where a power plant is installed for general power purposes.

3. According to the above paragraph, whether or not a steam heating system is considered a low pressure system is determined by the pressure   3.____

    A. generated by the boiler
    B. in the heating main
    C. at the inlet side of the reducing valve
    D. of the exhaust

4. According to the above paragraph, steam used for heating is sometimes obtained from steam   4.____

    A. generated principally to operate machinery
    B. exhausted from larger boilers
    C. generated at low pressure and brought up to high pressure before being used
    D. generated by engines other than boilers

5. As used in the above paragraph, the word *expressly* means   5.____

    A. rapidly   B. specifically
    C. usually   D. mainly

Questions 6-7.

DIRECTIONS: Questions 6 and 7 are to be answered in accordance with the paragraph below.

When one is making the selection of grinding wheel specifications, the first variable factor to consider is the wheel speed, which influences the grade and the bond of the wheel. It is recommended that the grade should be determined in this way: the higher the wheel speed with relation to work speed, the softer the wheel should be. When, for any reason, the wheel speed is reduced, then it may be expected that the wheel will wear faster, but this can be overcome by choosing a wheel of a harder grade, assuming that the grade was correct for the initial speed.

6. It can be said that the MOST important piece of information in the above paragraph is: 6.____

    A. The higher the relative wheel speed, the softer should be the wheel
    B. Wheel speed is a variable factor
    C. At low speeds wheels wear rapidly
    D. When a wheel slows down, it should be replaced by a harder grade

7. According to the above paragraph, no indication is made that   7.____

    A. there are other factors to be considered besides speed
    B. hard wheels at low speed wear faster than soft wheels at high speed
    C. the lower the speed the harder should be the grade
    D. the selection of the bond of the wheel is affected by speed

Questions 8-9.

DIRECTIONS: Questions 8 and 9 are to be answered ONLY according to the information in the following paragraph.

Metal spraying is used for many purposes. Worn bearings on shafts and spindles can be readily restored to original dimensions with any desired metal or alloy. Low-carbon steel shafts may be supplied with high-carbon steel journal surfaces, which can then be ground to size after spraying. By using babbitt wire, bearings can be lined or babbitted while rotating. Pump shafts and impellers can be coated with any desired metal to overcome wear and corrosion. Valve seats may be re-surfaced. Defective castings can be repaired by filling in blowholes and checks. The application of metal spraying to the field of corrosion resistance is growing, although the major application in this field is in the use of sprayed zinc. Tin, lead, and aluminum have been used considerably. The process is used for structural and tank applications in the field as well as in the shop.

8. According to the above paragraph, worn bearing surfaces on shafts are metal-sprayed in order to   8.____

    A. prevent corrosion of the shaft
    B. fit them into larger-sized impellers
    C. return them to their original sizes
    D. replace worn babbitt metal

9. According to the above paragraph, rotating bearings can be metal-sprayed using   9.____

    A. babbitt wire   B. high-carbon steel
    C. low-carbon steel   D. any desired metal

Questions 10-11.

DIRECTIONS: Questions 10 and 11 are to be answered ONLY according to the information in the following paragraph.

The wheels used for internal grinding should generally be softer than those used for other grinding operations because the contact area between the wheel and work is comparatively large. A soft wheel that will cut with little pressure should be used to prevent springing the spindle. The grade of the wheel depends upon the character of the work and the stiffness of the machine; and where a large variety of work is being ground, it may not be practicable to have an assortment of wheels adapted to all conditions. By adjusting the speed, however, a wheel not exactly suited to the work in hand can often be used. If the wheel wears too rapidly, it should be run faster; and if it tends to glaze, the speed should be diminished.

10. On the basis of the above passage only, it may BEST be said that   10.____

    A. the type and grade of wheel are independent of the sturdiness of the machine
    B. by increasing the wheel speed, parts can easily be internally ground
    C. wheels used for outside grinding usually have a smaller contact area between the wheel and work
    D. to carry on hand an assortment of wheels for all conceivable internal grinding jobs is economical

11. On the basis of the above passage only, it may BEST be said that   11.____

    A. in general, if a wheel wears too rapidly, the speed should be decreased
    B. by decreasing the wheel speed, a wheel not quite appropriate for the job may sometimes be used

C. where a large variety of work is being ground, the grade of wheel depends on the diameter of the wheel
D. if a wheel tends to glaze, it should run faster

Questions 12-15.

DIRECTIONS: Questions 12 through 15, inclusive, are to be answered ONLY in accordance with the following paragraph.

Cylindrical surfaces are the most common form of finished surfaces found on machine parts, although flat surfaces are also very common; hence, many metal-cutting *processes* are for the purpose of producing either cylindrical or flat surfaces. The machines used for cylindrical or flat shapes may be, and often are, utilized also for forming the various irregular or special shapes required on many machine parts. Because of the prevalence of cylindrical and flat surfaces, the student of manufacturing practice should learn first about the machines and methods employed to produce these surfaces. The cylindrical surfaces may be internal as in holes and cylinders. Any one part may, of course, have cylindrical sections of different diameters and lengths and include flat ends or shoulders; and frequently there is a threaded part or possibly some finished surface that is not circular in cross-section. The prevalence of cylindrical surfaces on machine parts explains why lathes are found in all machine shops. It is important to understand the various uses of the lathe because many of the operations are the same fundamentally as those performed on other types of machine tools.

12. According to the above paragraph, the MOST common form of finished surfaces found on machine parts is   12.____

   A. cylindrical   B. elliptical
   C. flat   D. square

13. According to the above paragraph, any one part of cylindrical surfaces may have   13.____

   A. chases   B. shoulders   C. keyways   D. splines

14. According to the above paragraph, lathes are found in all machine shops because cylindrical surfaces on machine parts are   14.____

   A. scarce   B. internal   C. common   D. external

15. As used in the above paragraph, the word *processes* means   15.____

   A. operations   B. purposes
   C. devices   D. tools

Questions 16-17.

DIRECTIONS: Questions 16 and 17 are to be answered ONLY in accordance with the following paragraph.

The principle of interchangeability requires manufacture to such specification that component parts of a device may be selected at random and assembled to fit and operate satisfactorily. Interchangeable manufacture, therefore, requires that parts be made to definite limits of error and to fit gages instead of mating parts. Interchangeability does not necessarily involve a high degree of precision; stove lids, for example, are interchangeable but are not particularly accurate, and carriage bolts and nuts are not precision products but are completely interchangeable. Interchangeability may be employed in unit production as well as mass production systems of manufacture.

16. According to the above paragraph, in order for parts to be interchangeable, they must be   16.____

    A. precision-machined   B. selectively-assembled
    C. mass-produced   D. made to fit gages

17. According to the above paragraph, carriage bolts are interchangeable because they are   17.____

    A. precision-made
    B. sized to specific tolerances
    C. individually matched products
    D. produced in small units

Questions 18-22.

DIRECTIONS: Questions 18 through 22 are to be answered in accordance with the following passage.

TITANIC AIR COMPRESSOR

Valves: The compressors are equipped with Titanic plate valves which are automatic in operation. Valves are so constructed that an entire valve assembly can readily be removed from the head. The valves provide large port area with short lift and are accurately guided to insure positive seating.

Starting Unloader: Each compressor (or air end) is equipped with a centrifugal governor which is bolted directly to the compressor crank shaft. The governor actuates cylinder relief valves so as to relieve pressure from the cylinders during starting and stopping. The motor is never required to start the compressor under load.

Air Strainer: Each cylinder air inlet connection is fitted with a suitable combination air strainer and muffler.

Pistons: Pistons are lightweight castings, ribbed internally to secure strength, and are accurately turned and ground. Each piston is fitted with four (4) rings, two of which are oil control rings. Piston pins are hardened and tempered steel of the full floating type. Bronze bushings are used between piston pin and piston.

Connecting Rods: Connecting rods are of solid bronze designed for maximum strength, rigidity, and wear. Crank pins are fitted with renewable steel bushings. Connecting rods are of the one-piece type, there being no bolts, nuts, or cotter pins which can come loose. With this type of construction, wear is reduced to a negligible amount, and adjustment of wrist pin and crank pin bearings is unnecessary.

Main Bearings: Main bearings are of the ball type and are securely held in position by spacers. This type of bearing entirely eliminates the necessity of frequent adjustment or attention. The crank shaft is always in perfect alignment.

Crank Shaft: The crank shaft is a one-piece heat-treated forging of best quality open-hearth steel, of rugged design, and of sufficient size to transmit the motor power and any additional stresses which may occur in service. Each crank shaft is counter-balanced (dynamically balanced) to reduce vibration to a minimum, and is accurately machined to properly receive the ball bearing races, crank pin bushing, flexible coupling, and centrifugal governor. Suitable provision is made to insure proper lubrication of all crank shaft bearings and bushings with the minimum amount of attention.

Coupling: Compressor and motor shafts are connected through a Morse Chain Company all-metal enclosed flexible coupling. This coupling consists of two sprockets, one mounted on, and keyed to, each shaft; the sprockets are wrapped by a single Morse Chain, the entire assembly being enclosed in a split aluminum grease packed cover.

18. The crank pin of the connecting rod is fitted with a renewable bushing made of   18._____

     A. solid bronze   B. steel
     C. slight-weight casting   D. ball bearings

19. When the connecting rod is of the one-piece type,   19._____

     A. the wrist pins require frequent adjustment
     B. the crank pins require frequent adjustment
     C. the cotter pins frequently will come loose
     D. wear is reduced to a negligible amount

20. The centrifugal governor is bolted DIRECTLY to the   20._____

     A. compressor crank shaft   B. main bearing
     C. piston pin   D. muffler

21. The number of oil control rings required for each piston is   21._____

     A. one   B. two   C. three   D. four

22. The compressor and motor shafts are connected through a flexible coupling. These couplings are _____ to the shafts.   22._____

     A. keyed   B. brazed   C. soldered   D. press fit

Questions 23-25.

DIRECTION: Questions 23 through 25, inclusive, are to be answered in accordance with the following paragraph.

Wherever a soil pipe has to be provided for in a partition, special care must be taken that the hubs do not project beyond the finish face of the plaster. Before framing a building, it is desirable to ascertain where the stacks are and to provide for them. Building regulations require the stacks to be of 4-inch cast-iron even in small dwellings. With a 4-inch stack, the hub is 6 1/8 inches in diameter; and, therefore, 2 by 6 studs must be used. Special care should be taken that no plaster comes in contact with a soil pipe for *subsequent* settlement may cause cracking.

23. As used in the paragraph above, *subsequent* means MOST NEARLY   23._____

     A. heavy   B. sudden   C. later   D. soon

24. According to the above paragraph, 4" cast-iron soil pipes are used because 24.____

    A. they will not project beyond the face of the plaster
    B. it is easier to plaster over 4" pipe
    C. they can be located easier
    D. they are required by law

25. According to the above paragraph, the reason plaster should NOT be in direct contact with soil pipe is because 25.____

    A. the plaster would be damaged by moisture
    B. rust will bleed through the plaster
    C. of the possibility of cracks due to settlement
    D. it is harder to plaster over 4" pipe

KEY (CORRECT ANSWERS)

1.	C		11.	B
2.	D		12.	A
3.	B		13.	B
4.	A		14.	C
5.	B		15.	A
6.	A		16.	D
7.	B		17.	B
8.	C		18.	B
9.	A		19.	D
10.	C		20.	A

21.	B
22.	A
23.	C
24.	D
25.	C

ARITHMETICAL REASONING
EXAMINATION SECTION
TEST 1

DIRECTIONS: Each question or incomplete statement is followed by several suggested answers or completions. Select the one that BEST answers the question or completes the statement. *PRINT THE LETTER OF THE CORRECT ANSWER IN THE SPACE AT THE RIGHT.*

1. The sum of the fractions 3/32, 3/16, 3/8, and 3/4 is equal to

    A. 1 13/32   B. 1 5/16   C. 1 7/8   D. 3

1.____

2. If a maintainer earns $11.52 per hour, and time and one-half for overtime, his gross salary for a week in which he works 5 hours over his regular 40 hours should be

    A. $460.80   B. $518.80   C. $547.20   D. $578.80

2.____

3. If the diameter of a shaft must be 2.620 inches plus or minus .002 inches, the shaft will be SATISFACTORY if it has a diameter of _____ inches.

    A. 2.518   B. 2.600   C. 2.617   D. 2.621

3.____

4. A bus part costs $275 per 100 when purchased from a vendor. The bus part could be made in the bus machine shop at a labor cost of $60 for 50 units, with material and other costs amounting to $25 for 25 units.
If 100 such parts were made in the bus shop, there would be a saving of

    A. $55   B. $95   C. $140   D. $165

4.____

5. The sum of 9/16", 11/32", 15/64", and 1 3/32" is MOST NEARLY

    A. 2.234"   B. 2.134"   C. 2.334"   D. 2.214"

5.____

6. The diameter of a circle whose circumference is 14.5" is MOST NEARLY

    A. 4.62"   B. 4.81"   C. 4.72"   D. 4.51"

6.____

7. A bus part cost $90 per 100 when purchased from a vendor. The bus part could be made in the bus machine shop at a labor cost of $20 for 50 units and material and other costs amounting to $10 for 25 units.
If 100 such parts are made in the bus shop, there would be a saving of

    A. $10   B. $30   C. $40   D. $60

7.____

8. A bus storage battery having a 300 ampere-hour capacity is 50% discharged.
If the bus running schedule for the day is such that the battery will be charging at an average rate of 30 amperes for 2 1/2 hours and discharging at an average rate of 9 amperes for 5 hours, then at the end of the day, the battery will be APPROXIMATELY

    A. at full charge   B. 75% charged
    C. 60% charged   D. 50% charged

8.____

9. If the total time allowance for replacing the glass in a broken bus window is 75 minutes, how many jobs of this kind would a maintainer be expected to do in 40 hours of work?   9.____

    A.   32   B.   40   C.   60   D.   72

10. A certain rod is tapered so that it changes diameter at a rate of 1/4 inch per foot of length. If the tapered rod is 3 inches long, then the difference in diameter between the two ends is MOST NEARLY   10.____

    A.   0.250"   B.   0.187"   C.   0.135"   D.   0.062"

11. How many 9 1/2 inch long pieces of copper tubing can be cut from a 20-foot length of tubing?   11.____

    A.   24   B.   25   C.   26   D.   27

12. Two splice plates must be cut from a piece of sheet steel that has an overall length of 14 3/8 inches. The plates are to be 7 5/8 inches and 5 1/4 inches long.
If 1/16 inch is allowed for each saw cut, then how much material would be left?   12.____

    A.   1 3/8"   B.   I 1/2"   C.   1 5/8"   D.   1 3/4"

13. A maintainer requires several lengths of tubing for oil lines as follows: 12 7/16 inches, 14 5/16 inches, 9 3/16 inches, 9 1/8 inches, 6 1/4 inches, and 5 inches.
The TOTAL length of tubing required is MOST NEARLY _____, feet.   13.____

    A.   2   B.   3   C.   4   D.   5

14. Two-thirds of 10 feet is MOST NEARLY   14.____

    A.   6'2"   B.   6'8"   C.   6'11"   D.   7'1"

15. You are directed to pick up a tray load of brake shoes. The combined weight of tray and brake shoes is 4,000 pounds. Assume that each brake shoe weighs 40 pounds and the tray weighs 240 pounds.
The number of brake shoes in the tray is MOST NEARLY   15.____

    A.   88   B.   94   C.   100   D.   106

16. A maintainer earns $12.44 per hour, and time and one-half for overtime over 40 hours. Each week, 15 percent of his total salary is deducted for social security and taxes. Also, each week a $18.00 deduction is made for a savings bond and a $9.00 deduction is made for a charitable organization.
If he works a total of 46 hours in a week, his take-home pay for that week is   16.____

    A. $609.56   B. $518.10   C. $491.12   D. $410.70

17. A rectangularly-shaped repair facility for light trucks is 160 feet wide and 260 feet long. A 10-foot space is provided along each wall for benches and equipment. A 60-foot wide area in the middle of the floor is to remain clear for its entire 260 foot length. The entrance to the shop is at one end of this open area.
Assuming that there are no columns to contend with, the MAXIMUM area available for parking of trucks is _____ sq. ft.   17.____

    A.   15,600   B.   19,200   C.   26,000   D.   41,600

18. A criterion is established that limits the yearly major repair expenses to 30% of the current value of the equipment. Equipment is depreciated at a rate of 20% of its original cost each year. A truck purchased on January 1, 2000 for $9,000 had a reconditioned engine installed in February 2003 at a total cost of $900.
The amount of money available for additional major repairs on this truck in 2003 is
18._____

    A. none   B. $180   C. $360   D. $720

19. Twenty carburetors are ordered for your shop by the Purchasing Department. The terms are list, less 30% less 10%, less 5%.
If the list price of a carburetor is $70 and all terms are met upon delivery, the charges to your budget will be
19._____

    A. $1,359.60   B. $1,085.40   C. $837.90   D. $630.80

20. The sum of the fractions 7/16", 11/16", 5/32", and 7/8" is MOST NEARLY
20._____

    A. 2.1753"   B. 2.1563"   C. 1.9522"   D. 1.9463"

21. If 750 feet of wire weighs 60 lbs., the number of pounds that 150 feet will weigh is MOST NEARLY
21._____

    A. 12   B. 10   C. 8   D. 6

22. A steel rod 19.750" long is to have three pieces cut from its length. One piece is to be 3.250" long, the second 6.500" long, and the third piece 5.375".
If .125" is allowed for each cut, the length of the material left over is
22._____

    A. 3.750"   B. 4.250"   C. 4.500"   D. 5.150"

23. If the distance between the north and south terminals is 10.8 miles and a train makes six roundtrips, then the total travel mileage would be NEAREST _____ miles.
23._____

    A. 22   B. 65   C. 130   D. 145

24. If the thickness of material worn from a car wheel is approximately 1/16 inch off the diameter in 20,000 miles of travel, the wheel diameter will be reduced from 33 inches to 32 3/4 inches after _____ miles.
24._____

    A. 60,000   B. 80,000   C. 100,000   D. 120,000

25. If the distance between the north and south terminals is 11.3 miles and a train makes five roundtrips, then the total travel mileage would be NEAREST _____ miles.
25._____

    A. 23   B. 55   C. 115   D. 130

KEY (CORRECT ANSWERS)

1.	A	11.	B
2.	C	12.	A
3.	D	13.	D
4.	A	14.	B
5.	A	15.	B
6.	A	16.	C
7.	A	17.	B
8.	C	18.	B
9.	A	19.	C
10.	D	20.	B

21.	A
22.	B
23.	C
24.	B
25.	C

SOLUTIONS TO PROBLEMS

1. $\frac{3}{32}+\frac{3}{16}+\frac{3}{8}+\frac{3}{4}=\frac{45}{32}=1\frac{13}{32}$

2. Gross salary = ($11.52)(40) + ($17.28)(5) = $547.20

3. 2.620 ± .002 means from 2.618 to 2.622. The only selection in this range is 2.621.

4. ($60)($\frac{100}{50}$)+($25)($\frac{100}{25}$) $220 if made in the bus shop. Savings = $275 - $220 = $55

5. 9/16" + 11/32" + 15/64" + 1 3/32" =143/64 = 2 15/64" ≈ 2.234"

6. Diameter = 14.5" ÷ π ≈ 4.62"

7. ($20)($\frac{100}{50}$)+($10)($\frac{100}{25}$) = $80 if made in the bus shop. Savings = $90 - $80 = $10

8. [150 + [(30)(2 1/2)] - [(9)(5)] = [150+75] - 45 = 180, and 180/300 = 60%

9. (40)(60) ÷ 75 = 32

10. (1/4")(3/12) = 1/16" ≈ .062"

11. (20)(12) = 240", and 240" ÷ 9 1/2" ≈ 25.3, rounded down to 25 pieces of tubing

12. 14 3/8" - 7 5/8" - 5 1/4" - 1/16" = 1 3/8"

13. 12 7/16" + 14 5/16" + 9 3/16" + 9 1/8" + 6 1/4" + 5" = 56 5/16" ≈ 5 ft.

14. (2/3)(10') = 6 2/3' = 6'8"

15. 4000 - 240 = 3760 lbs. Then, 3760 ÷ 40 = 94 brake shoes

16. Take-home pay = ($12.44)(40)+($18.66)(6) - .15[($12.44)(40) + ($18.66)(6)] - $18.00 - $9.00 = $491.126 ≈ $491.12

17. Subtracting the area for benches and equipment would leave an area of 240' by 140'. Now, deduct the 60' width. Final area = (240')(80') = 19,200 sq.ft.

18. In 2003, the value of the truck = $9000 - (3)(.20)($9000) = $3600 The limit of the expenses for repairs = (.30)($3600) = $1080 After installing engine, $1080 - $900 = $180 left for additional major repairs.

19. (20)($70)(.70)(.90)(.95) = $837.90

20. 7/16" + 11/16" + 5/32" + 7/8" = 69/32" ≈ 2.1563"

21. (150/750)(60) = 12 lbs.

22. 19.750" - 3.250" - 6.500" - 5.375" - .125" - .125" - .125" = 4.250" left over

23. (6)(10.8)(2) = 129.6 ≈ 130 miles

24. 33" - 32 3/4" = 1/4". Then, (1/4 ÷ 1/16)(20,000) = 80,000 miles

25. (5)(11.3)(2) = 113 miles, closest to 115 miles

TEST 2

DIRECTIONS: Each question or incomplete statement is followed by several suggested answers or completions. Select the one that BEST answers the question or completes the statement. *PRINT THE LETTER OF THE CORRECT ANSWER IN THE SPACE AT THE RIGHT.*

1. In looking over an alteration job on car bodies, you find that 96 pieces of 1" x 1" x 1'6" long square steel stock are needed to do this job. Steel weighs 480 lbs. per cu. ft. and costs $0.12 per lb.
   The total cost of this material is MOST NEARLY

   A. $40.00   B. $60.00   C. $80.00   D. $100.00   1.____

2. Assume that the breakdown cost of a particular motor job is as follows:
   Parts $160.00
   Labor   75.00
   Overhead   30.00
   The percentage of the total cost for labor is MOST NEARLY

   A. 20%   B. 25%   C. 28%   D. 32%   2.____

3. The engine hydraulic system and transmission on a certain type of tractor use the same type oil. This oil is delivered in 55 gallon drums.
   How many drums are needed to make all three changes on 10 of these tractors whose- capacities are the following:
   Engine   58 quarts
   Transmission   70 quarts
   Hydraulic system   22 gallons
   _____ drums.

   A. 100   B. 50   C. 54   D. 10   3.____

4. A new shop layout requires the following:
   1,000   sq.   ft.   for tool room
   3,000   sq.   ft.   for parts room
   10,000   sq.   ft.   for service bays
   5,500   sq.   ft.   for isles
   The building should be AT LEAST _____ yards wide and 70 yards long.

   A. 10   B. 20   C. 25   D. 30   4.____

5. When filling a diesel engine cooling system, the mix required is 80% antifreeze and 20% water. You are required to fill seven systems containing 30 gals. each. The number of 5 gallon cans of antifreeze that are required is MOST NEARLY

   A. 210   B. 168   C. 34   D. 26   5.____

6. The floors of 2 cars are to be painted with a special test paint. Assume that the floor area in each car is 600 square feet. A gallon of this paint will cover 400 square feet.
   The number of gallons of this paint that you should pick up at the storeroom to paint the two car floors would be

   A. 6   B. 5   C. 4   D. 3   6.____

7. Assume that you are sent to the storeroom for 1,000 of 600-volt contact tips which are to be distributed equally to 5 foremen, but you find that the storeroom can only supply you with 825.
If you distribute these 825 tips equally to the 5 foremen, the number of tips that each foreman will receive is

    A. 165   B. 175   C. 190   D. 200

7.____

8. You are asked to fill six 5-gallon cans of oil from a full drum containing 52 gallons.
When you have filled the six cans, the number of gallons of oil left in the drum will be MOST NEARLY

    A. 14   B. 16   C. 22   D. 30

8.____

9. A certain wire rope is made up of 6 strands, each strand containing 19 wires.
The TOTAL number of wires in this wire rope is

    A. 25   B. 96   C. 114   D. 144

9.____

10. The hook should be the weakest part of any crane, hoist, or sling.
According to this statement, if a particular hook has a rated capacity of 2 1/2 tons, then the MAXIMUM load that should be lifted with this hook is _____ pounds.

    A. 150   B. 3,000   C. 5,000   D. 5,500

10.____

11. Assume that 2 car wheels weigh 635 pounds each and are attached to an axle weighing 1,260 pounds.
The total weight of this assembly is MOST NEARLY _____ pounds.

    A. 1,270   B. 1,520   C. 1,895   D. 2,530

11.____

12. If an employee authorizes his employer to deduct 4% of his $300 weekly salary for a savings bond, the MINIMUM number of weekly deductions required to get enough money to buy a bond costing $36 is

    A. 3   B. 6   C. 8   D. 9

12.____

13. In weighing out a truckful of scrap metal, the scale reads 21,496 lbs.
If the empty truck weighs 9,879 lbs., the amount of scrap metal, in pounds, is MOST NEARLY

    A. 10,507   B. 10,602   C. 11,617   D. 12,617

13.____

14. Four trays of material are placed on the body of a delivery truck for delivery to the inspection shop. Each tray is 4 feet wide and 4 feet long.
If these trays are placed side by side on the floor of the delivery truck, together they will cover an area of the floor MOST NEARLY _____ square feet.

    A. 32   B. 48   C. 64   D. 72

14.____

15. Assume that you are operating a degreasing tank and its tray holds 5 gear cases. It takes 40 minutes to clean one tray of gear cases.
At the end of 6 hours of operation (excluding lunch break and loading and unloading time), the number of gear cases cleaned will be

    A. 30   B. 36   C. 45   D. 50

15.____

16. If a serviceman's weekly gross salary is $160 and 20% is deducted for taxes, his take-home pay is

    A. $120   B. $128   C. $140   D. $144

16.____

Questions 17-18.

DIRECTIONS: Questions 17 and 18 are to be answered on the basis of the following paragraph.

The car maintenance department is considering the purchase of a certain car part from Manufacturer X for $140. An equivalent part can be purchased from Manufacturer Y for $100. The part made by Manufacturer X must be reconditioned every 3 years, using material costing $30 and requiring 6 hours of labor. The part made by Manufacturer Y must be reconditioned every 1 1/2 years, using material costing $24 and requiring 5 hours of labor. The maintainer's rate of pay is $12 per hour.

17. The cost of operating with the part made by Manufacturer X (excluding the first cost) is MOST NEARLY _____ per year.

    A. $30   B. $32   C. $34   D. $42

17.____

18. The total cost of operating with the part made by Manufacturer Y over a period of 12 years, including the first cost of the part and assuming the part is scrapped at the end of 12 years, is MOST NEARLY

    A. $472   B. $572   C. $688   D. $772

18.____

19. The area of the steel plate shown in the sketch at the right is _____ sq. ft.

    A. 16
    B. 18
    C. 20
    D. 22

19.____

20. A car part made by a Manufacturer X has a purchase cost of $7,500 and a life of 5 years. It requires a yearly maintenance cost of $50. Manufacturer Y offers a similar part of this type for $4,800, with a life of 3 years and a yearly maintenance cost of $75.
By purchasing the part offering a better overall value, the yearly savings per unit purchased would be

    A. $115   B. $125   C. $135   D. $140

20.____

21. A car part can be overhauled at the rate of 12 parts per hour. Each part requires new material costing $6 each. If the labor cost is $14 per hour, one part can be overhauled for a total cost (labor plus material) of MOST NEARLY

    A. $6.64   B. $7.16   C. $7.46   D. $8.20

21.____

22. A car part costs $150 per 50 units when purchased in a finished condition from a vendor. The car part can be made in the shop at a total cost of $2.20 per unit, when made on a machine which can be purchased for $1,000. The MINIMUM number of parts which must be made on this machine before the savings equal the cost of the machine is

    A. 850   B. 1,000   C. 1,250   D. 1,500

22.____

23. A pound of a certain type of metal washer contains 360 washers.
If 1/4 of the material of each washer is removed by enlarging the center of each washer, the number of washers to the pound should then be MOST NEARLY

    A. 280   B. 300   C. 380   D. 480

23.____

24. A maintainer earns $10.84 per hour, and time and one-half for overtime. Ten percent of his total salary earned is deducted from his paycheck for social security and taxes. He also contributes $5.00 per week to a charitable organization. No other deductions are made.
If he works 2 hours over his basic 40 hours, his weekly take-home pay should be MOST NEARLY

    A. $466.12   B. $419.50   C. $414.50   D. $410.60

24.____

25. A car part costs $130 per 100 units if purchased from a vendor. The car part can be made on a machine which can be purchased for $1,000. Assume that this machine has a production life of 20,000 units with no salvage value, and that all shop costs amount to $80 per 100 units turned out in the shop.
The money that would be SAVED during the life of the machine would be

    A. $800   B. $8,000   C. $9,000   D. $18,000

25.____

KEY (CORRECT ANSWERS)

1.	B	11.	D
2.	C	12.	A
3.	D	13.	C
4.	D	14.	C
5.	C	15.	C
6.	D	16.	B
7.	A	17.	C
8.	C	18.	C
9.	C	19.	C
10.	C	20.	B

21.	B
22.	C
23.	D
24.	C
25.	C

SOLUTIONS TO PROBLEMS

1. Total cost ≈ (96)(.01)(480)(.12) ≈ $55, which is closest to $60. Note that 1" x 1" x 1'6" ≈ (1/12')(1/12')(3/2')= 1/96 ≈ .01 cu. ft.

2. Labor = $75 ÷ $265 ≈ 28%

3. (10)(14.5+17.5+22) = 540. Then, 540 ÷ 55 ≈ 10 drums

4. Total sq.ft. = 19,500, which is 2166 2/3 sq.yds.

   Then, 2166 2/3 ÷ 70 ≈ 30.95 or 31

5. Amount of antifreeze = (.80)(7)(.30) = 168 gallons.

   Then, 2166 2/3 ÷ 70 ≈ 30.95 or 31

6. (600+600) ÷ 400 = 3 gallons

7. 825 ÷ 5 = 165 for each foreman

8. 52 - (6)(5) = 22 gallons left

9. (19)(6) = 114 wires

10. (2 1/2)(2000) = 5000 pounds

11. (2)(635) + 1260 = 2530 pounds

12. ($300)(.04) = $12. Then, $36 ÷ $12 = 3 weekly deductions

13. 21,496 - 9,879 = 11,617 pounds

14. 4(4')(4') = 64 sq.ft.

15. 6 hrs ÷ 2/3 hr. = 9 trays = 45 gear cases cleaned

16. Take-home pay = ($160)(.80) = $128

17. ($30) + (6)($12) = $102 for 3 yrs = $34 per year

18. 100 + 7(24) + 7(60) = 688

19. Separate the figure into regions as follows:

    I: 1'x2' = 2 sq.ft.

    II: 3'x4' = 12 sq.ft.

    III: (3'x4') ÷ 2' =6 sq.ft.

    Total = 20 sq.ft.

20. Manufacturer X: $7500 + ($50)(5) = $7750, so the cost per year is $7750 ÷ 5 = $1550.
    Manufacturer Y: $4800 + (3)($75) = $5025, so the cost per year is $5025 ÷ 3 = $1675
    Using Manufacturer X, savings = $125 per year

21. Cost of 12 parts = (12)($6) + $14 = $86. Then, cost of one part = $86 ÷ 12 ≈ $7.16

22. Savings per unit is &150/50 - $2.20 = $.80. Then, $1000 ÷ $.80 = 1250

23. 1 - 1/4 - 3/4. Then, 360 ÷ 3/4 = 480

24. Take-home pay = [($10.84)(40)+($16.26)(2)][.90] - $5 ≈ $414.50

25. Amount if purchased from a vendor = $130(200) = $26,000

    Using the machine, amount = $1000 + ($80)(200) = $17,000. Amount saved = $9000

TEST 3

DIRECTIONS: Each question or incomplete statement is followed by several suggested answers or completions. Select the one that BEST answers the question or completes the statement. *PRINT THE LETTER OF THE CORRECT ANSWER IN THE SPACE AT THE RIGHT.*

1. A Cat 983 Traxcavator can make a complete loading cycle from bank to truck and back to bank in 25 seconds.
   If the bucket contains 4 cu. yds. of loose material, the MINIMUM amount of material that an operator should load in 4 hours is _____ cubic yards.

   A. 2,304   B. 2,100   C. 1,896   D. 576   1.____

2. An excavation is 12' x 18' x 15' and is to be dug by a Cat 983 Traxcavator with 3 cubic yards of solid material excavated per pass.
   The MINIMUM number of passes required to dig the hole is _____ passes.

   A. 40   B. 46   C. 120   D. 126   2.____

3. A Cat D8 tractor and 463 scraper can haul 22 cubic yards of cover material per trip.
   If it is required to cover an area 1,000 feet by 100 feet to a depth of 2 feet, the MINIMUM number of trips that will be required is MOST NEARLY

   A. 284   B. 337   C. 385   D. 421   3.____

4. Gravel weighs 2,800 pounds per cubic yard.
   In order to carry 42,000 pounds of gravel, the capacity of a truck must be AT LEAST _____ cubic yards.

   A. 10   B. 12   C. 15   D. 18   4.____

5. The average capacity of an Athey Wagon is 60 cubic yards. The Cat D8 tractor pulls 2 wagons.
   The MINIMUM number of trips to the fill that would be required to empty a barge loaded with 1,000 cubic yards of refuse is

   A. 9   B. 17   C. 30   D. 90   5.____

6. When pulling 2 Athey trailers, the operator of a Cat D8 tractor can make a roundtrip from the crane to the fill and back in 15 minutes.
   Assuming that delays and breaks allow the man to work productively for 75% of the shift, the MAXIMUM number of trips that the operator can make in an 8-hour shift is

   A. 43   B. 32   C. 24   D. 16   6.____

7. In plowing a street which is 24 feet wide, a motor grader can make an 8-ft. wide pass, with a 2-ft. overlap.
   If a roundtrip takes 4 minutes, the MINIMUM time needed to plow this street should be _____ minutes.

   A. 12   B. 16   C. 24   D. 32   7.____

8. A scraper is loaded with 23 cubic yards of sand weighing 100 pounds per cubic foot.
   The weight of the load, in tons, is MOST NEARLY

   A. 20   B. 30   C. 40   D. 60   8.____

9. Assume a crankcase oil change of 6 quarts for every 150 service hours.   9._____
   How many 42 gallon drums of oil are required for 8,400 total service hours?

   A. 5   B. 2   C. 1   D. 1 1/3

10. Assume that a ruler is marked in 10ths of a foot instead of in inches.   10._____
    5 tenths on this ruler would be

    A. 4"   B. 5"   C. 6"   D. 7"

11. A truck load of 1 1/2" stone from a 10 cubic yard truck will spread an area APPROXI-   11._____
    MATELY _____ long, 6" deep, and _____ wide.

    A. 50'; 10'   B. 10'; 5'   C. 54'; 10'   D. 45'; 5'

12. A dump truck with a body 10 ft. long, 5 ft. wide, and 4 ft. deep has a volume of _____   12._____
    cubic feet.

    A. 150   B. 200   C. 250   D. 300

13. A tractor is operated on a given landfill operation during the following time intervals in one   13._____
    day: from 8:15 A.M. to 11:45 A.M.; from 12:30 P.M. to 6:00 P.M.; from 6:45 P.M. to 11:30
    P.M.
    The total net operating time, expressed in hours and minutes, is MOST NEARLY
    _____ hours, _____ minutes.

    A. 13; 30   B. 13; 15   C. 13; 45   D. 12; 45

14. The area of ground contact (with standard track shoes) of a late model D8 Caterpillar   14._____
    Tractor is 4,296 sq. in. Expressed in square feet, this is MOST NEARLY

    A. 358   B. 29.8   C. 159.3   D. 21.37

15. A towing winch develops a bare drum line pull of 11.8 tons.   15._____
    This force represents, in pounds,

    A. 23,850   B. 28,300   C. 23,800   D. 23,600

16. The fuel tank gauge reads about 3/4 of a full tank.   16._____
    If the tank capacity is 72.5 gallons, the amount of fuel in the tank is MOST NEARLY

    A. 53.2   B. 53.8   C. 54.5   D. 55.0

17. If a dump truck capable of carrying 40 2/3 cubic yards is 3/4 loaded, it is carrying, in   17._____
    cubic yards,

    A. 28   B. 36 1/2   C. 30 1/2   D. 28 2/3

18. A load of sand filling a truck body 6 feet long, 5 feet wide, and 3 feet deep would contain   18._____
    _____ cubic feet.

    A. 14   B. 90   C. 33   D. 21

Questions 19-21.

DIRECTIONS: Questions 19 through 21 are to be answered on the basis of the diagrams of balanced levers shown below. P is the center of rotation, W is the weight on the lever, and F is the balancing force.

19. In Diagram 1, the force F required to balance the weight W lbs. on the lever shown is equal to _____ lbs.

    A. a/W   B. W/a   C. W   D. Wa

19._____

20. In Diagram 2, the force F required to balance the weight of 80 lbs. on the lever shown is _____ lbs.

    A. 4   B. 3   C. 16   D. 32

20._____

21. The mechanical advantage of the lever shown in Diagram 2 is

    A. 4   B. 5   C. 8   D. 12

21._____

22. The specific gravity of a liquid may be defined as the ratio of the weight of a given volume of the liquid to the weight of an equal volume of water. An empty bottle weighs 5 oz. When the bottle is filled with water, the total weight is 50 oz. When the bottle is filled with another liquid, the total weight is 95 oz.
The specific gravity of the second liquid is MOST NEARLY

    A. .50   B. .58   C. 1.7   D. 2.0

22._____

23. If one inch is approximately equal to 2.54 centimeters, the number of inches in one meter is MOST NEARLY

    A. 14.2   B. 25.4   C. 39.4   D. 91.4

23._____

24. One-quarter divided by five-eighths is

    A. 5/32   B. 1/10   C. 2/5   D. 5/2

24._____

25. A man works on a certain job continuously, with no time off for lunch.
If he works from 9:45 A.M. until 1:35 P.M. to finish the job, the total time which he spent on the job is MOST NEARLY _____ hours, _____ minutes.

    A. 3; 10   B. 3; 35   C. 3; 50   D. 4; 15

25._____

KEY (CORRECT ANSWERS)

1.	A	11.	C
2.	A	12.	B
3.	B	13.	C
4.	C	14.	B
5.	A	15.	D
6.	C	16.	C
7.	B	17.	C
8.	B	18.	B
9.	B	19.	C
10.	C	20.	C

21.	B
22.	D
23.	C
24.	C
25.	C

———

SOLUTIONS TO PROBLEMS

1. 4 hrs = (4)(60)(60) = 14,400 sec. Then, 14,400 ÷ 25 = 576 Thus, (576)(4 cu.yds.) = 2304 cu.yds.

2. (12')(18')(15') = 3240 cu.ft. = 120 cu.yds. Then, 120 ÷ 3 = 40

3. (1000')(100')(2') = 200,000 cu.ft. ≈ 7407.4 cu.yds.
   Finally, 7407.4 ÷ 22 = 336.7, rounded up to 337 trips.

4. 42,000 ÷ 2800 = 15 cu.yds.

5. (2)(60 cu.yds.) = 120 yds. Then, 1000 ÷ 120 = 8 1/3, which must be rounded up to 9 trips

6. 8 hrs ÷ 15 min = 32. Then, (32)(.75) = 24 trips

7. 24' ÷ 8' = 3; however, with a 2 ft. overlap, only 6' gets plowed. So, (24 ÷ 6)(4 min) = 16 min.

8. 23 cu.yds. = 621 cu.ft. Then, (621)(100) = 62,100 lbs.
   Finally, 62,100 ÷ 2000 ≈ 30 tons

9. 8400 ÷ 150 = 56. Then, (56)(6 qts) = 336 qts = 84 gallons
   Finally, 84 ÷ 42 = 2 drums

10. 5 tenths = (5/10)(12") = 6"

11. (54')(1/2')(10') = 270 cu.ft. = 10 cu.yds.

12. Volume = (10')(5')(4') = 200 cu.ft.

13. 3 hrs. 30 min. + 5 hrs. 30 min. + 4 hrs. 45 min. = 12 hrs. 105 min. = 13 hrs. 45 min.

14. 4296 sq.in. = 4296 ÷ 144 ≈ 29.8 sq.ft.

15. 11.8 tons = (11.8)(2000) = 23,600 lbs.

16. (72.5)(.75) = 54.375, closest to 54.5 gallons

17. (40 2/3)(3/4) = 30 1/2 cu.yds.

18. (6')(5')(3') = 90 cu.ft.

19. F = Wa/a = W lbs.

20. F = (80)(2) ÷ 10 = 16 lbs.

21. Mechanical advantage = 10/2 = 5

22. Specific gravity $= \dfrac{95-5}{50-5} = 2$

23. 1 meter = 100 cm. ≈ (100) ÷ (2.54) ≈ 39.4 in.

24. $1/4 \div 5/8 = \dfrac{1}{4} \cdot \dfrac{8}{5} = \dfrac{2}{5}$

25. 9:45 AM to 1:35 PM = 3 hrs. 50 min.

Diagnosing the Causes of Automotive Troubles
Contents

Page

Diagnosing the Causes of Automotive Troubles

The number of possible difficulties encountered with an automobile is endless, and no attempt will be made to present them all. Diagosing auto troubles requires thought and reasoning. If the principles and construction of the various parts of the car are understood, and one of the hundreds of possible troubles occurs, then simply reason it out. Determine what the trouble is, learn what might cause that trouble, and why the trouble is present. Decide whether it is in the ignition, fuel system, lubrication system or just where it is, and. then track it down by a process of elimination. Following is a list of various common troubles, each one of which is directly followed by its possible causes.

A.   ENGINE TROUBLES
1.   Engine fails to start
    a.   Lack of gasoline - empty tank or trouble in fuel system.
    b.   Carburetor needs priming.
    c.   Poor quality of gasoline - may contain water or be old and stale.
    d.   Too much gasoline - cylinder may be flooded; spark plugs may be soaked; gasoline needle valve not working.
    e.   No pressure in fuel tank.
    f.   Lack of ignition current - may be due to exhausted battery or broken or loose wiring.
    g.   Spark plugs - may be sooted from over-lubrication, or the points may be burnt or corroded.

2.   Engine starts but misses
    (The missing cylinder or cylinders may be located by short circuiting each spark plug with a screw driver. When the plug in the missing cylinder is short-circuited no difference will be noticed in the engine. Short-circuiting a good cylinder will cause another miss and slow the engine.)
    a.   Defective spark plugs.
    b.   Wet spark plugs, wiring or distributor.
    c.   Defective or dirty or wet distributor.
    d.   Improper or broken wiring connections.
    e.   Weak battery
    f.   Incorrect fuel mixture.
    g.   Defect ive condenser.
    h.   Engine cold on a cold day.
    i.   Valve leakage, which might be due to
        (1) Valves adjusted too tightly.
        (2) Need for grinding.
        (3) Broken spring or seat.
        (4) Carbon deposit.

3.   Engine starts but will not pull
    a.   Brakes dragging or hand brake set.
    b.   Low oil supply.
    c.   Defective lubrication system.
    d.   Water supply low, or defect in cooling system.
    e.   Mixture too lean or too rich.
    f.   Leaky valves or rings, causing loss of compression.

g. Spark retarded or improperly timed.
h. Slipping clutch.
i. Trouble in the ignition system.

4. Engine is hard to start
   a. Stiff engine due to cold weather or improper lubrication.
   b. Choke not functioning properly.
   c. Incorrect throttle setting.
   d. Lean mixture; leaky valves; weak battery.

5. Engine overheats
   a. Water or oil supply low.
   b. Defective or dirty cooling or lubrication system.
   c. Spark retarded or improperly timed.
   d. Mixture too rich or engine badly carbonized.
   e. Too much running on low gear.

6. Engine stalls
   a. If it stops suddenly without warning, either the ignition switch was turned off accidentally or there is trouble in the ignition system.
   b. If permanent stalling is preceded by intermittent missing or stalling, look for ignition trouble.
   c. If the engine "peters out" as though the throttle were suddenly closed all the way, look for carburetor trouble (usually dirt).
   d. If petering out is preceded by loss of power, backfiring, or missing (without muffler explosions) the trouble is most probably due to dirt in the fuel system.
   e. List of possible causes
      (1) Lack of gasoline.
      (2) Dirt or water in the fuel system.
      (3) Failure of fuel feed system.
      (4) Defects, improper connections, dirt or water in the ignition system.
      (5) Valves adjusted too tightly.
      (6) Mixture too rich.
      (7) Incorrect timing of valves or spark plugs.

7. Engine knocks
   a. Carbon knock - most noticeable when the car climbs in a steep grade in high gear. Usually not heard when engine is warming up.
   b. Spark too far advanced - noticeable with the throttle open and the engine pulling hard.
   c. Loose connecting-rod bearing - heard when the engine is running idly down hill, or when it is allowed to decelerate after speeding up.
   d. Loose main bearing - noticeable when running fast with the spark advanced.
   e. Loose flywheel - noticed when the ignition is shut off with the engine running, and then switched on when the engine has almost stopped.

  f. Loose pistons - most noticeable when the engine is speeded up while the car is standing.
  g. Loose piston pin.
  h. Lean mixture.
  i. Engine too hot or lacks oil,
  j. Valves stuck or need adjusting.

8. Engine backfires (This is always accompanied by missing.)
  a. Cold engine.
  b. Spark too far retarded.
  c. Fuel heating device not working.
  d. Lean mixture.
  e. Dirt in the carburator.
  f. Intake valve leaks, or too much clearance on exhaust valve.

9. Engine keeps running with switch off
   (This is caused by over heating, which may be due to:)
  a. Ignition system - defective switch.
  b. Poor oil - deposits carbon on the cylinder, and this carbon becomes red-hot, causing pre-ignition.

B. STARTING MOTOR TROUBLES
  1. Starting motor does not operate
    a. Battery - may be weak or exhausted, or a connection may be loose.
    b. Bendix drive or starting mechanism out of order.
    c. Open circuit in the wiring - broken or loose wiring connections.

  2. Starting motor operates, but not enough to turn over
    a. Weak battery.
    b. Engine may be unusually stiff.
    c. Poor contact at battery terminals.
    d. Trouble in the starting motor mechanism.

C. ENGINE LUBRICATION TROUBLES
  1. High oil consumption
    a. Leakage past pistons, or in the lubricating system.
    b. Oil too light or of poor quality.
    c. Pump pressure too high.
    d. High engine speeds.

  2. Low oil consumption
    a. Dilution of oil by fuel.
    b. Leakage of water into the oil,

  3. High and low oil pressures

  4. Oil gauge hand flutters
    a. Low oil supply.
    b. Leak in the piping.
    c. Pump strainer dirty.

          d.   Intermittent clogging in the lubrication system.

D.   CLUTCH TROUBLES

    1.   Clutch slips (Engine runs too fast in relation to car speed.)
- a. Too much oil on a lubricated clutch; oil present on a dry clutch.
- b. Clutch needs adjusting.
- c. Weak clutch.
- d. Badly worn clutch facings.

    2.   Clutch drags (Fails to release fully when thrown out.)
- a. Adjustment too tight.
- b. Rivets in the facing are protruding.
- c. Clutch bearing worn or broken.
- d. Clutch out of alignment.

    3.   Clutch spins (The driven member of the clutch fails to come to rest quickly when the clutch is thrown out.)
- a. Oil on clutch brake.
- b. Clutch adjusted too tightly.

    4.   Clutch grabs (A tendency of the clutch to take hold too suddenly.)
- a. Gummed oil on clutch faces.
- b. Adjustment too tight.
- c. Rivets protruding from clutch facing.
- d. Glazed lining.

E.   COOLING SYSTEM TROUBLES (Any defect in this system results in overheating the engine.)
1. Not enough water in the system.
2. Core passages of the radiator clogged -cleaned by flushing with a mixture of salsoda and water.
3. Faulty water pump.
4. Frozen water in the radiator.
5. Anti-freeze in the system in hot weather.
6. Leaks in the system.
7. Fan belt not working properly.

F.   BATTERY TROUBLES
1. Defective generator or circuit breaker.
2. Open circuits or poor connections.
3. Low electrolyte.
4. Sulphated or corroded battery terminals.
5. Battery does not hold charge.
- a. Car not run enough in the day time, or not a high enough speed, for the generator to charge the battery and replace the current consumed by the lights, starter, etc.
- b. Generator output not properly adjusted.
- c. Circuit breaker not operating properly.
- d. Overload on the electrical system, due to too many appliances (radio, lighters, etc.).
- e. Plates are sulphated.

f.   Active material of the plate grids is loose.

G.   CARBURETION TROUBLES

1.   Mixture too rich

    a.   Air cleaner dirty or clogged.

    b.   Improper choke adjustment.

    c.   Fuel pump pressure too high.

    d.   Nozzle oversize or improperly adjusted.

    e.   Leaking float, with not enough buoyancy to close the valve.

    f.   Float level too high - this is one of the most common causes for incorrect carburetion.

    g.   Leaking float valve.

    h.   Changing from heavy to light fuel, with the carburetor adjusted for the. heavier fuel.

    i.   Cold intake manifold.

    j.   Excessive back pressure due to clogged muffler or partly clogged exhaust pipe.

2.   Mixture too lean

    a.   Air leaks between the carburetor and the cylinders.

    b.   Float level set too low.

    c.   Fuel nozzle clogged or undersized.

    d.   Low pressure from fuel pump.

    e.   Incorrect valve timing, causing the inlet valves to close before allowing a full charge of gas into the cylinder.

    f.   Change from light to heavy fuel, with the carburetor adjusted to light fuel.

    g.   Excessively high temperatures of intake manifold or cooling system.

H.   REAR AXLE TROUBLES

1.   Wheels do not turn

    a.   Key holding the wheel may be broken.

    b.   Ring gear rivets sheared on differential housing.

    c.   Broken axle shaft, or pinion shaft coupling.

    d.   Broken universal joint or propeller shaft.

2.   Axle bucks or clashes

    a.   Worn pinion shaft thrust bearing or drive gear or pinion.

    b.   Worn universal joint or differential pinion.

    c.   Broken teeth or ring gear.

I.   STEERING TROUBLES

1.   Shimmy - excessive vibration of the front wheels from side to side or up and down, causing a jerky motion of the steering wheel.

    a.   Excessive caster, or, incorrect toe-in.

    b.   Low or unequal tire pressures.

    c.   Unbalanced front wheels.

    d.   Shock absorbers not acting properly.

    e.   Springs that are weak or have broken leaves.

    f.   Loose wheels or steering connections.

2. Pulling to one side
   a. Unequal camber or caster, or one rear wheel cambered.
   b. Unequal tire inflation.
   c. Dragging brakes or tight wheel bearings.

3. Wandering or weaving - gradual swinging of the car to one side or the other of the road.
   a. Insufficient or reversed caster.
   b. Excessive tightness or looseness in the steering system.
   c. Unequal camber or caster.
   d. Incorrect toe-in.
   e. Underinflation of rear tires.

4. Hard steering - especially in making turns.
   a. Excessive caster or tightness in steering system.
   b. Twisted axle, or improper camber.
   c. Low or unequal tire inflation.

J. TIRE TROUBLES

1. Tire scuffing - abrasion of the tread as it is dragged over the road surface instead of rolling on it. Caused by incorrect toe-in, or incorrect turning radius.
2. Excessive wear on one side of the tread - caused by incorrect camber.
3. Several worn spots are caused by a wobbly wheel or consistently making abrupt stops.
4. Uneven wear may be caused by springs that are too flexible, allowing variations in camber, caster or toe-in.
5. Excessive wear of the center of the tread may be due to improper alignment of the wheels or over-inflation.
6. Greater wear on the outer edges of the tread than in the center is usually due to under-inflation.

K. BRAKE TROUBLES

The most common brake trouble is slipping, which may be caused by oil, water or grease on the lining; by poor adjustment; by worn brakes linings. Sometimes the car tends to skid to one side when the brakes are applied. This means the brake on one wheel is dragging or binding, and is due to improper adjustment. Where all brakes tighten suddenly, the cause is most probably a broken near spring. Since the brakes control the safe operation of the car, they should be kept in the best possible condition. Any troubles in the brake system should be remedied immediately, and it should be kept in mind that "taking up" the brakes is sometimes a poor substitute for replacing the lining.

L. TROUBLES INDICATED BY THE EXHAUST SMOKE

1. Black and foul-smelling smoke is caused by too rich a mixture.
2. White or blue smoke means too much oil in the engine.
3. Gray smoke indicates too much fuel as well as excess oil.

BASIC FUNDAMENTALS OF ENGINES

CONTENTS

———

BASIC FUNDAMENTALS OF ENGINES

1. Engine Construction

The first step in understanding automotive engine construction and operation is to understand what goes on inside the engine. No matter how many cylinders an engine has, whether 1, 2, 6 or 12, the same actions take place in each cylinder. Since the diesel engine is mechanically similar to the gasoline engine we can learn about engine construction and operation by studying a single-cylinder engine (fig. 1). This engine is a 4-stroke-cycle (fig. 4), internal combustion, gasoline engine; these terms are explained in subsequent paragraphs.

a. Cylinder and Piston. A cutaway of a single cylinder gasoline engine is shown in figure 1. The upper, or head end is closed by a cylinder head, but the lower end is open. The piston is a hollow metal tube with the top end closed. It is a close-sliding fit in the cylinder, which means it can move up and down in the cylinder. This up-and-down movement, produced by the burning of fuel in the cylinder, results in the production of power from the engine.

b. Connecting Rod and Crank. The up-and-down movement of the piston is called *reciprocating motion.* This reciprocating motion must be changed to rotary motion so the wheels of the vehicle can be made to rotate. The change is accomplished by a crank on the crankshaft and a connecting rod which connects between the piston (fig. 2) and the crank. The connecting rod is connected to the piston by a piston pin. The pin passes through bearing surfaces in the piston and the connecting rod. The lower end of the connecting rod is attached to the crankpin on the crankshaft. As the piston moves up and down in the cylinder, the upper end of the connecting rod moves up and down with it. The lower end

of the connecting rod also moves up and down but, because it is attached to the crankpin on the crankshaft (fig. 3), it must also move in a circle with the crankpin. Each movement of the piston from top to bottom or from bottom to top is called a *stroke.* The piston takes two strokes as the crankshaft makes one complete revolution, an upstroke and a downstroke. When the pis-

Figure 1. Single-cylinder, 4-stroke cycle, internal combustion, gasoline engine—cutaway view.

PISTON

PISTON PIN

BOLT

CONNECTING } ROD }

CRANKPIN

CRANKSHAFT

{ LOWER ROD
{ BEARING CAP

WASHER

NUT

Figure 2. Piston, connecting rod, and piston pin.

ton is at the top of a stroke, it is said to be at top dead center (TDC). When the piston is at the bottom of a stroke, it is said to be at bottom dead center (BDC). These positions are called rock position (par. **5c**).

c. Valves. There are two valves (fig. 1) at the top of the cylinder. A valve is an accurately machined plug that fits into a machined opening at the top of the cylinder. When the valve is resting in this opening, it is said to be *seated*. When a valve is so positioned, it is *closed* and the opening is sealed off. When the valve is pushed off its seat, it is *opened*. The two valves in the cylinder are closed part of the time and opened part of the time. The valve mechanism that causes the valves to open and close is discussed in paragraph **2c**. One of the valves, called the *intake valve*, opens to admit a mixture of fuel and air into the cylinder. The other valve, called the *exhaust valve*, opens to allow the escape of burned gases after the fuel-and-air mixture has burned.

2. Engine Operation

a. Intake Stroke. The actions that take place within the engine cylinder may be divided into four basic parts, which are called *strokes*. The first stroke in the sequence is called the *intake* stroke (fig. 4). During this stroke, the piston is moving downward and the intake valve is open. This downward movement of the piston produces a partial void, or vacuum, in the cylinder, and air rushes into the cylinder past the opened instake valve. This is somewhat the same effect as when drinking through a straw. A partial vacuum is produced in the mouth and the liquid moves up through the straw to fill the vacuum (fig. 5). In the engine, the inrushing air passes through the carburetor before it enters the cylinder. The carburetor charges the air with gasoline vapor to produce a combustible mixture.

b. Compression Stroke. When the piston reaches bottom dead center at the end of the intake stroke and is therefore at the bottom of the cylinder, the intake valve closes. This seals the upper end of the cylinder. As the crankshaft continues to rotate, it pushes up, through the connecting rod, on the piston. The piston is therefore pushed upward and compresses the combustible mixture in the cylinder; this is called the *compression* stroke. The mixture is compressed to about a sixth or a seventh of its original volume. This is the same as taking a gallon of air and compressing it until a little more than a pint of air is left. Compressing the mixture in this way makes it still more combustible; the energy in the fuel is concentrated into a smaller space.

c. Power Stroke. As the piston reaches top dead center at the end of the compression stroke and therefore has moved to the top of the cylinder, the compressed fuel-air mixture is ignited. This ignition is produced by the ignition system. The ignition system causes an electric spark to occur suddenly in the cylinder. The spark sets fire to the fuel-air mixture. The mixture burns so rapidly that it might be said to explode. The pressure in the cylinder goes up to as much as 400 psi. This means that the force pushing on the end of a 3-inch piston would be more than 2,500 pounds. This force, or thrust, pushes the piston down. The thrust is carried through the connecting rod to the crankpin on the crankshaft. The crankshaft is given a powerful twist. This is called the *power* stroke. This turning effort, rapidly repeated in the engine and carried through gears and shafts,

PISTON

CRANKSHAFT

CONNECTING ROD

Figure 3. Relationship of piston, connecting rod, and crank on crankshaft as crankshaft turns one revolution.

will turn the wheels of a vehicle and cause it to move along the highway.

d. Exhaust Stroke. After the fuel-air mixture has burned, it must be cleared from the cylinder. This is done by opening the exhaust valve just as the power stroke is finished and the piston starts back up on the *exhaust* stroke. The piston forces the burned gases out of the cylinder past the opened exhaust valve. The four strokes (intake, compression, power, and exhaust) are continuously repeated as the engine runs.

e. Valve Mechanism Action. There are various ways of causing the intake and exhaust valves to open and close. One method is shown in figure 1. Here, a gear on the crankshaft is meshed with a second gear on another shaft. When the crankshaft turns, the other shaft must also turn. This second shaft is called the *camshaft* because it has a number of *cams on it*. These cams are simply raised sections, or collars, with high spots on them. When the camshaft rotates, the high spots (called *lobes*) move around and push away anything they

are in contact with. Riding on each cam is a cylindrical valve tappet. As the lobe moves up under the valve tappet, the valve tappet is raised. This upward movement causes the valve above it to be raised also. Thus, the valve is raised up off its seat in the cylinder so that the valve opens. When the lobe on the cam moves on around out of the way, the pressure of the spring under the valve forces the valve to move down and reseat. At the same time, the valve tappet is also forced downward so that it remains in contact with the cam. The gear on the camshaft is twice as large (has twice the number of teeth) as the gear on the crankshaft. This means that the camshaft will revolve half as fast as the crankshaft. In other words, the crankshaft must turn twice for the camshaft to turn once. Thus, the valves are opened only once every two crankshaft revolutions. This is the way it should be, since there is only one intake stroke (intake valve open) and only one exhaust stroke (exhaust valve open) every two crankshaft revolutions.

Figure 4. The four strokes in the 4-stroke cycle, gasoline engine.

Figure 5. Partial vacuum produced by suction.

f. Engine Accessory Systems. We have mentioned the carburetor which supplies vaporized fuel to the air passing into the engine cylinder on the intake stroke (*a* above). The carburetor is a unit in the fuel system. Another accessory system is the ignition system which ignites the compressed fuel-air mixture in the cylinder at the end of the compression stroke. A third accessory sys-

tem is the lubrication system; this supplies lubricating oil to the various moving parts in the engine. The oil lubricates all parts, such as the piston, bearings, crankpin, and valve stems, that rotate or slide in or on other parts. This oil permits the parts to move easily so that little power is lost and wear of parts is kept to a minimum. A fourth system is the cooling system. In the simple engine shown in figure 1, water is used as the cooling medium. Water circulates in jackets around the cylinder and in the cylinder head. This water removes part of the heat produced by the combustion of the fuel-air mixture. This action prevents the engine from overheating and thereby being damaged. All these accessory systems are described in detail in following chapters.

3. Comparison of Engine Types

a. Internal and External Combustion Engines. In the internal combustion engine, the combustion of the fuel takes place inside the engine cylinder. This is in contrast to external combustion engines, such as steam engines, where the combustion takes place outside of the engine. Figure 6 shows in simplified form an internal and an external combustion engine. The external combustion engine requires a boiler in which a fuel is burned. This combustion causes water to boil to produce steam. The steam passes into the engine cylinder under pressure and forces the piston to move downward. With the internal combustion engine, the combustion taking place inside the cylinder is directly responsible for forcing the piston to move downward. In both types of engine, valving is arranged to permit the piston to move back upward as the spent steam (external combustion engine) or burned gas (internal combustion engine) is exhausted.

Figure 6. Comparison of internal and external combustion engines.

b. Four-Stroke-Cycle and Two-Stroke-Cycle Engines. The engine described in paragraph 8 and illustrated in figures 1 and 4 is a 4-stroke-cycle engine. Four strokes of the piston, with two revolutions of the crankshaft and one revolution of the camshaft, are required for the complete cycle of events. This type of engine is also called a 4-stroke-Otto-cycle engine because it was Dr. N. A. Otto who, in 1876, first applied the principles of this engine. In the 2-stroke-cycle engine, the entire cycle of events (intake, compression, power, and exhaust) takes place in two piston strokes. This is accomplished by combining the four events so that they take place in two instead of four strokes, as explained in (1) and (2) below.

    (1) *Two-stroke cycle.* A 2-stroke-cycle engine is shown in figure 7. Every other stroke on this engine is a power stroke. Each time the piston moves down it is on the power stroke. Intake, compression, power, and exhaust still take place,

but they are completed in just two strokes. Intake and exhaust ports are cut into the cylinder wall instead of being placed at the top of the combustion chamber as in the 4-stroke-cycle engine. As the piston moves down on its power stroke, it first uncovers the exhaust port to let burned gases escape and then uncovers the intake port to allow a new fuel-air mixture to enter the combustion chamber. Then, on the upward stroke, the piston covers both ports and, at the same time, compresses the new mixture in preparation for ignition and another power stroke. In the engine shown in figure 7, the piston is so shaped that the incoming fuel-air mixture is directed upward, thereby sweeping out ahead of it the burned exhaust gases. Also, there is an inlet into the crankcase through which the fuel-

Figure 7. Events in a 2-stroke-cycle, internal combustion engine.

air mixture passes before it enters the cylinder. This inlet is opened as the piston moves upward, but it is sealed off as the piston moves downward on the power stroke. The downward moving piston slightly compresses the mixture in the crankcase, thus giving the mixture sufficient pressure to pass rapidly through the intake port as the piston clears this port. This improves the "sweeping-out," or scavenging, effect of the mixture as it enters and clears the burned gases from the cylinder through the exhaust port.

(2) *Comparison of 2-stroke-cycle and 4-stroke-cycle engines.* It might appear that a 2-stroke-cycle engine could produce twice as much horsepower as a 4-stroke-cycle engine of the same size, operating at the same speed. However, this is not the case. In order to scavenge the burned gases at the end of the power stroke and during the time both the intake and exhaust ports are open, the fresh fuel-air mixture rushes into and through the cylinder. A portion of the fresh fuel-air mixture mingles with the burned gases and is carried out the exhaust port. Also, due to the much shorter period the intake port is open (as compared to the period the intake valve in a 4-stroke-cycle engine is open), a relatively smaller amount of fuel-air mixture is admitted. Hence, with less fuel-air mixture, less power per power stroke is produced as compared to the power produced in a 4-stroke-cycle engine of like size operating at the same speed, and with other conditions being the same. To increase the amount of fuel-air mixture, auxiliary devices are used with 2-stroke-cycle engines to assure delivery of greater amounts of fuel-air mixture into the cylinder. Figure 7 shows one device which utilizes compression in the crankcase ((1) above). Other engines may use a blower or supercharger.

c. *Diesel Engines.* The diesel engine bears the name of Dr. Rudolph Diesel, a German engineer. He is credited with constructing, in 1897, the first successful diesel engine using liquid fuel.

His objective was an engine with greater fuel economy than the steam engine, which used only a small percentage of the energy contained in the coal burned under its boilers. Dr. Diesel originally planned to use pulverized coal as fuel, but his first experimental engine in 1893 was a failure. After a second engine also failed, he changed his plan and used liquid fuel. The engine then proved successful.

d. *Diesel Engine Compared to Gasoline Engine.*

(1) *General mechanical construction.* The diesel engine is mechanically similar to the gasoline engine but is somewhat heavier in construction. Both engine types utilize air, fuel, compression, and ignition. Intake, compression, power, and exhaust occur in the same sequence; arrangements of pistons, connecting rods, and crankshafts are similar. Both are internal combustion engines; that is, they extract energy from a fuel-air mixture by burning the mixture inside the engine.

(2) *Fuel intake and ignition of fuel-air mixture.* In principles of operation, the main difference between gasoline and diesel engines (figs. 8 and 9) is the two different methods of introducing the fuel into the cylinder and of igniting the fuel-air mixture. Fuel and air are mixed together before they enter the cylinder of a gasoline engine. The mixture is compressed by the upstroke of the piston and is ignited within the cylinder by a spark plug. (Devices other than spark plugs, such as "firing tubes," are sometimes utilized.) Air alone enters the cylinder of a diesel engine. The air is compressed by the upstroke of the piston and the diesel fuel is injected into the combustion chamber near the top of the upstroke (compression stroke). The air becomes greatly heated during compression and the diesel fuel ignites and burns as it is injected into the heated air. No spark plug is used in the diesel engine; ignition is by contact of the fuel with the heated air, although "glow plugs" are used in some models of diesel engines to assist in starting. Pressure developed by the compression stroke is much greater in the

EXHAUST

POWER

INJECTION

Figure 8. 4-stroke-cycle diesel engine.

COMPRESSION

INTAKE

GASOLINE

INTAKE STROKE

DIESEL

ON DOWNWARD STROKE OF PISTON, INTAKE VALVE OPENS AND ATMOSPHERIC PRESSURE FORCES AIR THROUGH CARBURETOR WHERE IT PICKS UP A METERED COMBUSTIBLE CHARGE OF FUEL. THE MIXTURE GOES PAST THE THROTTLE VALVE INTO CYLINDER SPACE VACATED BY THE PISTON

ON DOWNWARD STROKE OF PISTON, INTAKE VALVE OPENS AND ATMOSPHERIC PRESSURE FORCES PURE AIR INTO THE CYLINDER SPACE VACATED BY THE PISTON, THERE BEING NO CARBURETOR OR THROTTLE VALVE. CYLINDER FILLS WITH SAME QUANTITY OF AIR, REGARDLESS OF LOAD ON THE ENGINE.

COMPRESSION STROKE

ON UPSTROKE OF PISTON, VALVES ARE CLOSED AND MIXTURE IS COMPRESSED, USUALLY FROM 70 TO 125 PSI, DEPENDING ON COMPRESSION RATIO OF ENGINE.

ON UPSTROKE OF PISTON, VALVES ARE CLOSED AND AIR IS COMPRESSED TO APPROXIMATELY 500 PSI.

POWER STROKE

SPARK PLUG   NOZZLE

MAGNETO OR DISTRIBUTOR

FUEL INJECTION PUMP

COMPRESSED FUEL-AIR MIXTURE IS IGNITED BY ELECTRIC SPARK. HEAT OF COMBUSTION CAUSES FORCEFUL EXPANSION OF CYLINDER GASES AGAINST PISTON, RESULTING IN POWER STROKE.

HIGH COMPRESSION PRODUCES HIGH TEMPERATURE FOR SPONTANEOUS IGNITION OF FUEL INJECTED NEAR END OF COMPRESSION STROKE. HEAT OF COMBUSTION EXPANDS CYLINDER GASES AGAINST PISTON, RESULTING IN POWER STROKE.

EXHAUST STROKE

1300°F   900°F

UPSTROKE OF PISTON WITH EXHAUST VALVE OPEN FORCES BURNED GASES OUT, MAKING READY FOR ANOTHER INTAKE STROKE.

UPSTROKE OF PISTON WITH EXHAUST VALVE OPEN FORCES BURNED GASES OUT, MAKING READY FOR ANOTHER INTAKE STROKE.

Figure 9. Comparison of sequence of events in diesel and gasoline engines.

diesel engine, in which pressures as high as 500 psi are common. For each pound of pressure exerted on the air, there will be a temperature increase of about 2° F. At the top of the compression stroke (when pressure is highest), the temperature in the chamber will be about 1,000° F. This heat ignites the fuel almost as soon as it is injected into the cylinder, and the piston, actuated by the expansion of burning gases, then moves down on the power stroke. In a gasoline engine, the heat from compression is not enough to ignite the fuel-air mixture and a spark plug is therefore necessary.

(3) *Control of speed and power.* The speed and the power output of diesel engines are controlled by the quantity of fuel injected into the cylinder. This is opposed to the common gasoline engine, which controls speed and power output by limiting the amount of air admitted to the carburetor. The difference is that the diesel engine controls the quantity of fuel, whereas the gasoline engine regulates the quantity of air. In the diesel engine, a varying amount of fuel is mixed with a constant amount of compressed air inside the cylinder. A full charge of air enters the cylinder on each intake stroke. Because the quantity of air is constant, the amount of fuel injected determines power output and speed. As long as the amount of fuel injected is below the maximum established by the manufacturer in designing the engine, there is always enough air in the cylinder for complete combustion. A device in the carburetor of the gasoline engine controls the amount of air admitted. The amount of air and its velocity, in turn, control the quantity of fuel that is picked up and mixed with air to be admitted to the cylinder. The amount of mixture available for combustion determines power output and speed. It is apparent, therefore, that the controlling factor is the quantity and velocity of air passing through the carburetor.

(4) *Combustion process.* In the diesel engine, there is continuous combustion during the entire length of the power stroke, and pressure resulting from combustion

remains approximately constant throughout the stroke. In the gasoline engine, however, combustion is completed while the piston is at the upper part of its travel. This means that the volume of the mixture stays about the same during most of the combustion process. When the piston does move down and the volume increases, there is little additional combustion to maintain pressure. Because of these facts, the cycle of the gasoline engine is often referred to as having *constant-volume* combustion while the diesel cycle is said to have *constant-pressure* combustion.

4. Engine Measurements

a. Bore and Stroke. The size of an engine cylinder is usually indicated in terms of bore and stroke (fig. 10). *Bore* is the diameter of the cylinder. *Stroke* is the distance the piston moves in the cylinder, or the distance between top dead center and bottom dead center. When reference

Figure 10. Bore and stroke of an engine cylinder.

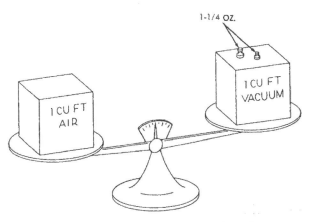

Figure 11. Illustrating the weight of air.

is made to these two measurements, the bore is always given first. For example, a 3⅝ x 4 cylinder means that the cylinder bore, or diameter, is 3⅝ inches and the length of the stroke is 4 inches.

b. Piston Displacement. Piston displacement is the volume of space that the piston displaces as it moves from bottom dead center to top dead center. The volume is figured by multiplying the length of stroke by the area of a circle having the diameter of the cylinder bore. Thus, a ⅝-inch-diameter circle has an area of 10.321 square inches, and therefore, this times 4 inches (length of stroke) equals 41.284 cubic inches, the piston displacement, that is, the number of cubic inches the piston displaces as it moves from bottom dead center to top dead center.

c. Vacuum in Cylinder on Intake Stroke. The piston, in moving down on the intake stroke, produces a partial vacuum in the cylinder. It is this vacuum that is responsible for air rushing in to fill the vacuum. A vacuum can be defined as an absence of air or other substances. It may be hard to think of air as a substance because it does not seem substantial, but it can be felt as a breeze or wind when it is moving.

(1) *The atmosphere.* Air does have weight, as can be proven with a balance scale and two 1-cubic-foot containers (fig. 11). If all air was drawn from one container so that it would be really empty (a vacuum), then it would weigh less than the other container. In fact, to balance the scales, 1¼ ounces would have to be placed on the empty container. At sea level, the weight of the air, pressing downward on the ground, produces a pressure of about 14.7 psi. This amount of pressure

means there is a great deal of air above us and there is a great amount of air surrounding the earth. This air, called the *atmosphere*, extends many miles above the earth. The atmosphere is a great ocean of air, and we live at the bottom of it, on the ground.

(2) *Atmospheric pressure.* The miles and miles of air extending above presses downward, or exerts pressure. Ordinarily this pressure is not noticed because we are accustomed to it. If the air was removed from a container and then the container was opened, this pressure would push air back into the container. This might be compared to what happens when an empty bottle is held under water and the cork is removed. The pressure of the water pushes water into the bottle. The higher we go into the air, as for instance when in an airplane, the less pressure is found. The reason for this is that as we ascend there is less air above us; we climb toward the top of the atmosphere. This means there is less air to press down on us and therefore the pressure is less. Six miles above the earth, for example, the pressure is only about 4.4 psi. Returning to earth, the air pressure increases. The nearer earth is approached, or the bottom of the ocean of air, the greater the pressure of the air. At sea level, this pressure is about 14.7 psi ((1) above).

(3) *Vacuum in the cylinder.* When the piston starts to move downward in the cylinder on the intake stroke, it produces a vacuum in the cylinder. If both the intake and exhaust valves were closed, then no substance could enter to fill this vacuum. The cylinder would remain empty. However, at the same time that the piston starts to move down, the intake valve is opened. Now, atmospheric pressure pushes air past the intake valve and into the cylinder. The cylinder therefore becomes filled with air (or with fuel-air mixture in gasoline engines).

d. Volumetric Efficiency. Although the atmosphere exerts considerable pressure and rapidly forces air into the cylinder on the intake stroke, it does take time for the air to flow through the carburetor and past the intake valve. If given enough time, enough air will flow into the cylinder to "fill it up." However, the air is given very little time to do this. For example, when the engine is running at 1,200 rpm, the intake stroke lasts only 0.025 second. In this very brief period, all the air that could enter does not have time to flow into the cylinder. The intake stroke ends too quickly. Nevertheless, engine design has taken this factor into consideration so that good operation will result even at high engine speed.

(1) *Measuring volumetric efficiency.* The measure of the amount of fuel-air mixture that actually enters the cylinder is referred to in terms of *volumetric efficiency.* Volumetric efficiency is the ratio between the amount of fuel-air mixture that actually enters the cylinder and the amount that could enter under ideal conditions. The greater the volumetric efficiency, the greater the amount of fuel-air mixture entering the cylinder. And the greater the amount of fuel-air mixture, the more power produced from the engine cylinder. At low speeds, more fuel-air mixture can get into the cylinder, and therefore the power produced during the power stroke is greater. Volumetric efficiency is high. But at high speeds, the shorter time taken by the intake stroke reduces the amount of fuel-air mixture entering the cylinder. Volumetric efficiency then is lower. In addition, the air is heated as it passes through hot manifolds on its way to the cylinder, and it therefore expands. This further reduces the amount of fuel-air mixture entering the cylinder, and further reduces volumetric efficiency.

(2) *Increasing volumetric efficiency.* Volumetric efficiency is higher at low engine speed because more fuel-air mixture gets into the cylinder ((1) above). Volumetric efficiency can also be improved by use of a blower, or air-compressing, device. On gasoline engines, this device is called a *supercharger.* It raises the air pressure above atmospheric pressure so that the air is pushed harder on its way into the cylinder. The harder push, or higher pressure, insures that more air will enter the cylinder. In a super-

PISTON AT BDC

PISTON AT TDC

Figure 12. Compression ratio is ratio between "A" and "B."

charged engine, the volumetric efficiency can run well over 100 percent. Since 100 percent efficiency means that the pressure inside the cylinder equals atmospheric pressure, a volumetric efficiency of more than 100 percent means the pressure inside the cylinder would be greater than atmospheric pressure at the end of the intake stroke. This increased volumetric efficiency increases engine power output. A supercharger is very important on airplane engines because the lowered air pressure (about 4.4 psi at a height of 6 miles) must be greatly increased if engine power output is to be maintained at high altitudes. Also, on 2-stroke-cycle engines, some form of device is required to increase the pressure of the ingoing fuel-air mixture (par. **3b**).

e. Compression Ratio. The compression ratio of an engine (fig. 12) is the volume in one cylinder with the piston at bottom dead center (displacement volume plus clearance volume) divided by the volume with the piston at top dead center (clearance volume). This figure indicates the actual amount that the air drawn into the cylinder will be compressed. For example, suppose that an engine cylinder has an air volume of 63 cubic inches with the piston at bottom dead center and a volume of 10 cubic inches with

13

the piston at top dead center. This gives a compression ratio of 63 divided by 10 or 6.3 : 1. That is, the air is compressed from 63 to 10 cubic inches, or to 1/6.3 of its original volume, on the compression stroke.

f. Effect of Increasing Compression Ratio. As compression ratio is increased, the fuel-air mixture drawn into the cylinder is compressed into a smaller space. This means a higher initial pressure at the start of the power stroke. It also means that the burning gases can expand a greater amount. Thus, there are higher pressures for a longer period on the power stroke. More power is obtained with each power stroke. Therefore, increasing compression ratio increases power output of an engine. Racing-car builders machine off cylinder heads so as to reduce the volume of the combustion chambers and thereby increase compression ratios. By this one act, the power output of an engine can be increased several horsepower. One important p r o b l e m brought about by increasing compression ratios is to find a fuel that will not cause difficulty from detonation.

5 . Timing

In a gasoline engine, the valves must open and close at the proper times with regard to piston position and stroke. In addition, the ignition system must produce the sparks at the spark plugs at the proper time so the power strokes can

Figure 13. Valve timing diagram on one engine.

start. Both valve and ignition system action must be properly timed if good engine performance is to be obtained.

a. Valve Timing. A new mixture must be trapped in the cylinder at the proper time during each cycle and, after combustion, the exhaust gases must be allowed to flow out of the cylinder. This means that the intake and exhaust valves must open and close in step with the piston movement. The opening and closing of the valves is controlled by the camshaft. The position of the piston is related to the position of the crankshaft since they are connected by the connecting rod. Thus, the crankshaft and camshaft must be in the proper relationship for correct valve timing. Figure 1 shows one method of driving the camshaft; a gear on the crankshaft drives a gear on the camshaft. These gears are called *timing gears*. The camshaft gear has twice as many teeth as the crankshaft gear (par. 2c). Thus, the camshaft turns once for every two crankshaft revolutions. As long as the relationship between the gears is not changed, the timing of the valve action will be in correct relationship to the piston movement. Figure 13 illustrates a valve timing diagram on one engine. Valve timing varies for different engines.

b. Exhaust Valve Timing. The exhaust valve opens before the piston reaches the end of the power stroke so that the pressure remaining in the cylinder will cause the exhaust gases to start rushing from the cylinder. If the valve did not open until the end of the power stroke, then there would be pressure in the cylinder at the start of the exhaust stroke that would impede the upward piston movement. Opening the exhaust valve well before bottom dead center on the power stroke causes some loss of pressure on the piston at the end of the power stroke. However, it does insure better removal of the burned gases which, plus the reduced pressure on the piston at the start of the exhaust stroke, more than balances this small loss.

c. Rock Positions. When the piston is at top dead center the crankshaft can move 15° to 20° without causing the piston to move up or down any perceptible distance. This is one of the two rock positions (fig. 14). When the piston moves up on the exhaust stroke, considerable momentum is imparted to the exhaust gases as they pass out through the exhaust valve port, but if the exhaust valve closes at top dead center, a small amount of the gases will be diluted. Since the piston has

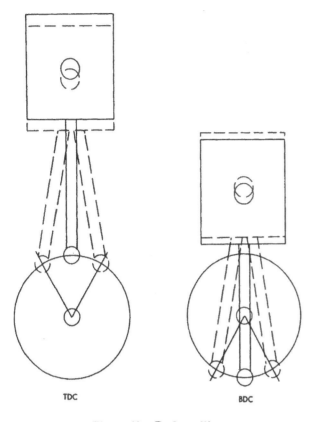

Figure 14. Rock positions.

little downward movement while in the rock position, the exhaust valve can remain open during this period and thereby permit a more complete scavenging of the exhaust gases.

d. Intake Valve Timing. Very little vacuum is produced in the cylinder as the piston passes through the rock position at top dead center. The exhaust gases, however, because of their momentum in passing through the exhaust valve port, produce an air current in the chamber. This air current is sufficient to cause a new mixture to start moving into the cylinder if the intake valve is open. For this reason the intake valve is opened slightly before the piston reaches top dead center. As the piston goes down on the intake stroke, the rapid decrease in pressure in the cylinder enables atmospheric pressure to impart considerable momentum to the incoming mixture. If the piston were to move slowly, the mixture would be able to enter fast enough to keep the pressure in the cylinder equal to that outside. But ordinarily, the piston will be moving so fast that it will reach the end of its downward stroke before a complete change has had time to enter. That is, the pressure in the cylinder will be below that of the atmosphere.

The intake valve therefore remains open a number of additional degrees of crankshaft rotation past bottom dead center (or through the lower rock position). This allows additional time for fuel-air mixture to flow into the cylinder.

e. Ignition Timing. Ignition timing refers to the timing of the spark at the spark plug gap with relation to the piston position during the compression and power strokes. Even though the compressed fuel-air mixture burns very rapidly, almost explosively, it does take some time for the mixture to burn and for the pressure increase from combustion to take place. Therefore, it is common for the ignition system to be so timed that the spark occurs before the piston reaches top dead center on the compression stroke. This gives the mixture sufficient time to ignite and start burning. If this time were not provided, that is, if the spark occurred at or after top dead center, then the pressure increase would not keep pace with the piston movement. The piston would be moving down on the power stroke as the mixture started to burn. The pressure, therefore, would not go very high and power would be lost. This power loss is avoided by timing the spark to occur before top dead center.

f. Ignition Advance. At the higher speeds, there is still less time for the fuel-air mixture to ignite and burn. In order to compensate for this, and thereby avoid power loss, the ignition system includes an advance mechanism that functions on speed. As engine speed increases, the advance mechanism causes the spark to occur earlier in the cycle. Thus, at high speed, the spark may occur as much as 30° before top dead center on the compression stroke. This means that the fuel-air mixture is ignited and starts to burn well before the power stroke actually starts. However, the piston is up over top dead center and moving down on the power stroke before the pressure rises to any great extent. This extra time gives the mixture ample time to burn well and deliver maximum push to the downward-moving piston. On most distributors, there is also a vacuum-advance mechanism which functions on intake-manifold vacuum. At part throttle, there is a partial vacuum in the intake manifold, and less fuel-air mixture is getting into the cylinder. With less fuel-air mixture, the mixture is less highly compressed and burns more slowly. Therefore, the vacuum-advance mechanism provides a spark advance which gives the mixture ample time to burn and increase pressure in the cylinder in the early part of the power stroke.

6. Engine Output

Engines vary in size and output. To compare engines, compare not only their size, but also the work they can do. These functions are explained in *a* through *j* below.

a. Work. Work is the movement of a body against an opposing force. When a weight is lifted from the ground, work is done on the weight. It is moved upward against the force of gravity. When a tank pushes over a tree, it does work on the tree as it forces it to the ground. If a 1-pound weight is lifted one foot, one *foot-pound* of work is done.

b. Energy. Energy is the ability to do work. As the speed of a tank is increased, the energy of movement of the tank is increased. It can thereby knock over a tree more easily. The higher a weight is lifted from the ground, the more energy is stored in the weight. Then, when it falls, it will strike the ground harder; that is, it will do more work on the ground. Suppose a stake is being driven in the ground. The greater the distance the weight falls, the more work it does on the stake and the farther it drives it into the ground.

c. Power. Power is the rate of work. It takes more power to work fast than to work slowly. Engines are rated in terms of the amount of work they can do per minute. A large engine that can do more work per minute is more powerful than a small engine which cannot work so hard. The work capacity of engines is measured in *horsepower*. A horsepower is a definite amount of power. Actually, it is the amount of power that an average horse was found to develop when working hard in tests made many years ago at the time steam engines were being developed. It was found that an average horse could lift a weight of 200 pounds a distance of 165 feet in 1 minute. The amount of work involved here is 33,000 foot-pounds (165 times 200). If 100 pounds were lifted 330 feet, or if 330 pounds were lifted 100 feet, the amount of work would be the same, 33,000 foot-pounds. When this amount of work is done in 1 minute, then 1 horsepower is required. If it took 2 minutes to do this amount of work, then 16,500 foot-pounds per minute, or ½ hp,

would be required. Or, if 33,000 foot-pounds of work were done in ½ minute, then 66,000 foot-pounds per minute, or 2 hp, would be required.

d. Prony Brake. A prony brake may be used to measure the actual horsepower that an engine can deliver. This device usually makes use of a series of wooden blocks fitted around a special flywheel that is driven by the engine (fig. 15). A tightening device is arranged so the blocks can be tightened on the flywheel. In addition, an arm is attached to this tightening device and one end of the arm rests on a scale. In operation, the wooden blocks are tightened on the flywheel. This loads up the engine and works it harder. Also, the pressure on the blocks tends to cause the arm to turn so that force is exerted on the scales. The length of the arm times the force exerted on the scales gives the engine torque in pound-feet (*f* below). The results of the prony brake test can be converted into brake horsepower by using the formula:

$$Bhp = \frac{2\,\pi\,\text{lnw}}{33{,}000}$$

where l is length of the arm in feet, n is the speed in rpm, and w is the load in pounds on the scale. For example, suppose the arm is 3 feet long, the load on the scale is 50 pounds, and the speed is 1,000 rpm. Substituting in the formula gives:

$$Bhp = \frac{2 \times 3.1416 \times 3 \times 1{,}000 \times 50}{33{,}000} = 28.56 \text{ brake horsepower}$$

e. Dynamometer. The dynamometer is essentially a dynamo of a special type which can be driven by an engine. This special dynamo can absorb all the power the engine can produce and indicate this power on dials or gages. Although the dynamometer is more complicated than a prony brake, it is generally considered to be more flexible and accurate. In addition to measuring

Figure 15. Simplified drawing of a prony brake

Figure 16. Applying twisting effort, or torque, on can lid.

engine power output, the dynamometer can also be used to drive the engine for purposes of measuring the friction of the engine itself or of the various accessories.

f. Torque Effect.

(1) Torque is twisting, or turning, effort. When the lid on a jar is loosened, a twisting force, or torque, is applied to it (fig. 16). Torque is measured in *pound-feet* (not to be confused with work, which is m e a s u r e d in foot-pounds). For i n s t a n c e, suppose a wrench is used to tighten a nut on a stud (fig. 17). If the handle of the wrench were 1-foot long and a 10-pound force is put on its end, 10 pound-feet of torque would be applied on the nut. If the handle were 2 feet long and 10-pound force is put on its end, 20 pound-feet of torque would be applied. Torque can be converted into work with the formula

ft-lb (work) = 2π n x lb-ft (torque) = 6.2832 n x lb-ft where n is the speed in revolutions per minute. For example, if an engine were checked on a prony brake and found to be delivering 100 pound-feet torque at 1,000 rpm then it would be

doing 628,320 foot-pounds of work every minute. This can be converted into horsepower by dividing it by 33,000 (*d* above). An illustration of a torque wrench in use is shown in figure 18.

(2) The engine exerts torque through gears and shafts connected to the wheels so that the wheels turn and the vehicle moves. The amount of torque ·that an engine produces varies with engine speed (fig. 19). Note that torque increases and then, at an intermediate speed, falls off. The reason for this variation is that, with increasing speed, the engine is turning faster and is thus capable of supplying a greater twisting effort, or torque. However, with further speed increases, volumetric efficiency falls off. Less fuel-air mixture gets to the cylin-

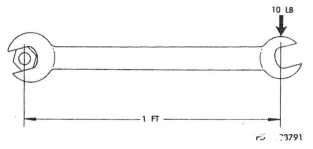

Figure 17. Applying torque with a wrench on a nut.

Figure 18. Torque wrench in use, tightening main bearing studs of an engine.

17

Figure 19. Relationship between torque and speed.

ders each intake stroke and thus the power strokes are not as powerful; torque falls off.

g. Torque-Horsepower-Speed (Rpm) Relationship.

(1) Figure 20 shows the comparison between the horsepower and torque of an engine. Torque increases with speed (up to rated speed) as shown in figure 19. Horsepower also shows a change with speed, and this is more marked than with torque. Horsepower is directly related to both torque and to speed. When both torque and speed are on the increase, as in the speed range of 1,200 to 1,600 rpm, then horsepower goes up sharply. When torque reaches maximum and then begins to taper off, the horsepower curve starts to drop. Finally, in the higher speed ranges, where torque falls off sharply, horsepower also falls off. The horsepower formula ($Hp = \frac{2\pi \, lw}{33,000}$) given in *d* above shows that horsepower depends on both speed and torque, since torque equals lw and n is speed. Substituting in the formula and dividing 2π (or 6.2832) into 33,000 gives

$$Hp = \frac{\text{torque x rpm}}{5,252}$$

which shows the relationship between horsepower, torque, and speed more directly.

(2) A *rated speed* is indicated in figures 19 and 20. This is the speed at which the governor is usually set in military vehicles. The rated speed is selected because, at higher engine speeds, wear on the engine increases rapidly and a disproportionate amount of fuel is used. Overspeeding, or driving the engine above rated speed, allows but a slight increase of horsepower.

h. Gross and Net Horsepower. The gross horsepower of an engine is the amount of power the engine delivers after it has been stripped of muffler, fan, generator, pump, and other accessories that require power to operate. Net horsepower is the power remaining and actually available to drive the vehicle. Net horsepower is the power available at the flywheel after the accessories have detracted from the gross horsepower.

i. Indicated Horsepower. Indicated horsepower is the horsepower actually developed inside the engine cylinders. It is called "indicated" horsepower because an indicating device is required to measure this horsepower. This device measures the pressures developed in the engine cylinders and, by a series of steps, translates this

Figure 20. Relationship between torque and horsepower.

data into indicated horsepower. Indicated horsepower is always considerably greater than horsepower delivered by the engine because power is lost from the engine in a number of ways (friction, heat-loss, etc.)

j. SAE Horsepower. The Society of Automotive Enginers (SAE) developed a simplified method of calculating horsepower, based on engine dimensions. This rating was used only for commercial licensing of vehicles. The formula is:

$$Hp = \frac{DN}{2.5}$$

where D is the cylinder diameter and N is the number of cylinders.

7. Engine Efficiency

The term *efficiency* means the relationship between results obtained and the effort required to obtain those results. It is expressed as: efficiency = $\frac{output}{input}$. Suppose, for example, a set of pulleys were used to raise a 450-pound weight 2 feet and this required a 100-pound pull for 10 feet (fig. 21). It would take 1,000 foot-pounds to get out 900 foot-pounds. The ratio would be $\frac{900}{1,000}$, or 0.90.

In other words, the efficiency of the pulleys would be 90 percent. There was a loss of 10 percent of the work put in. The system of pulleys shows a loss (or is only 90 percent efficient) because of friction. No machine or engine is 100 percent efficient; all lose energy, as explained in *a*, *b*, and *c* below.

a. Friction Loss. Friction is source of energy loss in any mechanical system. If a heavy plank is dragged across a rough floor, it offers some resistance to the movement. This resistance to movement would be less if the plank and floor were polished smooth. Resistance would be still less if the plank floated in water. This resistance to movement is called *friction*. Friction can be visualized as being caused by tiny irregularities, or high points, on the surfaces of the moving objects. These catch on each other and particles are torn off. All this requires force to overcome. If the plank and floor are made smooth, then the projecting points are much smaller and have less tendency to catch and tear off. Therefore, less force is required to pull the plank across the floor. And if the plank is floated in water, the surfaces can no longer rub against each other. There is, however, still some friction in the liquid. In the

engine, friction occurs at all moving parts, even though the parts are, in effect, floated in films of oil.

b. Mechanical Efficiency. The mechanical efficiency of the engine is the relationship between the power produced in the engine cylinders (indicated horsepower) and the power delivered by the engine (brake horsepower). Internal engine losses from friction and other factors always prevent brake horsepower from equaling indicated horsepower. A typical engine, for example, might develop 200 indicated horsepower as

Figure 21. System of pulley in which 1,000 foot-pounds must be expended to realize 900 foot-pounds of work.

against an actual brake horsepower of 180. This engine would have a mechanical efficiency of:

$$\frac{\text{Brake horsepower}}{\text{Indicated horsepower}}=\frac{180}{200}=90 \text{ percent}$$

c. *Thermal Efficiency.*

(1) Thermal efficiency is the relationship between the heat energy in the fuel and the engine power output (thermal means of or pertaining to heat). The term *thermal efficiency* relates the heat energy of the fuel and the work output. The heat energy is the amount of heat the fuel will produce as it burns. Much of this heat is lost to the cylinder walls and cooling system. Still more is lost in the hot exhaust gases as they pass out of the cylinder. This heat that is lost cannot do anything to cause the engine to produce power. Therefore, only a relatively small part of the heat in the burning fuel can contribute anything toward pushing down on the pistons and thereby causing the engine to produce power. In actual practice, because of the great amount of heat lost to the cooling water, lubricating oil, and in the exhaust gases, thermal efficiency may be as low as 20 percent. In other words, as much as 80 percent of the energy in the fuel is lost. However, the remaining 20 percent is sufficient to operate the engine normally. Practical limitations prevent thermal efficiencies of much above 25 percent.

(2) The overall thermal efficiency of an engine is the relationship between the fuel input and the power output. This relationship is commonly expressed in heat units called *British thermal units* (Btu). One Btu is equal to 778 ft-lb of work; therefore, the horsepower output of an engine can be readily converted into Btu per unit of time. The source of power in an engine is fuel, and the Btu content of regularly-used fuels has been determined by laboratory analysis:

$$\text{Thermal efficiency}=\frac{\text{power output in Btu}}{\text{fuel input in Btu}}$$

Example. An engine delivers 85 bhp for a period of 1 hour and in that time consumes 50 pounds (approx 7½ gals) of gasoline. Assuming that the gasoline has a value of 18,800 Btu per lb, we find the thermal efficiency of the engine:

Power delivered by engine is 85 bhp for 1 hour, or 85 hp-hours

1 hp-hour=

$$\frac{33,000 \text{ ft-lb per min}\times 60 \text{ min}}{778 \text{ ft-lb per Btu}}$$

=2,545 Btu

85 bhp×2,545 Btu=216,325 Btu output

50 lb×18,800 Btu per lb=940,000 Btu input per hour

$$\text{Overall thermal efficiency}=\frac{216,325}{940,000}$$

=0.230, or 23 percent

8. Advantages of Multicylinder Engines

a. *Power Increase.* In early automotive vehicles, 1-cylinder and some 3-cylinder engines were used, but the many advantages of a larger number of cylinders soon led to the adoption of 4-, 6-, 8-, 12-, and 16-cylinder engines. Although the power stroke of each piston theoretically continues for 180° of crankshaft rotation, best results can be obtained if the exhaust valve is opened when the power stroke has completed about four-fifths of its travel. Therefore, the period that power is delivered during 720° of crankshaft rotation, or one 4-stroke cycle, will be 145° multiplied by the number of cylinders in the engine. If an engine has two cylinders, power will be transmitted for 290° of the 720° of travel necessary to complete the four events of the cycle. The flywheel (par. 29) must supply power for the remaining 430° of crankshaft travel.

b. *Power Overlap.* As cylinders are added to an engine, each one must complete the four steps of the cycle during two revolutions of the crankshaft. The number of power impulses for each revolution also increases, producing smoother operation. If there are more than four cylinders, the power strokes overlap as shown in figure 22. The length of overlap increases with the number of cylinders. The diagram for the 6-cylinder engine shows a new power stroke starting each 120° of crankshaft rotation and lasting for four-fifths of a stroke, or 145°. This provides an overlap of 25°. In the 8-cylinder engine, a power stroke starts every 90° and continues for 145°, resulting in a 55° overlap of power. Because the cylinders fire at regular intervals, the power overlap will

NOTE:—THE CIRCLES SHOWN ABOVE REPRESENT 720 DEG NOT 360 DEG BECAUSE THE
CRANKSHAFT MUST ROTATE THROUGH 720 DEG TO COMPLETE
THE CYCLE ONCE FOR ALL CYLINDERS

Figure 22. Power in 1-, 4-, 6-, and 8-cylinder engines.

be the same regardless of firing order, and will apply to either in-line or V-type engines.

9. Classification of Engines

Automotive engines may be classified according to the type of fuel they use, type of cooling employed, or valve and cylinder arrangement. They all operate on the internal combustion principle, and the application of basic principles of contruction to particular needs or systems of manufacture has caused certain designs to be recognized as con-

ventional. The most common method of classification is by type of fuel used, that is, whether the engine burns gasoline or diesel fuel.

a. Cooling. Engines are classified as to whether they are air- or liquid-cooled. All engines are cooled by air to some extent, but air-cooled engines are those in which air is the only external cooling medium. Lubricating oil and

Figure 23. L-, I-, and F-head valve arrangements.

fuel helps somewhat to cool all engines, but there must be an additional external means of dissipating the heat absorbed by the engine during the power stroke.

(1) *Air-cooled.* Although air-cooled engines are not normally used in passenger cars and commercial trucks, they are used extensively in military vehicles as well as in aircraft. This type of engine is used where there must be an economy of space and weight. It does not require a radiator, water jacket, coolant, or a pump to circulate the coolant. The cylinders are cooled by conducting the heat to metal fins on the outside of the cylinder wall and head. To effect the cooling, air is circulated between the fins. When possible, the engine is installed so that it is exposed to the air stream of the vehicle; the baffles direct the air to the fins. If the engine cannot be mounted in the air stream, a fan is employed to force the air through the baffles.

(2) *Water-cooled.* Water-cooled engines require a water jacket to hold the coolant around the valve ports, combustion chambers, and cylinders; a radiator to dissipate the heat from the coolant to the surrounding air; and a pump to circulate the coolant through the engine. Water-

cooled engines also require a fan to pass air through the radiator because the speed of the vehicle does not always force enough air through the radiator to provide proper dissipation of heat.

b. Valve Arrangement. Engines may be classified according to the position of the intake and exhaust valves, that is, whether they are in the cylinder block or in the cylinder head. Various arrangements have been used, but the most common are L-head, I-head, and F-head (fig. 23). The letter designation is used because the shape of the combustion chamber resembles the form of the letter identifying it.

(1) *L-head.* In the L-head engines both valves are placed in the block on the same side of the cylinder. The valve-operating mechanism is located directly below the valves, and one camshaft actuates both the intake and exhaust valves. This type has supplanted the T-head, in which both valves were in the block but on opposite sides of the cylinder. The disadvantage of the T-head was that it required two complete valve-operating mechanisms.

(2) *I-head.* Engines using the I-head construction are commonly called *valve-in-head* or *overhead valve* engines, because the valves are mounted in the cylinder

head above the cylinder. This arrangement requires a tappet, a push rod, and a rocker arm above the cylinder to reverse the direction of valve movement, but only one camshaft is required for both valves. Some overhead valve engines make use of an overhead camshaft. This arrangement eliminates the long linkage between the camshaft and valve.

(3) **F-**_head_. In the **F**-head engine, the intake valves normally are located in the head, while the exhaust valves are located in the engine block. This arrangement combines, in effect, the L-head and the I-head valve arrangements. The valves in the head are actuated from the camshaft through tappets, push rods, and rocker arms (I-head arrangement), while the valves in the block are actuated directly from the camshaft by tappets (L-head arrangement).

c. Cylinder Arrangment. Automotive engines also vary in the arrangement of cylinders in the block, depending on the engine use. Cylinder arrangement in liquid-cooled engines is usually in-line or **V**-type; in air-cooled engines, it is **V**-type, radial, or horizontal-opposed.

(1) _In-line._ The vertical in-line cylinder arrangement is one of the most common used types. All the cylinders are cast or assembled in a straight line above a common crankshaft which is immediately below the cylinders. A variation is the inverted in-line type.

(2) **V-**_type_. In the **V**-type engine, two "banks" of in-line cylinders are mounted in a **V**-shape above a common crankshaft. This type is designated by the number of degrees in the angle between the banks of cylinders. Usually the angle of the V is 90° for 8-cylinder en-

gines; 75°, 60°, or 45° for 12-cylinder engines; and 45° or 135° for 16-cylinder engines. Crankshafts for **V**-type engines generally have only half as many throws as there are cylinders, as two connecting rods (one from each bank) are connected to each throw.

(3) _Radial._ The radial engine has cylinders placed in a circle around the crankshaft. The crankshaft has only one throw, and one piston is connected to this throw by a _master rod_. The connecting rods from the others pistons are fastened to the master rod, making the power flow first to the master rod and then to the crankshaft. The result is the same as if each rod were connected directly to the crankshaft. High-powered radial engines may have two rows of cylinders in which each row operates on its own throw of the crankshaft.

(4) _Horizontal-opposed._ The horizontal-opposed engine has its cylinders laid on their sides in two rows, with the crankshaft in the center. Because of its low overall height, much less headroom is required for mounting the engine. It can be put under the body of a bus, for example, or can be so mounted in a tank as to provide additional interior space in the tank. This engine is often called a _pancake_ engine, because it is relatively flat like a pancake.

(5) _Horizontal-opposed with vertical crankshaft._ In this engine, the cylinders are horizontal and opposed to each other, but the crankshaft is set vertically. This is the same type of engine mentioned in (4) above, except that the engine has been set up on end so that the crankshaft is vertical rather than horizontal.

BASIC FUNDAMENTALS OF
AUTOMOTIVE POWER TRAINS AND CHASSIS

TABLE OF CONTENTS

Basic Fundamentals of
Automotive Power Trains and Chassis

The mechanism that transmits the power of a vehicle's engine to the wheels and accessory equipment is called the power train. In a simple situation, a set of gears or a chain and sprocket could perform this task, but automotive vehicles are not designed for simple operating conditions. They are designed to have pulling power as well as to move at high speeds, to travel in reverse as well as forward, and to operate on rough terrain as well as on smooth roads. To meet these varying demands, a number of units have been added including clutches, transmissions, propeller shafts, universal joints, differentials, and live axles.

The chassis is the assembly of mechanisms that make up the major operating part of the vehicle. It usually includes everything except the vehicle body. This assembly includes the engine, the frame which supports the engine and the power train, the steering and braking systems, and the suspension system.

This chapter provides information on the various components, or subassemblies, that make up the automotive power train and chassis. In effect, it establishes the relationship between these various parts and shows how they work together in the automotive vehicle. To maintain and service these components, or subassemblies, you must know where to find them on a vehicle. You must also understand their purpose and how they operate. This chapter contains a general discussion of these subjects; the operation and maintenance manuals which accompany each piece of equipment will give you more detailed information.

I.   POWER TRAIN COMPONENTS

The common elements of the power train system assembled in a typical vehicle are shown in the following figure. The main components of the power train are described as follows:

<u>CLUTCH.</u>   By means of the clutch, the operator can disconnect the engine from the remainder of the power train. This is essential when starting the engine, thus allowing the vehicle to stand motionless while the engine is running. It also allows gradual engagement of the engine to the power train and gear ratio changing to meet varying road conditions.

<u>TRANSMISSION.</u>   An internal combustion engine cannot develop appreciable torque at low speeds; it develops maximum torque only at one speed, and the crankshaft of an engine must always rotate in the sane direction. Because of these limitations, a transmission is necessary in automotive vehicles. The transmission provides the mechanical advantage that enables the engine to propel the vehicle under adverse conditions of the load. It also provides the operator with a selection of vehicle speeds while the engine is held at speeds within the effective torque range, and it allows disengaging and reversing the flow of power from the engine to the wheels.

<u>PROPELLER SHAFT.</u>   A propeller shaft is used to transfer the power from the transmission located near the front of the vehicle to the differential near the rear.

UNIVERSAL JOINTS. It is necessary to provide flexibility in the power train if springs are to be used on the vehicle. As the load is increased or decreased, and as the vehicle travels over uneven surfaces, the vertical distance between the transmission output shaft and the axle will change. This flexibility is provided by the use of universal joints which permit transfer of torque at an angle.

SLIP JOINTS. As the load is changed, and as the vehicle travels over uneven ground, the distance from the axle to the transmission varies. Slip joints allow for this variation.

DIFFERENTIAL. A differential is required to compensate for the difference in distance the rear wheels travel when the vehicle rounds a turn. The differential permits application of power to the rear wheels while allowing each wheel to turn at a different speed when the vehicle is rounding a curve.

AXLES. An axle is a shaft supporting a vehicle on which the wheels turn. A live axle is one that supports part of the weight of a vehicle and also drives the wheels connected to it. A dead axle is one that carries part of the weight of a vehicle, but does not drive the wheels. The usual front axle of a vehicle is a dead axle and the rear axle is a live axle. In four-wheel drive vehicles, both front and rear axles are live axles, and in six-wheel drive vehicles, all three axles are live axles.

TYPICAL POWER TRAIN

THE CLUTCH

A clutch in an automotive vehicle is the mechanism in the power train that connects the engine crankshaft to, or disconnects it from, the transmission and thus the remainder of the power train. Since the internal combustion engine does not develop a high starting torque, it must be disconnected from the power train and allowed to operate without load until it develops enough torque to overcome the inertia of the vehicle when starting from rest. The application of the engine power to the load must be gradual to provide smooth engagement and to lessen the shock on the driving parts. After engagement, the clutch must transmit all the engine power to the transmission without slipping. Further, it is desirable to disconnect the engine from the power train during the time the gears in the transmission are being shifted from one gear ratio to another.

Clutches are located in the power train between the engine and the transmission assembly.

Clutches transmit power from the clutch driving plate to the driven member by friction. In the disk clutch, the driving plate or member, which is secured to the engine flywheel, is gradually brought into contact with the driven member (disk), which is attached to the transmission input shaft. The contact is made and held by strong spring pressure controlled by the operator with the clutch pedal. With only light spring pressure, there is little friction between the two members and the clutch is permitted to slip. As the spring pressure increases, friction also increases, and less slippage occurs. When the operator removes his foot from the clutch pedal and full spring pressure is applied, the speed of the driving plate and driven disk is the same, and all slipping stops. There is then a direct connection between the flywheel and transmission input shaft.

Malfunction Detection.   Several types of clutch troubles that may be encountered during vehicle operation are: slipping, chattering or grabbing when engaging, spinning or dragging when engaged, and clutch noises. As an operator, you would explain the malfunction on the Operator's Trouble Report and turn the report into the maintenance shop for corrective action.

Clutch Lubrication.   Although some clutches do not require lubrication, there are other types of clutches that require it at periodic intervals. The clutch-pedal control shaft and clutch linkage are among some of the lubricating points that would be greased at normal regular servicing intervals in accordance with the manufacturer's lubrication manual.

MANUAL TRANSMISSIONS

The transmission is part of the power train. It is located in the rear of the engine between the clutch housing and the propeller shaft. The transmission transfers engine power from the clutch shaft to the propeller shaft, and allows the operator a means of varying the gear ratio between the engine and the rear wheels.

Dual ratio, or two-speed, rear axles are sometimes used on trucks. They contain two different gear ratios which can be selected at will by the driver, usually by a manual-control lever. A dual-ratio rear axle serves the same purpose as the auxiliary transmission, and like the latter, it doubles the number of gear ratios available for driving the vehicle under the various loads and road conditions.

Operator's Maintenance.   It is the operator's responsibility to check with the manufacturer's instruction manual for instruction on the proper type and amount of recommended lubricant to be used in the transmission case. You must maintain the lubricant at the proper level. The normal level of lubricant to be placed in a transmission is usually at the bottom of the filler plug opening. By maintaining the proper level, gear teeth are protected, foaming is reduced, and thus the transmission will continue to perform properly.

Malfunction Detection.   Several types of transmission troubles that may be encountered in vehicle operation are: Hard shifting into gears; transmission slips out of <u>first</u> or <u>reverse;</u> transmission slips out of <u>second;</u> transmission slips out of high; no power through transmission; transmission noisy in gear; gear clash in shifting; and oil leaks. As an operator, you would explain the malfunction on the Operator's Trouble Report enabling the mechanic to check out the possible cause of trouble reported.

AUTOMATIC TRANSMISSIONS

The transmissions described previously are manual transmissions; that is, they require a clutch and a lever for shifting gears. The automatic transmission is used in almost all types of automotive and construction equipment. Automatic transmissions are composed of a fluid coupling or hydraulic torque converter and a system of planetary gears controlled automatically.

Fluid couplings.   Fluid couplings are widely used with automatic transmissions. By slipping at idling speeds and by holding to increase power as engine speed increases, fluid couplings act as a sort of automatic clutch. There is no mechanical connection between the engine and transmission, but power is transmitted through the use of oil.

The principle of fluid drive can best be illustrated through the use of a pair of electric fans facing each other. If one fan is operated with power, the air blast from this fan will cause the other fan to rotate.

There is considerable power loss through slippage at low speeds, but at intermediate or high driving speeds the power loss is very small. It ranges from 1 percent at 25 miles per hour to one quarter percent at 60 miles per hour.

Torque Converters.   A torque converter is a special form of fluid coupling. It is one of the most common types of automatic transmissions and is widely used in the latest models of automotive and construction equipment.

The torque converter consists of three basic elements: the pump (driving member), the turbine (driven member), and the stator (reaction member). All of these members have curved vanes. The stator is placed between the load and the power source to act as a fulcrum and is secured to the torque converter housing. The pump throws out oil in the same direction in which the pump is turning. As the oil strikes the turbine blade, it forces the turbine to rotate, and the oil is directed toward the center of the turbine. Then the oil leaves the turbine and moves in a direction opposite to that of the pump. As the oil strikes the stator, it is redirected to flow in the same direction as the pump, thereby adding its force to that of the pump. Torque is multiplied by the velocity and direction given to the oil by the pump, plus the velocity and direction of the oil entering the pump from the stator.

Planetary Gears.   Automatic transmissions use a system of planetary gears to enable the torque from the torque converter or fluid coupling to be used as efficiently as possible.

Planetary units are the heart of the modern automatic transmission. An understanding of the power flow through the planetary units is essential to an understanding of the operation of the automatic transmission.

Four basic parts make up the planetary gear system. These basic parts are the sun gear, the ring (or internal) gear, the planet pinions, and the planet carrier.

PLANETARY
SUN GEAR

PLANETARY
PINION

PLANETARY
CARRIER

PLANETARY
RING GEAR

The sun gear is so named because it is the center of the system. The term *planet* is used to describe these pinions and gears because they rotate around the sun gear. The ring gear, or internal gear, is so called because of its shape and because it has internal teeth.

There are several advantages inherent in the planetary gear system. One of the advantages is the compactness of the system. Another advantage is that there is more tooth contact to carry the load, in that each gear of the planetary system is usually in contact with at least two other gears of the system. The gears are always in mesh. There can be no tooth damage due to tooth clash or partial engagement. The big advantage is the one which makes it so popular: namely, the ease of shifting gears. Planetary gear sets in automatic transmissions are shifted without any skill on the part of the driver.

There are various ways in which power may be transmitted through the planetary gear set. A shaft from the engine may be connected to drive the sun gear, it may be connected to drive the planet carrier, or it may be connected to drive the ring gear. The propeller shaft also may be connected to any of these members. However, only power can be transmitted in the planetary gear system when (1) the engine is delivering power to one of the three members, (2) the propeller shaft is connected to one of the other members, and (3) the remaining member is held against rotation. All three conditions must be satisfied for power to be transmitted in the system. Automatic transmissions provide the means for holding a member through hydraulic servos or spring pressure.

Operation. Most automatic transmissions are basically the same. They combine a fluid torque converter with a planetary gear set, and control the shifting of the planetary gears with an automatic hydraulic control system.

6

To start the engine, the selector lever must be in the Neutral or Park position. It is good practice to apply the service brakes before starting the engine and keep them applied after the engine is running. In the automatic transmission, the fluid torque converter is attached to the engine crankshaft and serves as the engine flywheel. This means that whenever the engine runs, engine power flows into the converter and drives the converter output (turbine) shaft. There is no neutral in the torque converter. Neutral is provided in the planetary gear set by the release of bands and clutches.

With the engine running, you can *feel* the transmission go into gear and into neutral as the selector level is moved from Park or Neutral to Drive, Low, or Reverse. If the engine is running at fast (cold) idle, the vehicle will start to move as soon as the transmission goes into gear, unless the parking or service brakes are applied. If the engine is idling at normal (hot) idle, the vehicle will not move. You can, however, *feel* the transmission go into gear. Part of *this feel* is the audible decrease in engine rpm. The engine is now running under a load. The torque converter and the planetary gear set are actually transmitting engine torque to the driveshaft. The torque applied, however, is not sufficient to move the vehicle.

For all normal forward driving, the selector is moved to Drive. As the throttle is advanced from the idle position, the vehicle will start off smoothly and accelerate steadily. The transmission is designed to operate at a steady-throttle position. Most drivers depress the accelerator pedal to a definite position and hold it there steadily until the desired speed is attained. Depending on the accelerator pedal position, the transmission will upshaft automatically to intermediate and then to high.

The transmission automatically multiplies and/or transmits engine torque to the driveshaft as driving conditions demand. The speeds at which the coupling point and the gear shifts occur are controlled partially by the driver. The driver has only a partial control in the Drive position, because the transmission in the Drive position will shift the planetary gear set into the higher gears to prevent engine overspeeding regardless of throttle position.

The transmission can multiply engine torque as much as 5.4 times. The torque converter can multiply engine torque as much as 2.2 times. The planetary gear set in low gear multiplies the torque converter output torque 2.46 times. The maximum engine torque multiplication in the transmission is 2.2 x 2.46 or 5.41 times. This means that the transmission can receive an engine output torque of 100 ft-lbs and deliver 541 ft-lbs torque to the driveshaft. Of course, fric-tional losses have to be subtracted from the 541 ft-lbs.

The driver can force downshaft the transmission from high to intermediate at speeds up to about 65 mph. A detent on the downshift linkage warns the driver when the carburetor is wide open. Accelerator pedal depression through the detent will bring in the downshift.

With the throttle closed, the transmission will downshift automatically as the vehicle speed drops to about 10 mph. With the throttle open at any position up to the detent, the downshifts will come in automatically at speeds about 10 mph and in proportion to throttle opening. This prevents engine lugging on steep hill climbing.

When the selector lever is moved to L (low) with the transmission in high, the transmission will downshift to intermediate or to low depending on the road speed. At speeds below about 25 mph, the downshift will be from high to low.

With the selector in Low position, the transmission cannot upshift. On some vehicles the Low position is called Hill Control, since low gear provides maximum engine braking. When maximum engine braking is desired, the transmission must not upshift, because an upshift will reduce engine braking effort. When the selector is moved to Reverse, the hydraulic control system shifts the planetary gear set to reverse. When the selector lever is moved to Park, a spring force is applied against a pawl to engage the parking pawl with a parking gear on the output shaft. When the pawl is engaged, the transmission output shaft (and, therefore, the rear wheels) is mechanically locked to the transmission main case.

In summary:

1. An automatic transmission has the torque converter to act as an automatic clutch. This automatic clutch permits the vehicle to stand still at engine idle, but automatically goes to work at a full-throttle start so that the transmission can take maximum engine torque, multiply it more than four times and deliver it to the drive-shaft.
2. It is practically impossible to *kill* the engine under any driving condition.
3. At a start, engine speed is fast and vehicle speed is slow. With a steady throttle, engine speed remains fairly constant while vehicle speed increases to 65 mph. You found that the torque converter and planetary gear set *know* when engine torque should be multiplied, how much to multiply it, and when to transmit it to the drive-shaft.
4. The ratio changes (shifts) occur at full-engine torque within a fraction of a second and without extreme harshness.

<u>Operator's Maintenance.</u>   Periodic service by the operator includes checking the transmission oil level when the engine is idling and at normal operating temperature, the vehicle is level, and the transmission control lever is in Park. Remove dipstick and note oil level. If it is low, and sufficient transmission fluid (the oil used in all automatic transmission is special and is composed of mineral oil and additives). In the transmission, it is used as a combination power-transmission medium, hydraulic control fluid, heat transfer medium, bearing surface lubricant, and gear lubricant. In all cases, the manufacturer's recommendations should be followed when servicing and filling the transmission with transmission fluid.

Caution: Do not overfill the transmission because overfilling will cause foaming and shifting troubles.

<u>Malfunction Detection.</u>   Several types of automatic transmission troubles that may be encountered during vehicle operation are: No drive in any selected position; engine speed accelerates on standstill starts but vehicle acceleration lags; engine speed accelerates during upshifts; transmission will not upshift; upshift harsh; closed throttle (coast) downshift harsh; will not downshift; vehicle creeps excessively in drive; vehicle creeps in neutral; no drive in reverse, improper shift points; unusual transmission noise; and oil leaks. As an operator, you must explain the malfunction on the Operator's Trouble Report and turn the report into the maintenance shop for corrective action.

AUXILIARY TRANSMISSIONS

Auxiliary transmissions are mechanisms mounted in the rear of the regular transmission to provide an increased number of gear ratios. The types most commonly used, normally have only a low and a high (direct) range, incorporated into a transfer assembly. The low range provides an extremely low gear ratio on hard pulls. At all other times the high range is used, and the power passes through the main shaft. Gears are shifted by a separate gearshift lever in the driver's cab.

Transfer Cases.   Transfer cases are placed in the power trains of vehicles driven by all wheels. Their purpose is to provide the necessary offsets for additional propeller shaft connections to drive the wheels.

Transfer cases in heavier vehicles have two speed positions and a declutching device for disconnecting the front driving wheels. Two speed transfer cases serve also as auxiliary transmissions.

Some transfer cases are quite complicated. When they have speed changing gears, declutching devices, and attachments for three or more propeller shafts, they are even larger than the main transmission.

Some transfer cases contain an overrunning sprag unit (or units) on the front output shaft. (A sprag unit is a form of overruning clutch; power can be transmitted through it in one direction but not in the other.) On these transfer cases, the transfer is designed to drive the front axle slightly slower than the rear axle. During normal operation, when both front and rear wheels turn at the same speed, only the rear wheels drive the vehicle. However, if the rear wheels should lose traction and begin to slip, they tend to turn faster than the front wheels. As this happens, the sprag unit automatically engages so that the front wheels also drive the vehicle. The sprag unit simply provides an automatic means of engaging the front wheels in drive whenever additional tractive effort is required. There are two types of sprag-unit-equipped transfers: a single-sprag-unit transfer and a double-sprag-unit transfer. Essentially, both types work in the same manner.

Power Takeoffs.   Power takeoffs are attachments in the power train used for obtaining power to drive auxiliary accessories. They are attached to the transmission, auxiliary transmission, or transfer case.

Malfunction detection and operator maintenance for auxiliary transmissions are similar to those for the manual transmission.

PROPELLER SHAFT ASSEMBLY

The propeller shaft assembly consists of a propeller shaft, a slip joint, and one or more universal joints. This assembly provides a flexible connection through which power is transmitted from the transmission to the live axles.

The propeller shaft may be solid or tubular. A solid shaft is somewhat stronger than the hollow or tubular shaft of the same diameter, but the hollow shaft is stronger than a solid shaft of the same weight. Hollow shafts are used in the open.

A slip joint is provided at one end of the propeller shaft to take care of end play. The driving axle, being attached to the springs, is free to move up and down while the transmission is attached to the frame and cannot move. Any upward or downward movement of the axle, as the springs are flexed, shortens or lengthens the distance between the axle assembly and the transmission. To compensate for this changing distance, the slip joint is provided at one end of the propeller shaft.

The usual type of slip joint consists of a splined stub shaft, welded to the propeller shaft, which fits into a splined sleeve in the universal joint.

A universal joint is a connection between two shafts that permits one to drive the other at an angle. Passenger vehicles and trucks usually have universal joints at both ends of the propeller shaft.

Universal joints normally do not require any maintenance other than lubrication. Some universal joints (U-joints) have grease fittings and should be lubricated when the vehicle has a preventive maintenance inspection. Others may require disassembly and lubrication periodically. When lubricating U joints that have grease fittings, use a low pressure grease gun to avoid damaging seals.

FINAL DRIVES

A final drive is that part of the power train that transmits the power delivered through the propeller shaft to the drive wheels or to sprockets, in the case of tracklaying equipment. Because it is encased in the rear axle housing, the final drive is usually referred to as a part of the rear axle assembly. It consists of two gears called the ring gear and pinion. These are beveled gears, and they may be spur, spiral, or hypoid.

The function of the final drive is to change by 90 degrees the direction of the power transmitted through the propeller shaft to the driving axles. It also provides a fixed reduction between the speed of the propeller shaft and the axle shafts and wheels. In passenger cars this reduction varies from about 3 to 1 to 5 to 1. In trucks, it can vary from 5 to 1 to as much as 11 to 1.

The gear ratio of a final drive having bevel gears is found by dividing the number of teeth on the driven or ring gear by the number of teeth on the pinion. In a worm gear final drive, the gear ratio is found by counting the number of revolutions of the worm gear required for one revolution of the driven gear.

Most final drives are of the gear type. Hypoid gears are used in passenger cars and light trucks to eliminate the rear seat propeller shaft tunnel or to permit a lower body design. They permit the bevel driven pinion to be placed below the center of the ring gear, thereby lowering the propeller shaft. Worm gears allow a large speed reduction and are used to a limited extent on larger trucks. Spiral bevel gears are similar to hypoid gears. They are used in both passenger cars and trucks to replace spur gears that are considered too noisy.

DIFFERENTIALS

Associated with the final drive and contained in the rear axle housing is the differential. The purpose of the differential is easy to understand when you compare a vehicle to a company of men marching in mass formation. When the company makes a turn, the men in the inside file must take short steps, almost marking time, while men in the outside file must take long steps and walk a greater distance to make the turn. When a motor vehicle turns a corner, the wheels on the outside of the turn must rotate faster and travel a greater distance than the wheels on the inside. This causes no difficulty for front wheels of the usual passenger car because each wheel rotates independently. However, in order to drive the rear wheels at different speeds, the differential is needed. It connects the individual axle shaft for each wheel to the bevel drive gear. Therefore, each shaft can turn at a different speed and still be driven.

To overcome the situation where one spinning wheel might be undesirable, some trucks are provided with a differential lock. This is a simple dog clutch, controlled manually or automatically which locks one axle shaft to the differential case and bevel drive gear. Although this device forms a rigid connection between the two axle shafts and makes both wheels rotate at the same speed, it is used, very little. Too often the driver forgets to disengage the lock after using it. There are, however, automatic devices for doing almost the same thing. One of these, which is rather extensively used today, is the high-traction differential. This does not work, however, when one wheel loses traction completely. In this respect, it is inferior to the differential lock.

With the no-spin differential, one wheel cannot spin because of loss of tractive effort and thereby deprive the other wheel of driving effort. For example, one wheel is on ice and the other wheel is on dry pavement. The wheel on ice is assumed to have no traction. However, the wheel on dry pavement will pull to the limit of its tractional resistance at the pavement. The wheel on ice cannot spin because wheel speed is governed by the speed of the wheel applying tractive effort.

AXLES

A live axle is one that supports part of the weight of a vehicle and also drives the wheels connected to it. A dead axle is one that carries part of the weight of a vehicle but does not drive the wheels.

In 4-wheel drive vehicles, both front and rear axles are live axles, and in 6-wheel drive vehicles, all three axles are live axles. The third axle, part of a bogie drive, is joined to the rearmost axle by a trunnion axle. The axle trunnion is attached rigidly to the frame. Its purpose is to help in distributing the load on the rear of the vehicle to the two live axles which it connects.

There are four types of live axles used in automotive and construction equipment. They are: plain, semifloating, three-quarter floating, and full floating.

The plain live axle, or nonfloating rear axle, is seldom used in construction equipment today. The axle shafts in this assembly are called nonfloating because they are supported directly in bearings located in the center and ends of the axle housing. In addition to turning the wheels, these shafts carry the entire load of the vehicle on their outer ends. Plain axles also support the weight of the differential case.

The semifloating axle that is used on most passenger cars and light trucks has its differential case independently supported. The differential carrier relieves the axle shafts from the weight of the differential assembly and the stresses caused by its operation. For this reason the inner ends of the axle shafts are said to be floated. The wheels are keyed or bolted to outer ends of axle shafts and the outer bearings are between the shafts and the housing. The axle shafts therefore must take the stresses caused by turning or skidding of the wheels. The axle shaft in a semifloating live axle can be removed after the wheel and brake drum have been removed.

The axle shafts in a three-quarter floating axle may be removed with the wheels, which are keyed to the tapered outer ends of the shafts. The inner ends of the shafts are carried as in a semifloating axle. The axle housing, instead of the shafts, carries the weight of the vehicle because the wheels are supported by bearings on the outer ends of the housing. However, axle shafts must take the stresses caused by the turning, or skidding, of the wheels. Three-quarter floating axles are used in some trucks but in very few passenger cars.

The full floating axle is used in most heavy trucks. These axle shafts may be removed and replaced without removing the wheels or disturbing the differential. Each wheel is carried on the end of the axle tube on two ball bearings or roller bearings and the axle shafts are bolted to the wheel hub. The wheels are driven through a flange on the ends of the axle shaft which is bolted to the outside of the wheel hub. The bolted connection between axle and wheel does not make this assembly a true full floating axle, but nevertheless, it is called a floating axle. A true full floating axle transmits only turning effort, or torque.

MAINTENANCE

There are very lew adjustments that must be made to the power train during normal operations. As an operator, your primary duties will be limited to lubrication of the power train. You can reduce repairs by proper lubrication and periodic inspection of these power train units.

Proper lubrication depends upon the use of the right kind of lubricants which must be put in the right places in the amounts specified by the lubrication charts. The charts provided with the vehicle will show what units in the power train will require lubrication, and where they are located.

In checking the level of the lubricant in gear cases, keep these two important points in mind:

First, always carefully wipe the dirt away from around the inspection plug and then use the proper size wrench to remove the inspection plugs. A wrench too large will round the corners and prevent proper tightening of the plug. For the same reason, never use a pipe wrench or a pair of pliers for removing plugs.

Secondly, be sure the level of the lubricant is right - usually just below or on a level with the bottom of the inspection hole. Before checking the level, allow the vehicle to stand for a while on a level surface so the gear oil can cool and find its own level. Gear oil heated and churned by revolving gears expands and forms bubbles. Although too little gear oil in the gear boxes is responsible for many failures of the power train, do not add to much gear lubricant. Too much oil causes extra maintenance.

Excessive oil or grease can find its way past the oil seals or gear cases. It may be forced out of a transmission into the clutch housing and result in a slipping clutch; or it may get by the rear wheel bearings from the differential housing to cause brakes to slip or grab. Always clean differential and live axle housing vents to prevent leaking seals,

Universal joints and slip joints at the ends of propeller shafts are to be lubricated if fittings are provided. Some of these joints are packed with grease when assembled, others have grease fittings or small plugs, with screwdriver slots, that can be removed for inserting grease fittings. Do not remove these plugs until you consult the manual or your chief for instructions.

Some passenger cars and trucks have a leather boot or shoe covering the universal and slip joints. The boot prevents grease from being thrown from the joints and it also keeps dirt from mixing with the grease. A mixture of dirt and grease forms an abrasive that will wear parts in a hurry. Never use so much grease on these joints that the grease will be forced out of the boot. The extra grease will be lost and the added weight of the grease will tend to throw the propeller shaft out of balance.

When you are to give a vehicle a thorough inspection, inspect the power train for loose gear housings and joints. Look for bent propeller shafts that are responsible for vibrations, and examine the gear housing and joints for missing screws and bolts. Check to see that the U-bolts fastening the springs to the rear axle housing are tight. A loose spring hanger can throw the rear axle assembly out of line, and place additional strain on the propeller shaft and final drive. When making these inspections, always check the sheel lugs for tightness.

After tightening the gear housing, loose connections, and joints, road test the vehicle to see if the various units in the power train are working properly. Shift the gears into all operating speeds and listen for noisy sounds. Report all improper operation of the power train units on the Operator's Trouble Report enabling the mechanic to check out possible causes.

DRIVING WHEELS

Wheels attached to live axles are the <u>driving wheels.</u> The number of wheels and number of driving wheels is sometimes used to identify equipment. Wheels attached to the outside of the driving wheels make up <u>dual wheels.</u> Dual wheels give additional traction to the driving wheels and distribute the weight of the vehicle over a greater area of road surface. They are considered as single wheels in describing vehicles. For example, a 4x2 (four by two) could be a passenger car or a truck having 4 wheels with 2 of them driving. A 4x4 indicates a vehicle having 4 wheels with all 4 driving. In some cases, these vehicles will have dual wheels in the rear. You would describe such a vehicle as a 4x4 with dual wheels.

A 6x4 truck, although having dual wheels in the rear, is identified by 6 wheels, 4 of them driving. Actually, the truck has 10 wheels but the wheel attached to each driving wheel could be removed without changing the identity of the truck. If the front wheels of this truck were driven by a live axle, it would be called a 6x6.

II. BRAKE SYSTEMS

Good brakes are an absolute necessity for the safe operation of a motor vehicle. The modern day vehicle is capable of moving at extremely high speeds, and this results in an ever increasing demand for more efficient braking systems. Braking systems must not only be able to stop the vehicle, but must stop it in as short a distance as possible.

Friction is the resistance to relative motion between two surfaces in contact with each other. Thus, when a stationary surface is forced into contact with a moving surface, the resistance to relative motion or the rubbing action between the two surfaces will slow down the moving surface. In nearly all brake systems, the brake drums provide the moving surface and the brake shoes provide the stationary surface. The friction between the brake drums and the brake shoes slows the drum, wheel, and the friction between the tires and the road surface slows the vehicle, eventually bringing it to a complete stop.

INDIVIDUAL BRAKES

On modern equipment individual service brakes are provided for each wheel and are operated by a foot pedal. The equipment also has an emergency or parking brake. The parking brake is operated by a separate pedal or a hand lever.

Individual brakes are classified into three types: external contracting brake, internal expanding brake, and disk brake.

External Contracting Brakes.   External contracting brakes are sometimes used for parking brakes on motor vehicles and for controlling the speed of auxiliary equipment drive shafts.

In operation, the brake band (or shoe) of an external contracting brake is tightened around the rotating drum by moving the brake lever. The brake hand is made of comparatively thin, flexible steel, shaped to fit the drum, with a frictional lining riveted to the inner surface. This flexible brake band cannot withstand the high pressure required to produce the friction that will stop a heavily loaded or fast moving vehicle, but works well as a parking brake.

In an external contracting brake, the brake band is anchored opposite the point where the pressure is applied. In addition to supporting the band, the anchor provides a means for adjusting brake lining clearance. Other adjusting screws and bolts are provided at the ends of the band.

Internal Expanding Brakes. Internal expanding brakes are used almost exclusively as wheel brakes. This type of brake permits a more compact and economical construction. "The brake shoe and brake operating mechanism are supported on a backing plate or brake shield which is attached to the vehicle axle. The brake drum, attached to the rotating wheel, acts as a cover for the shoe and operating mechanism and furnishes a frictional surface for the brake shoe.

In operation, the brake shoe of an internal expanding brake is forced outward against the drum to produce the braking action. One end of the shoe is hinged to the backing plate by an anchor pin, while the other end is unattached and can be moved in its support by the operating mechanism. When force from the operating mechanism is applied to the unattached end of the shoe, the shoe expands and brakes the wheel. A retracting spring returns the shoe to the original position when braking action is no longer required.

The brake-operating linkage alone does not provide sufficient mechanical advantage for positive braking. Some means of supplementing the physical application of the braking system has to be used to increase pressure on the brake shoes. A self-energizing action is very helpful in accomplishing this, once setting of the shoes is started by physical effort. While there are variations of this action, it is always obtained by the shoes themselves, which tend to revolve with the revolving drum.

When the brake shoe is anchored (see figure below) and the drum revolves in the direction shown, the shoe will tend to revolve with the drum when it is forced against the drum. As a result, the shoe will exert considerable pressure against the anchor pin. Since the pin is fixed to the brake shield, this pressure will tend to wedge the shoe tightly in between the pin and the drum as shown. As the initial braking pressure is increased on the cam, the wedging action increases and the shoe is forced still more tightly against the drum to increase the friction. This self-energizing results in more braking action than could be obtained with the actuating pressure alone. Brakes making use of this principle to increase pressures on the braking surfaces are known as self-energizing (or servo) brakes.

External contracting brake

Internal expanding brake

It is most important that the operator control the total braking action at all times; therefore, the self-energizing action should increase only upon application of additional "actuating pressure at the brake pedal. The amount of self-energizing action available depends mainly on location of the anchor pin. As the pin is moved toward the center of the drum, wedging action increases until a point is reached where the shoe will automatically lock. The pin must be located outside this point so that the operator can control the braking.

When two shoes are anchored on the bottom of the backing plate, self-energizing action is effective on only one shoe. The other shoe tends to revolve away from its pivot, which reduces its braking action. When the wheel is revolving in the opposite direction, the self-energizing action is produced on the opposite shoe.

Two shoes are usually mounted so that self-energizing action is effective on both. This is accomplished by pivoting the shoes to each other and leaving the pivot free of the backing plate. The only physical effort required is for operating the first, or primary, shoe. Both shoes then apply additional pressure to the braking surfaces with no increase in the pressure on the operating linkage. The anchor pins are fitted into slots in the free ends of the brake shoes. This method of anchoring allows the movement of the shoes necessary to expand against the drum when the shoes are forced against the drum, and the self-energizing action of the primary shoe is transmitted through the pivot to the secondary shoe. Both shoes will tend to revolve with the drum and will be wedged against the drum by the one anchor pin. The other anchor pin will cause a similar action when the wheel is revolving in the opposite direction.

The operating mechanism for wheel brakes differs with the brake systems, and so do the brake shoe adjusting devices. The brake drums and brake shoes, however, are similar in all wheel brakes.

Most modern automotive brakes have a self-adjusting feature that automatically adjust the brakes when they need it as a result of brake lining wear.

Disk Brakes. The disk brake has a metal disk instead of a drum, and a pair of flat pads instead of curved brake shoes. The figure below shows a sectional view of a typical disk brake assembly. The two flat pads are located on the two sides of the disk. The assembly in which the flat pads are held is called the caliper assembly. In operation, the pads are forced against the two sides of the disk by the movement of pistons in the caliper assembly. The pistons are actuated by hydraulic pressure from the master cylinder. The effect is to clamp the rotating disk between the stationary pads as illustrated below. This is the same action you get when you pick up a

Sectional view of disk brake in released and applied position.

piece of paper; your lingers and thumb clamp on both sides of the paper to hold it. In the same way, the pads apply friction to the disk and attempt to stop its rotation. This provides the braking action.

MECHANICAL HANDBRAKES

In most automotive vehicles, the handbrake has its own hookup. Either external contracting brake bands are located on the drive shaft or some type of mechanical linkage operates the rear wheel brakes.

HYDRAULIC BRAKE SYSTEMS

A hydraulic brake system is primarily a liquid connection or coupling between the brake pedal and the individual brake shoes and drums. The system consists of one master cylinder connected by pipes and flexible tubing to the wheel cylinders. The wheel cylinders control the movement of the brake shoes at each wheel.

The brake fluid in hydraulic systems is composed of alcohol and caster oil or glycerin. This liquid neither freezes nor boils at temperatures encountered in year round operations. When the brake pedal in a hydraulic brake system is depressed, the hydraulic fluid forces the pistons in the wheel cylinder against the brake shoes. The shoes expand against the brake drum and stop the vehicle. Hydraulic brakes are self-equalizing brakes. If the actuating pistons were all the same size, each brake in the hydraulic system would receive an identical hydraulic force when the brakes are applied because a force exerted at any point upon a closed liquid is distributed equally through the liquid in all directions. Some brake systems have larger wheel cylinders in the front than in the rear. This is because, when stopping, more of the vehicle's weight is felt in front and, therefore, more front wheel braking effort is required.

The mechanical advantage of any brake system is the relation between the pressure applied by the operator on the brake pedal to the pressure exerted on the braking surfaces.

The master cylinder has two functions. It is a reservoir for the brake fluid, and it contains the piston and the valves which change mechanical force to hydraulic pressure when the brake pedal is depressed. The pressure on the brake pedal moves the piston within the master cylinder, forcing the brake fluid from the master cylinder through tubing and flexible hose to the wheel cylinders. As pressure on the pedal is increased, greater hydraulic pressure is build up within the brake cylinders, and thus greater force is put forth against the ends of the brake shoes. When pressure on the pedal is released, the springs on the brake shoes return the wheel cylinder pistons to their released positions. This action forces the brake fluid back through the flexible hose and tubing to the master cylinder.

Most older model cars are equipped with the single system master cylinder. This system is, however, being replaced with dual system master cylinders.

The operation of a dual system master cylinder is basically the same as a single master cylinder. The dual system master cylinder, however, has two pistons, two separate fluid reservoirs, and two output ports. Thus, the dual system master cylinder has two separate hydraulic pressure systems. One of the hydraulic systems normally is connected to the front brakes, and the other system is the rear brakes. If either the front or rear hydraulic system fails, the other system remains operational.

The master cylinder, like other parts in the brake system, is subject to wear, leaks, and deposits or corrosion on the cylinder wall and piston. Master cylinder reservoir fluid level should be checked periodically and clean brake fluid added, as needed, to maintain fluid level approximately 1/2" from the top of the reservoir.

The brake lines transmit fluid and pressure from the master cylinder to the wheel cylinders, which in turn change the hydraulic pressure into mechanical force. The wheel cylinders are mounted on the brake backing plate. Inside each cylinder are two pistons that move in opposite directions by hydraulic pressure, which pushes the brake shoes against the brake drum. The brake shoes are made of iron, steel, or cast aluminum. They support the brake lining and transmit force to the lining, which is attached to the face of the shoe and make contact with the inner surface of the brake drums. During contact with one another the lining and the drum create the frictional surface that gives the braking effect.

AIRBRAKE SYSTEMS

Air, like all gases, is easily compressed. Compressed air exerts pressure and this pressure will be equal in all directions. Air under pressure can be conveniently stored and carried through lines or tubes. Considerable force is available for braking since operating air pressure may be as high as 100 psi. All brakes on a vehicle, and on a trailer (when one is used), are operated together by means of a brake valve.

The compressor is driven from the engine crankshaft or one of the auxiliary shafts. The three common methods of driving the compressor from the engine are gear, belt, and chain.

The compressor may be lubricated from the engine crankcase or be self-lubricated. Cooling may be either by air or liquid from the engine.

The purpose of the compressor governor is to automatically maintain the air pressure in the reservoir between the maximum pressure desired (100-105 psi) and the minimum pressure required for safe operation (80-85 psi) by starting and stopping compression.

The two steel tanks which are components of most air brake systems are called reservoirs. These tanks are used to cool, store, and remove moisture from the air and give a smooth flow of air to the brake system.

A safety valve consists of an adjustable spring-loaded ball check valve in a body. It is used to protect the system against excessive pressures and is usually mounted on a reservoir. The safety valve is normally set at 150 psi but can be varied to suit the vehicle requirements.

A pressure gauge is attached to any line which registers reservoir pressure and is mounted to the dashboard of the vehicle.

The brake valve is the operator's control of the air brake system. When the brake valve is engaged, air from the reservoir flows through the valve to the brakes. The three types of brake valves used in the air brake systems are pedal, treadle, and hand. When you press the pedal of an airbrake system, air under pressure in a reservoir is released to the brake lines by an air valve. This air goes to the brake chambers located close to the wheel brakes, which contain flexible diaphragms. The force of the air admitted to these chambers causes the diaphragms to operate the brake shoes through a mechanical linkage.

An air pressure gage will let you know if you have proper air pressure within the reservoir (60 lbs. pressure is minimum). This gage is usually found on the instrument panel of a truck or bus. If the pressure fails to build up or exceeds the maximum limits after building up, secure the truck until the fault is corrected.

Independent control of trailer brakes is valuable under adverse conditions when it is sometimes desirable to apply the brakes on the trailer without applying the brakes on the truck or tractor. The independent trailer control valve, conveniently located in the cab, provides the operator with perfect control of his trailing load at all times.

VACUUM BRAKES

In the vacuum brake system, depressing the brake pedal opens a valve between the power cylinder, which contains a piston, and the intake manifold to which the power cylinder is connected. To apply the brakes, air is exhausted from the cylinder ahead of the piston, while atmospheric pressure acts on the rear side of the piston to exert a powerful pull on the rod attached to the piston.

When the brake valve is closed, the chamber ahead of the piston is shut off from the intake manifold and is open to the atmosphere. The pressure is then the same on both sides of the piston; therefore, no pull is exerted upon the pull rod. The brake shoe return springs then release the brakes and return the piston to its original position in the power cylinder.

Hydrovac is a trade name for a one-unit vacuum power braking system. It combines into one assembly a hydraulic control valve, a vacuum power cylinder, and a hydraulic slave cylinder. This assembly is connected to both the master cylinder and the wheel brakes, eliminating the need for mechanical connections with the brake pedal.

When you press the brake pedal, fluid is forced from the master cylinder through the check valve to the slave cylinder and on to the wheel cylinders. The foot pedal pressure, acting through the master cylinder, acts also against the slave cylinder piston, assisting the vacuum pistons and push rods to press upon the brake shoes.

OPERATOR MAINTENANCE

Periodic brake service by the operator includes the use of proper brake fluid; checking brake fluid level; inflating tires properly; checking for loose connections or parts; checking for leaks in the system; draining air reservoirs daily; and checking the self-contained lubricating oil system of air compressors daily.

MALFUNCTION DETECTION

The types of brake trouble that may be encountered in vehicle operation are: brake pedal goes to the floorboard with no resistance; one brake drags; all brakes drag; vehicle pulls to one side when braking; soft or spongy pedal; excessive pedal effort required; noisy brakes; air in the system; loss of brake fluid; brakes heat up during driving and fail to release; leaky brake cylinder; grabbing brake action; and brake pedal can be depressed without slowing the vehicle. As an operator, you must explain the malfunction on the Operator's Trouble Report and turn it into the maintenance shop for necessary correction.

STEERING MECHANISMS

All steering mechanisms have the same basic parts. The steering linkage ties the front wheels together and connects them to the steering gear case at the lower end of the steering column, which in turn connects the gear case to the steering wheel.

The arms and rods of the steering linkage have ball or ball and socket ends to provide a swivel connection between them. These jointed ends are provided with grease fittings, dust seals or boots, and many of them have end-play adjustment devices. These joints and devices must be adjusted and lubricated regularly.

The <u>tie-rod</u> is usually located behind the axle and keeps the front wheels in proper alignment. To provide for easier steering and maximum leverage, the tie-rod may be separated into two lengths and connected to the steering gear near the center of the vehicle.

The <u>drag link</u> between the steering arm and the pitman arm may be long or short, depending on the installation.

The <u>pitman arm,</u> splined to the shaft extending from the steering gear case, moves in an arc, its position depending on which way the steering wheel is turned. It is approximately vertical when the front wheels are straight ahead. Therefore, the length of the drag link is determined by the distance between the steering arm and the vertical position of the pitman arm. Unlike the tie-rods, the length of the drag link is not adjustable.

The steering gear case contains the gears that control the movement of the pitman arm and steering linkage.

POWER STEERING

Power steering has been used for a number of years on heavy-duty applications, but it is only in recent years that power steering has been applied to any extent on automotive vehicles. The principle of power steering is very simple. A booster arrangement is provided which is set in operation when the steering wheel is turned. The booster then takes over and does most of the work of steering. Power steering has used compressed air, electrical mechanisms, and hydraulic pressure. Hydraulic pressure is used on the vast majority of power-steering mechanisms today.

In the hydraulic power-steering system, a continuously operating pump provides hydraulic pressure. As the steering wheel is turned, valves are operated to admit this hydraulic pressure to a cylinder. Then, the pressure causes a piston to move - and the piston does most of the steering work.

There are actually two general types of power-steering systems. In one, the integral type, the power operating assembly is located in the steering gear case. In the other, the linkage type, the power operating assembly is part of the steering linkage.

In the linkage-type power-steering system, the power cylinder or booster cylinder is not part of the steering gear. Instead, the power cylinder is connected into the steering linkage. In addition, the valve assembly is included in the steering linkage, either as a separate assembly or united with the power cylinder.

WHEEL ALIGNMENT

Steering control depends greatly upon the position of the wheels in relation to the rest of the vehicle and the surface over which it travels. Any changes from the specified setting of the wheels affect steering and the riding control of the vehicle. Therefore, the proper <u>wheel alignment</u> is important for vehicle control.

<u>Steering geometry</u> is the term manufacturers use to describe steering and front wheel alignment. Steering geometry includes <u>pivot inclination,</u> wheel <u>caster,</u> wheel <u>chamber, toe-in,</u>

and <u>toe-out.</u> These terms refer to angles in the front wheel alignment which may change because of driving over rough terrain, striking stationary objects, and accident damage.

OPERATOR MAINTENANCE

During maintenance servicing by the operator, the service that the steering linkage normally requires is periodic lubrication of the connecting joints between the links which contain bushings.

When vehicles are equipped with manually operated steering, check the steering gear housing for sufficient lubrication and add recommended manufacturer's gear lubricant, if necessary. For vehicles equipped with power steering, check belt tension which can cause low oil pressure and hard steering. Check fluid level. If the fluid level is low, add fluid to bring it up to the recommended level. Use only special power steering fluid recommended. If the level is low, the possibility exists that there is a leak. Check all hose and power-steering connections for signs of leaks. Leakage may occur at various points in the power-steering unit if the seals are defective. Report conditions to the maintenance shop for replacement of any defective seal, or it may only be necessary to tighten the connections to eliminate leaks.

MALFUNCTION DETECTION

The types of steering trouble that may be encountered in vehicle operation are: excessive play in the steering system; hard steering; vehicle wanders; vehicle pulls to one side when braking; front wheel shimmy at low speeds; front-wheel tramps (high speed shimmy); steering kickback; tires squeal on turns; improper tire wear; and noises. As an operator, you would explain the malfunction on the Operator's Trouble Report and turn it into the maintenance shop for corrective actions.

III.   SUSPENSION SYSTEMS

A suspension system is a system of <u>anchoring</u> and <u>suspending</u> the wheels or tracks from the frame by means of springs. The suspension system is an important feature of military vehicles; it supports the weight and allows them to be driven under varying loads and speed conditions over bumpy roads and rough terrain without great risk of damage.

The usual components of a suspension system are the <u>springs</u> and <u>shock absorbers.</u> Some suspension systems also have <u>torsion bars.</u>

SPRINGS

Springs support the frame and the body of the vehicle, as well as the load the vehicle carries. They allow the wheels to withstand the shocks of uneven road surfaces and provide a flexible connection between the wheels and the body. The best spring is the one which absorbs road shock rapidly and returns to its normal position slowly. Such a spring, however, is very rare, if not an impossibility. Extremely flexible, or soft springs allow too much movement of the vehicle superstructure, while still, hard springs do not allow enough movement.

The springs do not support the weight of the wheels, rims, tires, and axles. These parts make up the unsprung weight of the vehicle. The unsprung weight decreases the action of the springs and is, therefore, kept to a minimum to permit the springs to do the job of supporting the vehicle frame and load.

The three types of spring suspension usually found in vehicles are: the <u>longitudinal,</u> the lengthwise mounting, which is the most common; the <u>independent,</u> which is generally used in front suspensions; and <u>transverse,</u> which is the crosswise mounting.

The <u>multiple leaf spring</u> consists of a number of steel strips or leaves of different lengths, fastened together by a bolt through the center. Each end of the largest or master leaf is rolled into an eye which serves as a means of attaching the spring to the spring hanger and spring shackle. Leaf rebound clips surround the leaves at two or more intervals along the spring to keep them from separating on the rebound after the spring has been depressed. The clips allow the spring leaves to slide but prevent them from separating and throwing the entire rebound stress on the master leaf. Thus the spring acts as a flexible beam. Leaf springs may be suspended lengthwise (parallel to the frame), or cross-wise.

When installed <u>lengthwise,</u> both ends of the spring are attached to the frame and the center is clamped to the axle or spring seat. In some trucks and cars the rear springs are clamped under the axle, instead of over it to lower the center of gravity. A low center of gravity will help prevent a heavily loaded truck from upsetting.

Springs installed <u>crosswise</u> have the ends attached to the axle, and the frame rests on the center of the spring. Torque arms or radius rods are required with this type of spring suspension to absorb the driving thrust of the wheels. The driving thrust and brake action of wheels tend to twist the springs from the spring hangers and shackles connecting them to the frame or axles.

Spring hangers are fittings to which the spring ends are attached. A bolt or pin passes through the bushing in the spring eye and is secured to the spring hanger on the frame. The bushing and shackle bolt or pin, therefore, provide the bearing surface which supports the load on the spring.

The <u>spring bushings</u> may be made of bronze or rubber. They may be pressed or screwed into the spring eye, depending on the design. The steel bolts or pins that pass through the bushing are also either plain or threaded. Threaded bushings and shackle bolts offer a greater bearing surface and are replaced more easily when they become worn.

When a leaf spring is compressed, it must straighten out or break. Therefore, <u>spring shackles</u> are required at one or both ends of the spring. Spring shackles provide a swinging support and allow the spring to straighten out when compressed. One shackle is used in either the front or rear support of springs installed lengthwise. Two shackles are used in supporting springs installed crosswise.

You will see many types of spring shackles. The link shackle and U-shackle are the most common. Link shackles are used in heavy vehicles, and the U-type is more common for use on passenger cars and light trucks.

You will find link shackles used to support a transverse spring on the dead front axle of some wheeled tractors. Most wheeled tractors do not even have springs, and all load cushioning is obtained through large, low pressure tires.

Track-type tractors are equipped with one large leaf spring supported without spring shackles. It is fastened to the engine support and rests on the frames supporting the tracks and rollers. Brackets on the track frames keep the spring from shifting. The main purpose of the spring is to relieve the running gear of stresses during operation.

Some vehicles are equipped with leaf springs at the rear wheels only; others are so equipped both front and rear.

Coil springs are most generally used on independent suspension systems. They provide a very smooth riding quality. Their use has normally been limited to passenger vehicles. Recently, however, they have been used to a limited extent on trucks. The spring seat and hanger, shaped to fit the coil ends, hold the spring in place. Spacers made of rubberized fabric are placed at each end of the coil to prevent squeaking. The rubber bumper, mounted in the spring supporting member, prevents metal to metal contact when the spring is compressed. Most vehicles are equipped with coil springs at the two front wheels, while some others have them at both front and rear.

SHOCK ABSORBERS

Springs alone are never satisfactory in a light vehicle suspension system. A stiff spring gives a hard ride because it does not flex and rebound when the vehicle passes over a bump. On the other hand, too flexible a spring rebounds too much, and the vehicle rides roughly. To smooth the riding qualities of the vehicle, shock absorbers are used. They prevent excessive jolting *of* the vehicle by balancing spring stiffness and flexibility. They allow the springs to return to rest slowly after having been compressed. Although single-acting shock absorbers check only spring rebound, double-acting shock absorbers check spring compression as well as spring rebound, permitting the use of the more flexible springs.

FRONT AXLE SUSPENSION

Most passenger car front wheels are individually supported with independent suspension systems. The ones you are likely to encounter are the coil spring and the torsion bar suspension systems. These are used with independent front axles and shock absorbers.

REAR AXLE SUSPENSION

Driving wheels are mounted on a live driving axle that is suspended by springs attached to the axle housing. Leaf springs are generally used for suspending live axles. Coil springs are used on a number of passenger cars with torque tube drive.

OPERATOR MAINTENANCE

Under normal operation, and given proper maintenance, suspension systems would not need adjustments or replacement for many miles. The spring assemblies of the suspension system should be checked regularly to ensure that shackles are tight and that bushings within the shackles are not worn excessively or frozen tight. Occasionally, spraying lubricating oil on the spring leaves helps to prevent squeaking at the ends of the spring leaves. Following the lubrication chart furnished for a particular vehicle, check and lubricate the front suspension system including linkage, kingpin, and ball joints. During your checks you may find shock absorber bushings worn; if so, it is best to have the bushings replaced, or in some instances a complete replacement of the shock absorbers is needed.

<u>MALFUNCTION DETECTION</u>

Some types of suspension troubles that may be encountered in vehicle operation are: hard steering, vehicle wander, vehicle pulls to one side during normal driving, front-wheel shimmy, front-wheel tramp (high speed shimmy), steering kickback, hard or rough ride, sway on turns, spring breakage, sagging springs, and noises. As an operator, you would explain the malfunction on the Operator's Trouble Report and turn the trouble report into the maintenance shop for corrective action.

IV.   FRAME

The chassis is the assembly of mechanisms that make up the major operating part of the vehicle. It is usually assumed to include everything except the vehicle body. The individual operating assembles are mounted on the <u>frame,</u> which must be strong enough to support the weight of the vehicle and its rated load without distortion. The frame must be rigid enough to keep the units of the vehicle in proper alignment and to protect them against the stresses ane strains of road and surface shocks.

The frame is generally constructed of cold-rolled open-hearth steel, but sometimes of alloy steel to lighten the weight of the vehicle. The <u>side members</u> or <u>rails</u> are the heaviest parts of the frame. The <u>cross members</u> are fixed to the side members rigidly enough to prevent weaving and twisting of the frame. Angular pieces of metal called <u>gusset plates</u> are riveted or welded at the point where members are joined for added strength .

The number, size, and arrangement of cross members depend on the type of vehicle for which the frame is designed. Usually, a front cross member supports the radiator and front end of the engine as well as stiffens the frame. The rear cross members furnish support for the fuel tanks and rear trunk on passenger cars, and the two-bar connections for trucks. Additional cross members are added to the frame to support the rear of the engine and power train and to secure the rigidity required.

The cross members of most small vehicles are designed in either X or K form. The front cross members are wider and of heavier construction than the back members because they support the engine and the front wheels. The side members are shaped to accommodate the body and support its weight. They narrow toward the front of the vehicle to permit a shorter turning radius for the wheels and widen under the main part of the body where the body is secured to the frame. Trucks and trailers usually have frames with straight side members to accommodate several designs of bodies and to give the vehicle added strength to withstand heavier loads. Heavy duty trucks and trailers have I-beam frames.

Brackets and hangers which are bolted or riveted to the frame to support the shock absorbers, fenders, running boards and springs are usually made of case or pressed steel.

GLOSSARY OF
AUTOMOTIVE TERMS

CONTENTS

GLOSSARY OF
AUTOMOTIVE TERMS
A

A-PILLAR - The roof support on either side of a car's windshield.

AC - Alternating current, or current that reverses its direction at regular intervals.

ACCELERATING PUMP - A device in the carburetor that supplies an additional amount of fuel, temporarily enriching the fuel-air mixture when the throttle is suddenly opened.

ACCELERATION - The process of increasing velocity. Average rate of change of increasing velocity, usually in feet per second.

ACKERMAN STEERING - The steering-system design that permits the front wheels to round a turn without sideslip by turning the inner wheel in more than the outer wheel.

ACTIVE SUSPENSION - An extremely sophisticated, computer-controlled suspension system that uses powered actuators instead of conventional springs and shock absorbers. The actuators position a car's wheels in the best possible manner to deal with road disturbances and handling loads.

AERODYNAMIC DRAG - The drag produced by a moving object as it displaces the air in its path. Aerodynamic drag is a force usually measured in pounds; it increases in proportion to the object's frontal area, its drag coefficient, and the square of its speed.

AIR BLEED - A passage in the carburetor through which air can seep or bleed into fuel moving through a fuel passage.

AIR BRAKES - Vehicle brakes actuated by air pressure.

AIR CLEANER - A device, mounted on the carburetor or connected to the carburetor, "through which air must pass before entering the carburetor air horn. A filtering device in the air cleaner removes dust and dirt particles from the air.

AIR-COOLED ENGINE - An engine cooled by air circulating between cylinders and around cylinder head as opposed to the liquid-cooled engine cooled by a liquid passing through jackets surrounding the cylinders.

AIR DAM - A front spoiler mounted beneath the bumper and shaped to reduce the airflow under the car. Air dams can increase the airflow to radiators, reduce aerodynamic drag, and/or reduce lift.

AIR FILTER - A filter through which air passes, and which removes dust and dirt particles from the air. Air filters are placed in passages through which air must pass, as in crankcase breather, air cleaner, etc.

AIR HORN - That part of the air passage in the carburetor which is on the atmospheric side of the venturi. The choke valve is located in the air horn.

AIR-PAC BRAKES - A type of braking system using a vacuum.

AMMETER - An electric meter that measures current, in amperes, in an electric circuit.

AMPERE - Unit of electric-current-flow measurement. The current that will flow through a 1-ohm resistance when 1 volt is impressed across the resistance.

AMPHIBIOUS VEHICLE - A vehicle with a hull that permits it to float in water, and tracks or wheels that permit it to travel on land.

ANGLE OF APPROACH - The maximum angle of an incline onto which a vehicle can move from a horizontal plane without interference; as, for instance, from front bumpers.

ANGLE OF DEPARTURE - The maximum angle of an incline from which a vehicle can move onto a horizontal plane without interference; as, for instance, from rear bumpers.

ANTI-DIVE - A tuned-in front suspension characteristic that converts braking-induced forces in the suspension links into a vertical force that tends to lift the body, thereby reducing dive under braking.

ANTIFREEZE - A substance added to the coolant system in a liquid-cooled engine to prevent freezing.

ANTIFRICTION BEARING - A bearing of the type that supports the imposed load on rolling surfaces (balls, rollers, needles), minimizing friction.

ANTIKNOCK - Refers to substances that are added to automotive fuel to decrease the tendency to knock when fuel-air mixture is compressed and ignited in the engine cylinder.

ANTI-LOCK BRAKING SYSTEM - A braking system that senses when any of the wheels have locked up, or are about to, and automatically reduces the braking forces to keep the wheels rolling. Commonly called ABS, such a system can control all four wheels or only two.

ANTI-ROLL BAR - A suspension element (used at the front, the rear, or both ends of a car) that reduces body roll by resisting any unequal vertical motion between the pair of wheels to which it is connected. An anti-roll bar does not affect suspension stiffness when both wheels are deflected equally in the same direction. Often incorrectly called a sway bar.

ANTI-SQUAT - Similar to anti-dive, this suspension characteristic uses acceleration-induced forces in the rear suspension to reduce squat.

APEX - The point(s) or region on the line through a corner that touches the corner's inner radius.

ARMATURE - The rotating assembly in a direct current generator or motor. Also, the iron piece in certain electrical apparatus that completes a magnetic (and in many cases, an electric) circuit.

ASPECT RATIO - Generally the ratio between two dimensions of an object. In tire terminology, it applies to the unloaded sidewall height of the tire divided by its overall width. A lower aspect ratio implies a shorter, wider tire. When used to describe a wing, it is the span of the airfoil (the long dimension perpendicular to the airflow) divided by its chord (the dimension parallel to the airflow).

ATMOSPHERE - The mass of air that surrounds the earth.

ATMOSPHERIC PRESSURE - The weight of the atmosphere per unit area.

ATOM - The smallest particle, or part, of an element, composed of electrons and protons and also of neutrons (with exception of hydrogen).

ATOMIZATION - The spraying of a liquid through a nozzle so that the liquid is broken into tiny globules or particles.

AUTOMATIC CHOKE - A choke that operates automatically in accordance with certain engine conditions (usually temperature and intake manifold vacuum)(also electrically controlled).

AUTOMATIC TRANSMISSION - A transmission that reduces or eliminates the necessity of hand-shifting of gears to secure different gear ratios in the transmission.

AXIAL - In a direction parallel to the axle. Axial movement is movement parallel to the axis.

AXIS - A center line. The line about which something rotates or about which something is evenly divided.

AXLE - A cross support on a vehicle on which supporting wheel, or wheels, turn. There are two general types: live axles that also transmit power to the wheels and dead axles that transmit no power.

AXLE TRAMP - It is a form of wheel hop that occurs on cars with live axles, caused by the axle repeatedly rotating slightly with the wheels and then springing back.

B

B-PILLAR - The roof support between a car's front door window and rear side window, if there is one.

BACKFIRING - Pre-explosion of fuel-air mixture so that explosion passes back around the opened intake valve and flashes back through the intake manifold.

BACKLASH - The backward rotation of driven gear that is permitted by clearance between meshing teeth of two gears.

BAFFLE - A plate or shield to divert the flow of liquid or gas.

BALANCE SHAFT - A shaft designed so that, as it rotates, it vibrates in a way that reduces or cancels some of the vibration produced by an engine. Not essential to an engine's operation, balance shafts are nonetheless becoming increasingly common as a means of engine refinement. Balance-shafted four-cylinder engines use two shafts turning in opposite directions on either side of the engine's crankshaft. A single balance shaft is used when fitted to three-cylinder and V-6 engines.

BALL BEARING - A type of bearing which contains steel balls that roll between inner and outer races.

BALL JOINT - A flexible joint consisting of a ball in a socket, used primarily in front suspensions because it can accommodate a wide range of angular motion.

BATTERY - A device consisting of two or more cells for converting chemical energy into electrical energy.

BATTERY CHARGING - The process of supplying a battery with a flow of electric current to produce chemical actions in the battery; these actions reactivate the chemicals in the battery so they can again produce electrical energy.

BDC - Bottom dead center; the position of the piston when it reaches the lower limit of travel in the cylinder.

BEAM AXLE - A rigid axle supporting the non-driven wheels. Also called a dead axle.

BEARING - A part in which a journal pivot, or pia.turns or revolves. A part on or in which another part slides.

BELTLINE - The line running around a car's body formed by the bottom edges of its glass panels.

BENDIX DRIVE - A type of drive used in a starter which provides automatic coupling with the engine flywheel for cranking and automatic uncoupling when the engine starts.

BEVEL GEAR - One of a pair of meshing gears whose working surfaces are inclined to the center lines of the driving and driven shafts. Bevel gears are used to transmit motion through an angle.

BLACKOUT LIGHTS - A lamp installed on a vehicle for use during blackouts, which can be seen from the air only at very close range.

BLOCK - See Cylinder

Block. BLOW-BY - Leakage of the compressed fuel-air mixture or burned gases from combustion, passing piston and rings and into the crankcase.

BLOWER - A mechanical device for compressing and delivering air to engine at higher than atmospheric pressure.

BODY - The assembly of sheet-metal sections, framework, doors, windows, etc., which provides an enclosure for passengers or carriage space for freight.

BOGIE - A suspension unit consisting of tandem axles jointed by a single cross support (trunnion axle) that also acts as a vertical pivot for the entire unit.

BOND - To bind together.

BOOST PRESSURE - The increase above atmospheric pressure produced inside the intake manifold by any supercharger. It is commonly
measured in psi, inches of mercury, or bar.

4

BORE - The diameter of engine cylinder hole. Also diameter of any hole; as, for example, the hole into which a bushing is fitted.

BOSS - An extension or strengthened section, such as the projections within a piston which support the piston pin.

BRAKE BAND - A flexible band, usually of metal with an inner lining of brake fabric, which is tightened on a drum to slow or stop drum rotation.

BRAKE BIAS - The front/rear distribution of a car's braking power. For the shortest stopping distance, brake bias should match the car's traction at each end during hard braking.

BRAKE DRUM - Metal drum mounted on car wheel or other rotating members; brake shoes or brake band, mechanically forced against it, causes it to slow or stop.

BRAKE FLUID - A compounded fluid used in hydraulic braking system; it transmits hydraulic force from the brake master cylinder to the wheel cylinder and should be impervious to heat or freezing.

BRAKE HORSEPOWER - The power actually delivered by the engine which is available for driving the vehicle.

BRAKE LINING - A special woven fabric material with which brake shoes or brake bands are lined; it withstands high temperatures and pressures.

BRAKE MODULATION - The process of varying pedal pressure to hold a car's brakes on the verge of lockup. Ideally, the brakes will unlock with only a slight reduction in the pressure needed to lock them. Typically, however, a considerable pressure reduction is required.

BRAKE SHOES - The curved metal part, faced with brake lining, which is forced against the brake drum to produce braking or retarding action.

BRAKE SYSTEM - The system on a vehicle that slows or stops it as a pedal or lever is operated.

BRAKE TORQUING - A procedure generally used in performance tests to improve the off-the-line acceleration of a car equipped with an automatic transmission. It is executed by firmly depressing the brake with the left foot, applying the throttle with the car in gear to increase engine rpm, then releasing the brakes. Brake torquing is particularly effective with turbocharged cars because it helps overcome turbo lag.

BRAKES - The mechanism that slows or stops a vehicle or mechanism when a pedal or other control is operated. Also called the brake system.

BREATHING (ENGINE) - A term used to describe an engine's ability to fill its cylinders with air-fuel mixture and then discharge the burnt exhaust gases. In general, the more air-fuel mixture an engine burns, the more power it produces.

BRONZE - An alloy consisting essentially of copper and tin.

BRUSHES - The carbon or carbon and metal parts in a motor or generator that contact the rotating armature commutator or rings.

BUSHING - A sleeve placed in a bore to serve as a bearing surface. A simple suspension bearing that accommodates limited rotary motion, typically made of two coaxial steel tubes bonded to a sleeve of rubber between them. The compliance of the bushing in different directions has a great effect on ride harshness and handling.

BYPASS - A separate passage which permits a liquid, gas, or electric current to take a path other than that normally used.

C

C-PILLAR - The roof support between a car's rearmost side window and its rear window. On a vehicle with four side pillars, the rearmost roof support may be called a D-pillar.

CAB - Separate driver's compartment provided on trucks.

CAD/CAM - Computer-aided design and computer-aided manufacturing -the harnessing of computers to generate drawings, perform complex structural and design analyses, and directly program numerically controlled machines to produce automotive parts.

CAM - A moving part of an irregular form designed to move or alter the motion of another part.

CAMBER - To curve or bend; the amount in inches or degrees that the front wheels of an automotive vehicle are tilted from a true vertical at the top.

CAM PROFILE - The shape of each lobe on a camshaft. The profile determines the amount, or *duration,* of time the valve is open; it also largely determines the valve's maximum opening, or lift.

CAMSHAFT - A shaft fitted with several cams, whose lobes push on valve lifters to convert rotary motion into linear motion. The opening and closing of the valves in all piston engines is regulated by one or more camshafts.

CAPACITANCE - That property of a circuit which tends to increase the amount of current flowing in a circuit for a given voltage or to delete in its entirety.

CAPACITOR (CONDENSER) - A device for inserting the property of capacitance into a circuit; two or more conductors separated by a dielectric.

CARBON FIBER - Threadlike strands of pure carbon that are extremely strong in tension (that is, when pulled) and are reasonably flexible. Carbon fiber can be bound in a matrix of plastic resin by heat, vacuum, or pressure to form a composite that is strong, light - and very expensive.

CARBON-PILE REGULATOR - A type of regulator for regulating or controlling voltage or amperage in a circuit, which makes use of a stack, or pile, of carbon disks.

CARBURETOR - The device in a fuel system which mixes fuel and air and delivers the combustible mixture to the intake manifold.

CASTER - The amount in degrees that the steering knuckle pivots are tilted forward or backward from a true vertical.

CATALYTIC CONVERTER - Often simply called a *catalyst* - a stainless-steel canister fitted to a car's exhaust system that contains a thin layer of catalytic material spread over a large area of inert supports. The material used is some combination of platinum, rhodium, and palladium; it induces chemical reactions that convert an engine's exhaust emissions into less harmful products. So-called three-way catalysts are particularly efficient; their operation, however, demands very precise combustion control, which can be produced only by a feedback fuel-air-ratio control system.

CELL - A combination of electrodes and electrolyte which converts chemical energy into electrical energy. Two or more cells connected together form a battery.

CENTER DIFFERENTIAL - A differential used in four-wheel-drive systems to distribute power to the front and rear differentials.

CENTER OF GRAVITY - The imaginary point in any object about which it is in perfect balance no matter how it is turned or rotated around that point.

CENTRIFUGAL ADVANCE - The mechanism in an ignition distributor by which the spark is advanced or retarded as the engine speed varies.

CENTRIFUGAL FORCE - The force acting on a rotating body, which tends to move its parts outward and away from the center of rotation.

CHARGE INDICATOR - The device on a vehicle that indicates, by a needle, whether or not the battery is receiving a charge from the generator.

CHARGING RATE - The rate of flow, in amperes, of electric current flowing through a battery while it is being charged.

CHASSIS - An assembly of mechanisms, attached to a frame, that make up the major operating part of an automotive vehicle (less body). In cars with unitized construction, the chassis comprises everything but the body of the car.

CHOKE - A device in the carburetor that chokes off, or reduces, the flow of air into the intake manifold; this produces a partial vacuum in the intake manifold and a consequent richer fuel-air mixture.

CIRCUIT - A closed path or combination of paths through which passage of the medium (electric current, air, liquid, etc.) is possible.

CIRCUIT BREAKER - In electric circuits, a mechanism designed to break or open the circuit when certain conditions exist; especially the device in automotive circuits that,opens the circuit between the generator and battery to prevent overcharging of the battery. (One of the three units comprising a generator regulator.)

CLOCKWISE - Direction of movement, usually rotary, which is the same as movement of hands on the face of a clock.

CLUTCH - The mechanism in an automotive vehicle, located in the power train, that connects the engine to, or disconnects the engine from, the remainder of the power train.

COIL - In electrical circuits, turns of wire, usually on a core and enclosed in a case, through which electric current passes.

COIL SPRING - A type of spring made of an elastic metal such as steel, formed into a wire or bar and wound into a coil. Coil springs have many automotive applications but are particularly important as suspension springs.

COMBAT VEHICLE - A type of vehicle, usually armored, for use in armed combat.

COMBUSTION - A chemical action, or burning; in an engine, the burning of a fuel-air mixture in the combustion chamber.

COMBUSTION CHAMBER - The space at the top of the cylinder and in the head in which combustion of the fuel-air mixture takes place. It is formed by the top of the piston and a cavity in the cylinder head. Since most of the air-fuel mixture's combustion takes place in this space, its design and shape can greatly affect the power, fuel, efficiency, and emissions of the engine.

COMMUTATION - The process of converting alternating current which flows in the armature windings of direct current generators into direct current.

COMMUTATOR - That part of rotating machinery which makes electrical contact with the brushes and connects the armature windings with the external circuit.

COMPLIANCE - A slight resiliency, or *give,* designed into suspension bushings to help absorb bumps. Good compliance allows the wheels to move rearward a bit as they hit bumps but doesn't allow them to move laterally during cornering.

COMPOSITE - Any material that consists of two or more components, typically one or more of high strength and one an adhesive binder. The most common composite is fiberglass, which consists of thin glass fibers bonded together in a plastic matrix. The structural properties of composites can be altered by controlling the orientation and configuration of the high-strength components.

COMPRESSION - Act of pressing into a smaller space or reducing in size or volume by pressure.

COMPRESSION RATIO - The ratio between the volume in the cylinder with the piston at bottom dead center and with the piston at top dead center. The ratio between the combined volume of a cylinder and a combustion chamber when the piston is at the bottom of its stroke, and the volume when the piston is at the top of its stroke. The higher the compression ratio, the more mechanical energy an engine can squeeze from its air-fuel mixture. Higher compression ratios, however, also make detonation more likely.

COMPRESSION RINGS - The upper rings on a piston; the rings designed to hold the compression in the cylinder and prevent blow-by.

COMPRESSION STROKE - The piston stroke from bottom dead center to top dead center during which both valves are closed and the gases in the cylinder are compressed.

CONCENTRIC - Having a common center, as circles or spheres, one within the other.

CONDENSER - See Capacitor.

CONDUCTOR - A material through which electricity will readily flow.

CONNECTING ROD - Linkage between the crankshaft and piston, usually attached to the piston by a piston pin and to the crank journal on the crankshaft by a split bearing and bearing cap.

CONSTANT-VELOCITY JOINT - A particular kind of universal joint designed so that there is no cyclic fluctuation between the speeds of its input and output shafts.

CONTACT PATCH - The portion of a tire tread that is in contact with the road. On modern tires, it varies from nearly a circle to a wide ellipse.

CONTROL ARM - A suspension element that has one joint at one end and two joints at the other end, typically the chassis side. Also known as a wishbone or an A-arm.

CONVERTIBLE - A car whose top can be completely lowered.

COOLANT - The liquid that circulates in an engine cooling system which reduces heat generated by the engine.

COOLING FAN - The fan in the engine cooling system that provides a forced circulation of air through the radiator or around the engine cylinders so that cooling is effected.

COOLING FINS - Thin metal projections on air-cooled-engine cylinder and head which greatly increases the heat-radiating surfaces and helps provide cooling of engine cylinder.

COOLING SYSTEM - A system which reduces heat generated by the engine and thereby prevents engine overheating; includes, in liquid cooled engine, engine water jackets, radiator, and water pump.

CORE - An iron mass, generally the central portion of a coil or electromagnet or armature around which the wire is coiled.

CORNERING LIMIT - The maximum speed at which a car can negotiate a given curve.

COUNTERCLOCKWISE - Direction of movement, usually rotary, which is opposite in direction to movement of hands on the face of a clock.

COUPE - A closed car with two side doors and less than 33 cubic feet of rear interior volume, according to measurements based on SAE standard J1100. A two-door car is, therefore, not necessarily a coupe.

COWL - The front portion of the vehicle body or cab which partially incloses the dash panel and forms the windshield frame.

CRANK - A device for converting reciprocating motion into rotary motion, and vice versa.

CRANKCASE - The lower part of the engine in which the crankshaft rotates. In automotive practice, the upper part is lower section of cylinder block while lower section is the oil pan.

CRANKCASE BREATHER - The opening or tube that allows air to enter the crankcase and thus permit crankcase ventilation.

CRANKCASE DILUTION - Dilution of the lubricating oil in the oil pan by liquid gasoline seeping down the cylinder walls past the piston rings.

RANKCASE VENTILATION - The circulation of air through the crankcase which removes water and other vapors, thereby preventing the formation of water sludge and other unwanted substances.

CRANKING MOTOR - See Starter.

CRANKSHAFT - The main rotating member or shaft of the engine, with cranks to which the connecting rods are attached. Together, thecrankshaft and the con rods transform the pistons' reciprocating motion into rotary motion.

CRASH - Generally a high-speed parking maneuver. Often, the driver at fault will refer to it as a *shunt* or an *incident.*

CROSS-DRIVE TRANSMISSION - A special type of transmission used in tanks and other heavy vehicles which combines the actions of a transmission with torque converter, steering system, and differential.

CURRENT REGULATOR - A magnetic-controlled relay by which the field circuit of the generator is made and broken very rapidly to secure even current output from the generator and prevent generator overload from excessive output. (One of the three units comprising a generator regulator.)

CUTOUT RELAY - An automatic magnetic switch attached to the generator to cut out generator circuit and prevent overcharging of battery. See Circuit Breaker.

CYCLE - A series of events with a start and finish, during which a definite train of events takes place. In the engine, the four piston strokes (or two piston strokes on 2-stroke cycle engine) that complete the working process and produce power.

CYLINDER - A tubular-shaped structure. In the engine, the tubular opening in which the piston moves up and down. Typically made of cast iron and formed as a part of the block.

CYLINDER BLOCK - That part of an engine to which, and in which, other engine parts and accessories are attached or assembled.

CYLINDER HEAD - The part of the engine that encloses the cylinder bores. Contains water jackets (on liquid-cooled engine) and valves (on I-head engines). The aluminum or iron casting that houses the combustion chambers, the intake and exhaust ports, and much or all of the valvetrain. The head (or heads, if an engine has more than one bank of cylinders) is always directly above the cylinders.

CYLINDER LINER - The circular housing that the piston moves in when the cylinder is not an integral part of the block. Also known as a *sleeve*.

D

DBA - A unit of measure for decibels, the measure of sound intensity or pressure named after Alexander Graham Bell. It is a logarithmic measurement; every 3dB increase represents a doubling of the sound pressure. The *A* in dBA indicates that the measurement was taken with an A-weighted scale; sound pressure varies across the audible spectrum, and the A-weighted scale approximates the human ear's sensitivity to various frequencies.

DC - Direct current, or current that flows is one direction only.

DAMPER - A device for reducing the motion or oscillations of moving parts, air, or liquid.

DASH PANEL - The partition that separates the driver's compartment from the engine compartment. Sometimes called firewall.

DE DION SUSPENSION - A suspension system in which the rear, driven wheels are bolted to a transverse, 1ightweight, rigid member. Power is delivered to the wheels by universal-jointed half-shafts attached to a body-mounted differential.

DEAD AXLE - An axle that simply supports and does not turn or deliver power to the wheel or rotating member.

DEAD PEDAL - A footrest found to the left of the leftmost pedal. It provides a place for the driver to brace his left leg during hard cornering.

DECELERATION - The process of slowing down. Opposite to acceleration.

DEGASSER - A device used in connection with carburetors for shutting off the flow of fuel during deceleration so that gases from incomplete combustion during deceleration are prevented.

DETONATION - A condition in which, after the spark plug fires, some of the unburned air-fuel mixture in the combustion chamber explodes spontaneously, set off only by the heat and pressure of air-fuel mixture that has already been ignited. Detonation, or *knock*, greatly increases the mechanical and thermal stresses on the engine.

DIAPHRAGM - A flexible membrane, usually made of fabric and rubber in automotive components, clamped at the edges and usually spring-loaded; used in fuel pump, vacuum pump, distributor, etc.

DIESEL ENGINE - An engine using the diesel cycle of operation; air alone is compressed and diesel fuel is injected at the end of the compression stroke. Heat of compression produces ignition.

DIFFERENTIAL - A special gearbox designed so that the torque fed into it is split and delivered to two outputs that can turn at different speeds. Differentials within axles are designed to split torque evenly; however, when used between the front and rear axles in four-wheel-drive systems (a center differential), they can be designed to apportion torque unevenly.

DIFFERENTIAL WINDING - In electrical machinery, a winding that is wound in a reverse direction or different direction than the main operating windings. The differential winding acts to modify or change the action of the machine under certain conditions.

DISC BRAKES - Properly called caliper disc brakes - a type of brake that consists of a disc that rotates at wheel speed, straddled by a caliper that can squeeze the surfaces of the disc near its periphery. Disc brakes provide a more linear response and operate more efficiently at high temperatures and wet conditions than drum brakes.

DISTRIBUTOR - See Ignition Distributor.

DIVE - the dipping of a car's nose that occurs when the brakes are applied. Dive is caused by a load transfer from the rear to the front suspension; this transfer occurs because the car's center of gravity, through which all inertial forces pass, is higher than its contact patches, the points where the braking forces are exerted on the ground.

DOLLY - A two-wheel trailer coupled to a semitrailer to support and steer its front end when it is converted into a full trailer.

DOHC - Double overhead camshaft - a DOHC engine has two camshafts in each cylinder head; one camshaft operates the intake valves, the other actuates the exhaust valves.

DOWNFORCE - A vertical force directed downward, produced by airflow around an object - such as a car body.

DRAG COEFFICIENT - A dimensionless measure of the aerodynamic sleekness of an object. A sleek car has a drag coefficient, or *Cd,* of about 0.30; a square, flat plate's is 1.98. Also signified by Cx.

DRAG LINK - An intermediate link in the steering system between the Pitman arm and an intermediate arm or drag-link arm.

DRIVABILITY - The general qualitative evaluation of a power-train's operating qualities, including idle smoothness, cold and hot starting, throttle response, power delivery, and tolerance for altitude changes.

DRIVELINE - Everything in the drivetrain, less the engine and the transmission.

DRIVESHAFT - The shaft that transmits power from the transmission to the differential.

DRIVETRAIN - All of a car's components that create power and transmit it to the wheels; i.e., the engine, the transmission, the differential(s), the hubs, and any interconnecting shafts.

DRUM BRAKES - A type of brake that has an iron casting shaped like a shallow drum that rotates with the wheel. Curved brake shoes are forced into contact with the inner periphery of this drum to provide braking.

DUAL IGNITION - Ignition system using two spark plugs for each cylinder so that a dual spark effect takes place driving each power stroke.

DUAL-RATIO AXLES - Axle in truck which contains a mechanism for changing driving ratio of the wheels to either high or low ratio. Two-speed differential.

DYNAMOMETER - A device for measuring power output on an engine.

E

EGR - Exhaust-gas recirculation - a method of reducing NOx (oxides of nitrogen) exhaust emissions by recirculating some of the engine's exhaust gas into the intake manifold. The exhaust gas serves as inert filler that absorbs heat during the combustion process and reduces the peak temperature reached during combustion.

ECCENTRIC - Off center.

EDDY CURRENTS - Currents which are induced in an iron core and circulate in the core.

EFFICIENCY - Ratio between the effect produced and the power expended to produce the effect.

ELECTRIC BRAKES - A brake system which uses electric current for energization.

ELECTRICAL SYSTEM - In the automotive vehicle, the system that electrically cranks the engine for starting, furnishes high-voltage sparks to the engine cylinders to fire compressed fuel-air charges, lights the lights, operates heater motor, ratio, etc. Consists, in part, of starter, wiring, battery, generator, generator regulator, ignition distributor, and ignition coil.

ELECTRICITY - A form of energy that involves the movement of electrons from one place to another, or the gathering of electrons in one area.

ELECTRODE - Either terminal of an electric source; either conductor by which the current enters and leaves an electrolyte.

ELECTROLYTE - The liquid in a battery or other electrochemical device, in which the condution of electricity is accompanied by chemical decomposition.

ELECTROMAGNET - Temporary magnet constructed by winding a number of turns of insulated wire into a coil or around an iron core; it is energized by a flow of electric current through the coil.

ELECTRON - Negative charged particle that is a basic constituent of matter and electricity. Movement of electrons is an electric current.

ENERGY - The capacity for performing work.

ENGINE - An assembly that burns fuel to produce power, sometimes referred to as the power plant.

ENGINE-CONTROL SYSTEM - A computerized brain that regulates an engine's operation by monitoring certain engine characteristics (rpm, coolant temperature, intake airflow, etc.) through a network of sensors and then controlling key variables (fuel metering, spark timing, EGR, etc.) according to pre-programmed schedules.

EPA FUEL ECONOMY - Laboratory fuel-economy tests administered by the Environmental Protection Agency using simulated weight and drag to re-create real driving conditions. The city fuel-economy test, also used to test emissions compliance, is based on a drive through typical Los Angeles urban traffic of about twenty years ago. The highway test uses a higher, steadier speed, averaging 49.4 mph.

EVAPORATION - The action that takes place when a liquid changes to a vapor or gas.

EXHAUST MANIFOLD - The network of passages that gathers the exhaust gases from the various exhaust ports and routes them toward the catalysts and mufflers of the exhaust system. A manifold with free-flowing passages of a carefully designed configuration, called a *header*, can improve breathing.

EXHAUST PORT - The passageway in the cylinder head leading from the exhaust valves to the exhaust manifold.

EXHAUST STROKE - The piston stroke from bottom dead center to top dead center during which the exhaust valve is opened so that burned gases are forced from the engine cylinder.

EXHAUST VALVE - The valve which opens to allow the burned gases to escape from the cylinder during the exhaust stroke.

F

FAN - See Cooling Fan.

FEEDBACK FUEL-AIR-RATIO CONTROL - A feature of a computer-controlled fuel system. By using a sensor to measure the oxygen content of the engine's exhaust, the system keeps the fuel-air ratio very close to the proportion for chemically perfect combustion. Such tight control of the fuel-air ratio is mandatory for the proper operation of three-way catalysts.

F-HEAD - A type of engine with valves arranged to form an F; one valve is in the head, the other in the cylinder block.

FIBERGLASS - A composite material that relies on small glass fibers for its strength.

FIELD - In a generator or electric motor, the area in which a magnetic flow occurs.

FIELD COIL - A coil of wire, wound around an iron core, which produces the magnetic field in a generator or motor when current passes through it.

FIELD FRAME - The frame in a generator or motor into which the field coils are assembled.

FIELD WINDING - See Field Coil.

FIFTH WHEEL - The flat, round heavy steel plates (upper and lower) together with a kingpin for coupling semitrailer to truck-tractor. The lower plate is mounted on the truck-tractor, the upper on the semitrailer.

FILTER - A device through which gas or liquid is passed; dirt, dust, and other impurities are removed by the separating action.

FINAL DRIVE - That part of the power train on tractors, truck-tractors tanks, and tank-like vehicles that carries the driving power to the wheels or sprockets to produce the vehicle motion as they turn.

FINAL-DRIVE RATIO - The reduction ratio, found in the gearset of a drivetrain, that is furthest removed from the engine. Typically, the differential ratio.

FLOAT - In the carburetor, the metal shell that is suspended by the fuel in the float bowl and controls a needle valve that regulates the fuel level in the bowl.

FLOAT CIRCUIT - In the carburetor, the circuit that controls entry of fuel and fuel level in the float bowl.

FLOORPAN - The largest and most important stamped metal part in a car's body. Usually assembled from several smaller stampings, the floorpan forms the floor and fixes the dimensions for most of the car's external and structural panels. It is also the foundation for many of the car's mechanical parts.

FLUID COUPLING - Any device that transfers power through a fluid between its inputs and outputs. A fluid coupling basically consists of two fans in a sealed, oil-filled housing. The input fan churns the oil, and the churning oil in turn twirls the output fan. Such a coupling allows some speed difference between its input and output shafts. FLYWHEEL - The rotating metal wheel, attached to the crankshaft, that helps level out the power surges from the power strokes and also serves as part of the clutch and engine-cranking system.

FOOT- POUND - A unit of work done in raising 1 pound avoirdupois against the force of gravity to the height of 1 foot.

FORCE - The action that one body may exert upon another to change its motion or shape.

FOUR-STROKE-CYCLE ENGINE - An engine that requires four piston strokes (intake, compression, power, exhaust) to make the complete cycle of events in the engine cylinder.

FOUR VALVES PER CYLINDER - A valvetrain with a total of four valves in the combustion chamber, typically two intakes and two exhausts. Compared to the more common two-valve-per-cylinder engine designs, a four-valve layout offers improved breathing and allows the sparkplug to be located closer to center of the combustion chamber.

FOUR-WHEEL DRIFT - A somewhat imprecise term that describes a cornering situation in which all four tires are operating at large slip angles.

FOUR-WHEEL STEERING - A steering system that actively steers the rear wheels as well as the fronts to improve handling and maneuverability.

FOURTEEN-WHEEL STEERING - A stunning, high-speed maneuver that occurs when a large semi truck experiences four simultaneous blowouts while driving down a steep hill in the rain.

FRAME - An assembly of metal structural parts and channel sections that support the engine and body and that is supported by the vehicle wheels.

FREQUENCY - The number of vibrations, cycles, or changes in direction in a unit of time.

FRICTION - The resistance to motion between two bodies in contact with each other.

FUEL - The substance that is burned to produce heat and create motion of the piston on the power stroke in an engine.

FUEL FILTER - A device placed in the fuel line of the fuel system to remove dirt and other harmful solids.

FUEL GAGE - An indicating device in the fuel system that indicates the amount of fuel in the fuel tank.

FUEL INJECTION - Any system that meters fuel to an engine by measuring its needs and then regulating the fuel flow, by electronic or mechanical means, through a pump and injectors. Throttle-body injection locates the injector(s) centrally in the throttle-body housing, while port injection allocates at least one injector for each cylinder near its intake port.

FUEL LINE - The tube or tubes connecting the fuel tank and the carburetor and through which the fuel passes.

FUEL PASSAGE - Drilled holes in the carburetor body and tubes through which fuel passes from the float bowl to the fuel nozzles.

FUEL PUMP - The mechanism in the fuel system that transfers fuel from the fuel tank to the carburetor.

FUEL TANK - The storage tank for fuel on the vehicle.

FULCRUM - The support, as a wedge-shaped piece or a hinge, about which a lever turns.

FULL TRAILER - An independent and fully contained vehicle without motive power.

FUSE - A circuit-protecting device which makes use of a substance that has a low melting point. The substance melts if an overload occurs, thus protecting other devices in the system.

G

G - The unit of measure for lateral acceleration, or *roadholding*. One g is equivalent to 32.2 feet per second, the rate at which any object accelerates when dropped at sea level. If a car were cornering at 1.0g - a figure that very few production cars are able to approach - the driver's body would be pushing equally hard against the side of the seat as against the bottom of it.

GASKET - A flat strip, usually of cork or metal, or both, placed between two surfaces to provide a tight seal between them.

GASOLINE - A hydrocarbon, obtained from petroleum, is suitable as an internal combustion engine fuel.

GEAR RATIO - The relative speeds at which two gears turn; the proportional rate of rotation.

GEARS - Mechanical devices to transmit power or turning effort, from one shaft to another; more specifically, gears which contain teeth that engage or mesh upon turning.

GEARSET - A group of two or more gears used to transmit power.

GEARSHIFT - A mechanism by which the gears in a transmission system are engaged.

GENERATOR - In the electrical system, the device that changes mechanical energy to electrical energy for lighting lights, charging the battery, etc.

GENERATOR REGULATOR - In the electrical system, the unit which is composed of the current regulator voltage regulator, and circuit breaker relay.

GOVERNOR - A mechanism that controls speed or other variable. Specifically, speed governors used on automotive vehicles to prevent excessive engine speed by controlling actions in the carburetor.

GREENHOUSE - The portion of a car's body that rises above the belt-line of the car.

GROUND - Connection of an electrical unit to the engine or frame to return the current to its source.

GROUND EFFECT - The phenomenon that occurs when the airflow between a moving object and the ground creates downforce.

GUSSET PLATE - A plate at the joint of a frame structure of steel to strengthen the joint.

H

HALF-SHAFT - An articulating, rotating shaft used in independent-suspension systems to transmit power from a differential to a wheel.

HALF TRACK - A vehicle using tracks instead of wheels at the rear.

HANDBRAKE - A brake operated by hand. Also referred to as the parking brake.

HANDLING - A general term covering all the aspects of a car's behavior that are related to its directional control.

HARSHNESS - The aspect of a car's ride roughness that is characterized by small, sharp jolts.

HEADLIGHT - Lights at the front of the vehicle designed to illuminate the road ahead when the vehicle is traveling forward.

HEAT - A form of energy.

HEEL-AND-TOE - A performance-oriented technique of downshifting while braking that requires the driver to use all three pedals of a manual-transmission car simultaneously. To perform a heel-and-toe downshift, the driver brakes with the toe of his right foot and -while continuing to brake - uses the heel or the side of the same foot to blip the throttle and raise engine rpm as he downshifts. The left foot operates the clutch pedal in the normal fashion. The sequence is as follows: brake with the right toe; depress the clutch with the left foot; shift to neutral; while continuing to brake, blip the throttle with the side or the heel of the right foot to raise rpm; shift to a lower gear; let the clutch out; release the brakes. The technique is difficult to master, but after practice it can be performed in less than a second. This process is best for smooth power flow and long transmission life.

HEIM JOINT - An extremely rigid articulating joint, commonly known as a *spherical rod- end,* used in any precision linkage. Heim joints are often used in the suspension links of race cars because they locate wheels very precisely.

HELICAL - In the shape of a helix, which is the shape of a screw thread or coil spring.

HELICAL GEAR - A type of gear in which the teeth are cut at a slanting angle to the gear's circumference. A helical design produces an even, constant tooth loading in a gearset, thereby reducing noise.

HEMI - A term used to describe any engine that has hemispherical combustion chambers in its cylinder head. Although a four-valve design is more efficient, a hemi head provides room for a pair of large valves and offers good breathing characteristics.

HIGH-SPEED CIRCUIT - In the carburetor, the passages through which fuel flows when the throttle valve is fully opened.

HIGH TENSION - Another term for high voltage. In the electrical system, refers to the ignition secondary circuit since this circuit produces high-voltage surges to cause sparking at the spark plugs.

HILL HOLDER - A device in the transmission that automatically prevents the vehicle from rolling backwards down a hill when the vehicle is brought to a stop.

HORN - An electrical signaling device on the vehicle.

HORSEPOWER - The common unit of measurement of .an engine's power. One horsepower equals 550 foot-pounds per second, the power needed to lift 550 pounds one foot off the ground in one second - or one pound 550 feet up in the same time.

HOTCHKISS DRIVE - Type of rear live axle suspension in which the springs serve as torque members.

HOTCHKISS SUSPENSION - A live-axle rear suspension in which leaf springs handle both the axle's springing and its location.

HULL - In a tank, the protective shell that encloses the vehicle components and occupants.

HYDRAMATIC - A type of automatic transmission containing a fluid coupling and automatic controls for shifting from one gear ratio to another.

HYDRAULIC BRAKES - A braking system that uses a fluid to transmit hydraulic pressure from a master cylinder to wheel cylinders, which then cause brakeshoe movement and braking action.

HYDRAULIC LIFTER - A valve lifter that, using simple valving and the engine's oil pressure, can adjust its length slightly - thereby maintaining zero clearance in the valvetrain. Hydraulic lifters reduce valvetrain noise and are maintenance-free.

HYDRAULIC STEERING - A steering system that uses a fluid to produce an assisting hydraulic pressure on the steering linkage, thus reducing the steering effort on the part of the driver.

HYDRAULIC TRAVERSING MECHANISM - A turret traversing system that makes use of hydraulic pressure to furnish the motive power to traverse the turret.

HYDRAULIC VALVE TAPPET - A valve tappet that, by means of hydraulic pressure, maintains zero valve clearance so that valve noise is reduced.

HYDROMETER - A device to determine the specific gravity of a liquid. This indicates the freezing point of the coolant in a cooling system or, as another example, the state of charge of a battery.

HYDROVAC BRAKES - A type of braking system using vacuum to assist in brake operation. The vacuum action reduces the effort required from the driver to operate the vehicle brakes.

I

IDLE - Engine speed when accelerator pedal is fully released; generally assumed to mean when engine is doing no work.

IDLE CIRCUIT - The circuit in the carburetor through which fuel is fed when the engine is idling.

IDLER GEAR - A gear placed between a driving and a driven gear to make them rotate in the same direction. It does not affect the gear ratio.

IDLING ADJUSTMENT - Adjustment made on the carburetor to alter the fuel-air mixture ratio or engine speed on idle.

IGNITION - The action of setting fire to; in the engine, the initiating of the combustion process in the engine cylinders.

IGNITION ADVANCE - Refers to the spark advance produced by the distributor in accordance with engine speed and intake manifold vacuum.

IGNITION COIL - That component of the ignition system that acts as a transformer and steps up battery voltage to many thousand volts; the high voltage then produces a spark at the spark plug gap.

IGNITION DISTRIBUTOR - That component of the ignition system that closes and opens the circuit between the battery and ignition coil, and distributes the resultant high-voltage surges from the coil to the proper spark plugs.

IGNITION SWITCH - The switch in the ignition system that can be operated to open or close the ignition primary circuit.

IGNITION TIMING - Refers to the timing of the spark at the spark plug as related to the piston position in the engine cylinder.

I-HEAD - A type of engine with valves in the cylinder head.

IMPELLER - The rotor of a centrifugal pump which causes the fuel-air in an engine to be thrown into a diffuser chamber to effect thorough mixing and good distribution.

INDEPENDENT SUSPENSION - Any suspension in which the camber of a wheel is not directly affected by the vertical motion of the opposite wheel.

INDICATED HORSEPOWER - A measurement of engine power based on power actually developed in the engine cylinders.

INDUCTION - The action or process of producing voltage by the relative motion of a magnetic field and a conductor.

INJECTOR - The mechanism, including nozzle, which injects fuel into the engine combustion chamber on diesel engines.

IN-LINE ENGINE - An engine in which all engine cylinders are in a single row, or line.

INSERT - A form of screw thread insert to be placed in a tapped hole into which a screw or bolt will be screwed. The insert protects the part into which the hole was tapped, preventing enlargement due to repeated removal and replacement of the bolt.

INSTRUMENTS - The displays on the dashboard that communicate information about the mechanical operation of the car to the driver. Mechanically controlled instruments almost always feature analog displays (usually needles-and-numbers dials). Electronically controlled instruments use analog displays, digital readouts, or even graphics panels.

INSULATION - Substance that stops movement of electricity (electrical insulation) or heat (heat insulation).

INSULATOR - A substance (usually of glass or porcelain) that will not conduct electricity.

INTAKE CHARGE - The mixture of fuel and air that flows into the engine.

INTAKE MANIFOLD - The network of passages that directs air or air-fuel mixture from the throttle body to the intake ports in the cylinder head. The flow typically proceeds from the throttle body into a chamber called the plenum, which in turn feeds individual tubes, called runners, leading to each intake port. Engine breathing is enhanced if the intake manifold is configured to optimize the pressure pulses in the intake system.

INTAKE PORT - The passageway in a cylinder head leading from the intake manifold to the intake valve(s).

INTAKE STROKE - The piston stroke from top dead center to bottom dead center during which the intake valve is open and the cylinder receives a charge of fuel-air mixture.

INTAKE VALVE - The valve in the engine which is opened during the intake stroke to permit the entrance of fuel-air mixture into the cylinder.

INTEGRAL - Whole; entire; lacking nothing of completeness.

INTERCOOLER - A heat exchanger that cools the air (or, in some installations, the intake charge) that has been heated by compression in any type of supercharger. An intercooler resembles a radiator; it houses large passages for the intake flow, and uses either outside air or water directed over it to lower the temperature of the intake flow inside.

INTERFERENCE - In radio, any signal received that overrides or prevents normal reception of the desired signal. In mechanical practice, anything that causes mismating of parts so they cannot be normally assembled.

INTERNAL COMBUSTION ENGINE - An engine in which the fuel is burned inside the engine, as opposed to an external combustion engine where the fuel is burned outside the engine, such as a steam engine.

INTERNAL GEAR - A gear in which the teeth point inward rather than outward as with a standard spur gear.

J

JACKSHAFT - An intermediate driving shaft.

JET - A metered opening in an air or fuel passage to control the flow of fuel or air.

JOUNCE - The motion of a wheel that compresses its suspension.

JOUNCE BUMPER - An elastic cushion used to stiffen the suspension gradually as it approaches the end of its jounce travel.

JOURNAL - That part of a shaft that rotates in a bearing.

K

KEVLAR - A very flexible, strong, light, and abrasion-resistent artificial fiber, manufactured by Du Pont, that can be combined with a plastic resin to produce an efficient composite material for chassis and body components.

KICKDOWN - A downshift in an automatic transmission caused by depressing the throttle.

KINGPIN - The pin by which a stud axle is articulated to an axle-beam or steering head; also the enmeshing pin in a fifth wheel assembly.

KINGPIN INCLINATION - The number of degrees that the kingpin, which supports the front wheel, is tilted from the vertical.

KNOCK - In the engine, a rapping or hammering noise resulting from excessively rapid burning or detonation of the compressed fuelair mixture.

KNOCK SENSOR - A sensor mounted on the engine that is designed to detect the high-frequency vibrations caused by detonation. By employing a knock sensor, a computerized engine-control system allows an engine to operate very near its detonation limit -thereby improving power and efficiency.

KNUCKLE - A joint or parts carrying a hinge pin which permit one part to swing about or move in relation to another.

L

LAMINATED - Made up of thin sheets, leaves, or plates.

LAMINATED LEAF SPRING - Spring made up of leaves of graduated size.

LANDING GEAR - Retractable support under the front end of a semitrailer to hold it up when it is uncoupled from the truck tractor.

LATERAL LINK - A suspension link that is aligned to resist sideways motions in a wheel.

LEADING LINK - A suspension link that is aligned to resist longitudinal motions in a wheel; it is mounted to the chassis behind the wheel.

LEAF SPRING - A long, flat, thin, flexible piece of spring steel or various composite materials that deflects by bending when forces act upon it. Leaf springs are used primarily in suspensions.

LEAN MIXTURE - A fuel-air mixture that has a high proportion of air and a low proportion of fuel.

LEVER - A rigid bar or beam of any shape capable of turning about one point, called the fulcrum; used for transmitting or changing force or motion.

LEVERAGE - The mechanical advantage obtained by use of lever; also an arrangement or combination of levers.

L-HEAD - A type of engine with valves in the cylinder block.

LIFT - A vertical force directed upward, produced by the airflow around a moving object - such as a car body.

LIFT-THROTTLE OVERSTEER - A handling characteristic that causes the rear tires to lose some of their cornering grip when the throttle is released during hard cornering.

LIGHT - In the electric circuit, an electrical device that includes a wire in a gas-filled bulb which glows brightly when current passes through it - often called a lamp.

LIGHTING SWITCH - In the electrical circuit, a switch that turns light on or off.

LIMITED-SLIP DIFFERENTIAL - A differential fitted with a mechanism that limits the speed and torque differences between its two outputs. Limited slip ensures that some torque is always distributed to both wheels, even when one is on very slippery pavement.

LINE - The path through a corner that best accommodates a late braking point, a high cornering speed, and the fastest-possible exit speed out of a corner.

LINK - A suspension member that has a single joint at each end.

LIVE AXLE - A rigid axle incorporating a differential and axle shafts to power the two wheels it is supporting.

LOCKUP - The juncture at which a tire starts to skid during braking. A tire's maximum braking force is developed when it is on the verge of lockup, so a car's shortest stopping distances are produced when its front and rear tires approach lockup simultaneously. This is very hard to achieve under varying conditions of load and traction, so one end typically locks up before the other. Front-wheel lockup is inherently more stable than rear-wheel lockup.

LOCKUP DIFFERENTIAL - A differential whose two outputs can be locked together, eliminating any differential action but maximizing traction under slippery conditions.

LOCKUP TORQUE CONVERTER- A torque converter fitted with a lock-up clutch that can be engaged to eliminate the slip between the torque converter input and output, thereby improving fuel efficiency and performance.

LOOSE - A slang term for oversteer.

LUBRICATION - The process of supplying a coating of oil between moving surfaces to prevent actual contact between them. The oil film permits relative movement with little frictional resistance.

LUNETTE - An eye that hooks into a pintle assembly to tow vehicles.

M

MAGNET - Any body that has the ability to attract iron.

MAGNETIC FIELD - The space around a magnet which the magnetic lines of force permeate.

MAGNETIC FLUX - The total amount of magnetic induction across or through a given surface.

MAGNETIC POLE - Focus of magnetic lines of force entering or emanating from magnet.

MAGNETISM - The property exhibited by certain substances and produced by electron (or electric current) motion which results in the attraction of iron.

MAGNETO - A device that generates voltage surges, transforms them to high-voltage surges, and distributes them to the engine cylinder spark plugs.

MAIN BEARING - In the engine, the bearings that support the crankshaft.

MANIFOLD - See Intake Manifold or Exhaust Manifold.

MASTER CYLINDER - In the hydraulic braking system, the liquid-filled cylinder in which hydraulic pressure is developed by depression of the brake pedal.

MASTER ROD - In a radial engine, the rod to which all other connecting rods are attached, or articulated.

MATTER - Anything which has weight and occupies space.

MECHANICAL EFFICIENCY - In an engine, the ratio between brake horsepower and indicated horsepower.

MECHANISM - A system of parts or appliances which acts as a working agency to achieve a desired result.

MEMBER - Any essential part of a machine or structure.

MESHING - The mating or engaging of the teeth of two gears.

METERING ROD - A small rod, having a varied diameter, operated within a jet to vary the flow of fuel through the jet.

MID-ENGINE - A chassis layout that positions the engine behind the passenger compartment but ahead of the rear axle.

MOLECULE - The smallest particle into which a chemical compound can be divided.

MONOCOQUE - A type of body structure that derives its strength and rigidity from the use of thin, carefully shaped and joined panels, rather than from a framework of thick members. Also called *unit* or *unitized construction.*

MOTOR - A device for converting electrical energy into mechanical energy.

MOTORCYCLE - Two-wheeled vehicle similar to a bicycle but motor-driven.

MOTOR TRICYCLE - Similar to a motorcycle except the rear wheel has been replaced by two wheels.

MUFFLER - In the exhaust system, a device through which the exhaust gases must pass; in the muffler, the exhaust sounds are greatly reduced.

MULTILEAF SPRING - A leaf spring with several leaves bundled together by steel bands.

MULTILINK SUSPENSION - A rear suspension consisting of at least four links, or *arms*, and no struts. Because multilink suspensions assign specific wheel-locating duties to each element, they provide great flexibility for optimizing both ride and handling.

MUTUAL INDUCTION - Induction associated with more than one circuit, as two coils, one of which induces current in the other as the current in the first changes.

N

NEEDLE VALVE - Type of valve with rod-shaped, needle-pointed valve body which works into a valve seat so shaped that the needle point fits into it and closes the passage; the needle valve in the carburetor float circuit is an example.

NEGATIVE - A term designating the point of lower potential when the potential difference between two points is considered.

NEGATIVE TERMINAL - The terminal from which electrons depart when a circuit is completed from this terminal to the positive terminal of generator or battery.

NEUTRAL STEER - A cornering condition in which the front and rear slip angles are roughly the same. Although seemingly an ideal state of balance, perfect neutral steer is not as stable as slight understeer.

NORTH POLE - The pole of a magnet from which the lines of force are assumed to emanate.

NO-SPIN DIFFERENTIAL - A special type of differential which prevents the spinning of one of the driving wheels even if it is resting on smooth ice.

NOZZLE - An orifice or opening in a carburetor through which fuel feeds into the passing air stream on its way to the intake manifold.

O

OCTANE RATING - A measure of the antiknock value of engine fuel.

ODOMETER - The part of the speedometer that measures, accumulatively, the number of vehicle miles traveled.

OHM - A measure of electrical resistance. A conductor of one ohm resistance will allow a flow of one ampere of current when one volt is imposed on it.

OHMMETER - A device for measuring ohms resistance of a circuit or electrical machine.

OIL - A liquid lubricant derived from petroleum and used in machinery to provide lubrication between moving parts. Also, fuel used in diesel engines.

OIL CONTROL RINGS - The lower rings on the piston which are designed to prevent excessive amounts of oil from working up into the combust ion chamber.

OIL COOLER - A special cooling radiator, through which hot oil passes. Air also passes through separate passages in the radiator, providing cooling of the oil.

OIL GAGE - Indicating device that indicates the pressure of the oil in the lubrication system. Also a bayonet-type rod to measure oil in the crankcase.

OIL PAN - The lower part of the crankcase in which a reservoir of oil is maintained.

OIL PUMP - The pump that transfers oil from the oil pan to the various moving parts in the engine that require lubrication.

OIL STRAINER - A strainer placed at the inlet end of the oil pump to strain out dirt and other particles, preventing these from getting into moving engine parts.

ON-CENTER FEEL - The responsiveness and feel of the steering when the wheel is approximately centered. In a car with good on-center feel, the steering wheel tends to return to center when slightly deflected, assisting straight-line stability.

OPPOSITE LOCK - A technique in which the steering wheel is turned in the direction away from where the car is turning. Opposite lock is used to control a car when it is oversteering and its tail is swinging wide.

OVERDRIVE - Any gearset in which the output shaft turns faster than the input shaft. Overdrive gears are used in most modern transmissions because they reduce engine rpm and improve fuel economy. Occasionally, a separate gearbox with an overdrive gearset is coupled to a conventional transmission.

OVERFLOW TANK - Special tank in cooling system (a surge tank) for hot or dry country to permit expansion and contraction of engine coolant without loss.

OVERHEAD CAM - The type of valvetrain arrangement in which the engine's camshaft(s) is in its cylinder head(s). When the camshaft(s) is placed close to the valves, the valvetrain components can be stiffer and lighter, allowing the valves to open and close more rapidly and the engine to run at higher rpm. In a single-overhead-cam (SOHC) layout, one camshaft actuates all of the valves in a cylinder head. In a double-overhead-camshaft (DOHC) layout, one camshaft actuates the intake valves, and one camshaft operates the exhaust valves.

OVERHEAD VALVE - Valve mounted in head above combustion chamber. Valve in I-head engine.

OVERLOAD BREAKER - In an electrical circuit, a device that breaks or opens a circuit if it is overloaded by a short, ground, use of too much equipment, etc.

OVERRUNNING CLUTCH - A type of drive mechanism used in a starter which transmits cranking effort but overruns freely when engine tries to drive starter. Also, a special clutch used in several mechanism that permits a rotating member to turn freely under some conditions but not under other conditions.

OVERSQUARE - A description of an engine whose bore is larger than its stroke.

OVERSTEER - A handling condition in which the slip angles of the rear tires are greater than the slip angles of the front tires. An oversteering car is sometimes said to be *loose* because its tail tends to swing wide.

P

PANHARD ROD - A long lateral link that provides lateral location of a rigid axle. It usually sits roughly parallel to the axle, with one end attached to the body and the other attached to the axle.

PARABOLIC REFLECTOR - A reflector that sends all reflected light originating at the focal point outward in parallel rays.

PARALLEL CIRCUIT - The electrical circuit formed when two or more electrical devices have like terminals connected together (positive to positive and negative to negative) so that each may operate independently of the other.

PARKING BRAKE - See Handbrake.

PENT-ROOF - A combustion chamber whose upper surface resembles a shallow peaked roof. Usually used with four valves per cylinder.

PERIOD - The time required for the completion of one cycle.

PERMANENT MAGNET - Piece of steel or alloy in which molecules are so alined that the piece continues to exhibit magnetism without application of external influence.

PHASE - That portion of a whole period which has elapsed since the activity in question passed through zero position in a positive direction.

PILOT - A short plug at the end of a shaft to align it with another shaft or rotating part.

PINION - The smaller of two mating or meshing gears.

PINTLE ASSEMBLY - A swivel-type assembly used to engage with a lunette for towing trailers.

PISTON - In an engine, the cylindrical part that moves up and down in the cylinder.

PISTON DISPLACEMENT - The volume displaced by the piston as it moves from the bottom to the top of the cylinder in one complete stroke.

PISTON PIN - The cylindrical or tubular metal pin that attaches the piston to the connecting rod (also called wrist pin).

PISTON RING - One of the rings fitted into grooves in the piston. There are two types, compression rings and oil-control rings.

PISTON ROD - See Connecting Rod.

PITCH - The rotation of a car about a horizontal axis, which causes its nose or tail to bob up and down. Dive and squat are pitching motions.

PITMAN ARM - The arm that is a part of the steering gear; it is connected by linkage to the wheel steering knuckle.

PIVOT INCLINATION - See Kingpin Inclination.

PLANETARY GEARS - A gearset in which all of the gears are in one plane, grouped around each other like the planets around the sun. The central gear is called the *sun gear.* In mesh with it is a circular grouping of gears, called *planet gears* mounted on a rotating carrier. The planet gears also engage teeth on the inner periphery of the *ring gear.* By holding any one of the three gear elements motionless, different ratios can be produced between the other two. Planetary gearsets are common in automatic transmissions.

PLENUM CHAMBER - A chamber, located between the throttle body and the runners of an intake manifold, used to distribute the intake charge evenly and to enhance engine breathing.

POLAR MOMENT OF INERTIA - The resistance of an object to rotational acceleration. When the mass of an object is distributed far from its axis of rotation, the object is said to have a high polar moment of inertia. When the mass distribution is close to the axis of rotation, it has a low polar moment of inertia. A mid-engined car has most of its mass within its wheelbase, contributing to a low polar moment of inertia, which, in turn, improves cornering turn-in.

POPPET - A spring-loaded ball engaging a notch. A ball latch.

PORT FUEL INJECTION - A type of fuel injection with at least one injector mounted in the intake port(s) of each cylinder. Usually the injector is mounted on the air intake manifold close to the port. Port fuel injection improves fuel distribution and allows greater flexibility in intake-manifold design, which can contribute to improved engine breathing.

POSITIVE - A term designating the point of higher potential when the potential difference between two points is considered.

POTENTIAL - A characteristic of a point in an electric field or circuit indicated by the work necessary to bring a unit positive charge from infinity; the degree of electrification as compared to some standard (the earth, for example).

POTENTIAL DIFFERENCE - The arithmetical difference between two electrical potentials; same as electromotive force, electrical pressure, or voltage.

POUND-FEET - The unit of measurement for torque. One pound-foot is equal to the twisting force produced when a one-pound force is applied to the end of a one-foot-long lever.

POWER - The rate at which work is performed. Power is proportional to torque and rpm and is measured in horsepower.

POWER BAND - The subjectively defined rpm range over which an engine delivers a substantial fraction of its peak power. The power band usually extends from slightly below the engine's torque peak to slightly above its power peak.

POWER DIVIDER - A mechanism placed between dual rear axles to apportion driving effort between the two pairs of wheels to provide the maximum tractive effort.

POWER PLANT - The engine or power-producing mechanism on the vehicle.

POWER STEERING - Vehicle steering by use of hydraulic pressure to multiply the driver's steering effort so as to improve ease of steering.

POWER STROKE - The piston stroke from top dead center to bottom dead center during which the fuel-air mixture burns and forces the piston down so the engine produces power.

POWER-TAKE-OFF - An attachment for connecting the engine to power driven auxiliary machinery when its use is required.

POWERTRAIN - An engine and transmission combination.

PREIGNITION - Premature ignition of the fuel-air mixture being compressed in the cylinder on the compression stroke.

PRIMER - An auxiliary fuel pump operated by hand to feed additional fuel into the engine to produce a richer mixture for starting.

PRISMATIC LENS - A lens with parallel grooves or flutes which deflect and distribute light rays.

PROFILE - The aspect ratio of a tire.

PROGRESSIVE-RATE SPRING - A spring with an increasing spring constant.For example, if the first inch of spring motion requires 100 pounds of force, the second inch would require more than an additional 100 pounds, and the third inch would require still more. Progressive-rate springs become stiffer as they are compressed, unlike single-rate springs, which have a fixed spring rate.

PROPELLER SHAFT - The driving shaft in the powertrain that carries engine power from the transmission to the differential; also, the shaft that turns the propeller in amphibian vehicles.

PROTON - Basic particle of matter having a positive electrical charge, normally associated with the nucleus of the atom.

PSI - Pounds per square inch, the common unit -of measurement for pressure. Normal atmospheric pressure at sea level is 14.7 psi.

PUMP - A device that transfers gas or liquid from one place to another.

PUSH - A slang term for understeer.

PUSHROD - A general term for any rod that transfers force in compression. In a valvetrain, pushrods are used to transfer reciprocating motion from the cam followers to a more distant part of a valvetrain, typically the rocker arms.

R

RPM - Revolutions per minute, a measure of rotational speed.

RACK-AND-PINION - A steering mechanism that consists of a gear in mesh with a toothed bar, called a *rack*. The ends of the rack are linked to the steered wheels with tie rods. When the gear is rotated by the steering shaft, it moves the rack from side to side -turning the wheels.

RADIAL - Pertaining to the radius of a circle.

RADIAL ENGINE - An engine with each cylinder located on the radius of a circle and with all cylinders disposed around a common crankshaft.

RADIATOR - A device in the cooling system that removes heat from the coolant passing through it, permitting coolant to remove heat from the engine.

RADIUS - Distance from the center of a circle or from center of rotation.

REBOUND - The motion of a wheel that extends the suspension. The opposite of jounce.

RECIROULATING-BALL - A steering mechanism in which the steering shaft turns a worm gear that, in turn, causes a toothed metal block to move back and forth. Ball bearings in a recirculating track reduce friction between the worm gear and the block. As the block moves, its teeth rotate a gear connected to a steering arm, which then moves the steering linkage.

RECTIFIER - An electrical device that changes alternating current to direct current.

REDLINE - The maximum recommended revolutions per minute for an engine. In cars equipped with a tachometer - an instrument that measures engine rpm - the redline is usually indicated by, surprisingly enough, a red line. Some tachometers mark the redline with a colored sector. Others have two 1ines: the lower one marking the maximum allowable sustained engine rpm, the higher line indicating the absolute maximum rpm.

RELAY - In the electrical system, a device that opens or closes a second circuit in response to voltage or amperage changes in a controlling circuit.

RESIDUAL MAGNETISM - The magnetism retained by a material after all magnetizing forces have been removed.

RESISTANCE - The opposition offered by a substance or body to the passage through it of an electric current.

RESISTOR - In an electrical system, a device made of resistance wire, carbon, or other resisting material, which has a definite value of resistance and serves a definite purpose in the system by virtue of that resistance.

RHEOSTAT - A resistor for regulating the current by means of variable resistance.

RICH MIXTURE - Fuel-air mixture with a high proportion of fuel.

RIDE HEIGHT - A measurement between the ground and some fixed reference point on a car's body (the reference point varies according to the whims of the particular automaker). This dimension can be used to measure the amount of suspension deflection or the height of the body from the ground.

RIDE STEER - A generally undesirable condition in which a wheel steers slightly as its suspension compresses or extends. Also called *bump steer*.

RIGID AXLE - A simple non-independent suspension, consisting of a rigid transverse member with wheel hubs solidly bolted to it. The axle can be attached to the body by leaf springs, or by a combination of suspension arms and links.

RIM - That part of a vehicle wheel on which the tire is mounted.

RING-AND-PINION GEAR - Any gearset consisting of a small gear (the pinion gear) which turns a large-diameter annular gear (the ring gear).

RING GEAR - A gear in the form of a ring such as the ring gear on a flywheel or differential.

ROADHOLDING - The ability of a car to grip the pavement. Technically described as *lateral acceleration*, because cornering is actually a continuous deviation from a straight path. Measured in gs.

ROAD-LOAD HORSEPOWER - The amount of power at the driving wheels
needed to move a car down the road at a steady speed. This power varies according to the car's speed, aerodynamic drag, and mechanical friction, as well as the tires' rolling resistance. Road-load horsepower is distinct from engine power because the output of the engine is sapped by various mechanical losses between the engine's output at its flywheel and the driving wheels.

ROCK POSITION - The piston and connecting rod position (top or bottom dead center) at which the crank can rock or rotate a few degrees without appreciable movement of the piston.

ROD - See Connecting Rod.

ROD CAP - The lower detachable part of the connecting rod which can be taken off by removing bolts or nuts so the rod can be detached from the crankshaft.

ROLL - The rotation of a car's body about a longitudinal axis. Also less accurately called *sway* or *lean*, it occurs in corners because the car's center of gravity is almost always higher than the axis about which it rotates.

ROLLER BEARING - A type of bearing with rollers positioned between two races.

ROTOR - A part that revolves in a stationary part; especially the rotating member of an electrical mechanism.

RUBBER-ISOLATED CROSSMEMBER - A laterally aligned structural member that is attached to the body or the frame via vibration-absorbing rubber isolators. By bolting suspension or driveline components to such crossmembers, automotive engineers can reduce the transmission of noise and/or ride harshness to the body.

S

SAE - Society of Automotive Engineers - the professional association of transportation-industry engineers. The SAE sets most auto-industry standards for the testing, measuring, and designing of automobiles and their components.

SAE HORSEPOWER - A measurement based upon number of cylinders and cylinder diameter.

SCOOTER - A small version of a motorcycle.

SCRUB RADIUS - The distance from the point where the steering axis intersects the ground to the longitudinal line that runs through the center of the tire's contact patch. Also called *steering offset.*

SEALED-BEAM - A special type of headlight in which the reflector and lens are sealed together to enclose and protect the filaments.

SEDAN - As used by CAR AND DRIVER, the term *sedan* refers to a fixed-roof car with at least four doors or any fixed-roof two-door car with at least 33 cubic feet of rear interior volume, according to measurements based on SAE Standard J1100.

SELF-INDUCTION - A property of a circuit which causes it to magnetically affect voltage and current in the circuit.

SEMI-ELLIPTIC LEAF SPRING - A slightly curved leaf spring that is attached to a car's body at its ends and to a suspension component near its middle. One of the two body attachments is a shackle, which allows for changes in the spring's length as it flexes up and down.

SEMITRAILER - A type of trailer supported at the rear by attached wheels and at the front by the truck-tractor; the truck-tractor can be coupled and uncoupled by means of fifth wheel.

SEMI-TRAILING-ARM SUSPENSION - An independent rear-suspension system in which each wheel hub is located only by a large, roughly triangular arm that pivots at two points. Viewed from the top, the line formed by the two pivots is somewhere between parallel and perpendicular to the car's longitudinal axis.

SEPARATOR - In the storage battery, the wood, rubber, or glass mat strip used as insulator to hold the battery plates apart.

SERIES CIRCUIT - The electrical circuit formed when two or more electrical devices have unlike terminals connected together (positive to negative) so that the same current must flow through all.

SERIES (TIRE) - The numerical representation of a tire's aspect ratio. A 50-series tire has an aspect ratio of 0.50.

SHACKLE - A swinging support that permits a leaf spring to vary in length as it is deflected.

SHIFT GATE - The mechanism in a transmission linkage that controls the motion of the gearshift lever. The shift gate is usually an internal mechanism; however, in some transmissions - including Ferrari five-speeds and Mercedes-Benz automatics - the shift gate is an exposed guide around the shift lever.

SHIM - A strip of copper or similar material, used under a bearing cap for example, to adjust bearing clearance.

SHIMMY - Abnormal sidewise vibration, particularly of the front wheels.

SHOCK ABSORBER - A device that converts motion into heat, usually by forcing oil through small internal passages in a tubular housing. Used primarily to dampen suspension oscillations, shock absorbers respond to motion; their effects, therefore, are most obvious in transient maneuvers. Shock absorbers have no effect during steady-state conditions.

SHORT CIRCUIT - In electrical circuits, an abnormal connection that permits current to take a short path or circuit, thus by-passing important parts of the normal circuit.

SHROUD - Forward subassembly of a body or cab containing dash, cowl, and instrument panel. Also, a hood placed around a fan to improve fan action.

SHUNT - Parallel connections, in a portion of an electrical circuit.

SIDE CAR - A car attached to a motorcycle for carrying a passenger or cargo.

SINGLE-RATE SPRING - A spring with a constant spring rate. For example, if a 100-pound force deflects the spring by one inch, an additional 100 pounds will deflect it one more inch, and so on until the spring either bottoms or fails.

SKIDPAD - A large area of smooth, flat pavement used for various handling tests. Roadholding is measured by defining a large-diameter circle (CAR AND DRIVER uses 300 feet) on the skidpad and measuring the fastest speed at which the car can negotiate the circle without sliding off.

SLIP ANGLE - The angular difference between the direction in which a tire is rolling and the plane of its wheel. Slip angle is caused by deflections in the tire's sidewall and tread during cornering. A linear relationship between slip angles and cornering forces indicates an easily controllable tire.

SLIP JOINT - In the power train, a variable-length connection that permits the propeller shaft to change effective length.

SLUSHBOX - Slang for an automatic transmission.

SOHC - Single overhead camshaft - an SOHC engine uses one camshaft in each cylinder head to operate both the exhaust valves and the intake valves.

SOLENOID - A coil of wire that exhibits magnetic properties when electric current passes through it.

SOUTH POLE - The pole of the magnet into which it is assumed the magnetic lines of force pass.

SPACE FRAME - A particular kind of tube frame that consists exclusively of relatively short, small-diameter tubes. The tubes are welded together in a configuration that loads them primarily in tension and compression.

SPARK PLUG - The assembly that includes a pair of electrodes which has the purpose of providing a spark gap in the engine cylinder.

SPECIFIC GRAVITY - The ratio of the weight of a substance to weight of an equal volume of chemically pure water at 39.2° F.

SPEED - Rate of motion.

SPEEDOMETER - An indicating device, usually connected to the transmission , that indicates the speed of motion of the vehicle.

SPIDER - In planetary gear sets, the frame, or part, on which the planetary gears are mounted.

SPIRAL BEVEL GEAR - A bevel gear having curved teeth.

SPLINE - Slot or groove cut in a shaft or bore; a splined shaft onto which a hub, wheel, etc., with matching splines in its bore is assembled so the two must engage and turn together.

SPOILER - An aerodynamic device that changes the direction of airflow in order to reduce lift or aerodynamic drag and/or improve engine cooling.

SPRAG UNIT - A form of overrunning clutch; power can be transmitted through it in one direction but not in the other.

SPRINGS - Flexible or elastic members that support the weight of a vehicle.

SPUR GEAR - A gear with radial teeth parallel to the axis.

SQUAT - The opposite of dive, squat is the dipping of a car's rear end that occurs during hard acceleration. Squat is caused by a load transfer from the front to the rear suspension.

STARTER - In the electrical system, the motor that cranks the engine to get it started.

STARTING SYSTEM - The electrical system, including the starter battery, cables, switch and controls, that has the job of starting the engine.

STATIC ELECTRICITY - Accumulated electrical charges, usually considered to be those produced by friction.

STEERING AXIS - The line that intersects the upper and lower steering pivots on a steered wheel. On a car with a strut suspension, the steering axis is defined by the line through the strut mount on top and the ball joint on the bottom.

STEERING FEEL - The general relationship between forces at the steering wheel and handling. Ideally, the steering effort should increase smoothly as the wheel is rotated away from center. In addition, the steering effort should build as the cornering forces at the steered wheels increase. Finally, the friction built into the steering mechanism should be small in comparison with the handling-related steering forces.

STEERING GAIN - The relationship between yaw and the steering wheel's position and effort. All three should be proportional and should build up smoothly.

STEERING GEAR - That part of the steering system, located at the lower end of the steering shaft, which carries the rotary motion of the steering wheel to the vehicle wheels for steering.

STEERING GEOMETRY - Difference in angles between the two front wheels and the car frame during turns; the inside wheel turns more sharply than the other wheel turns since it must travel on an arc of a smaller radius. Also called *toe-out during turns*.

STEERING LINKAGE - Linkage between steering gear and vehicle wheels.

STEERING RESPONSE - A subjective term that combines steering feel and steering gain.

STEERING SYSTEM - The system of gears and linkage in the vehicle that permits the driver to turn the wheels for changing the direction of vehicle movement.

STORAGE BATTERY - A lead-acid electrochemical device that changes chemical energy into electric energy. The action is reversible; electric energy supplied to the battery stores chemical energy.

STRAIGHT-LINE TRACKING - The ability of a car to resist road irregularities and run in a straight line without steering corrections.

STROKE - The movement, or the distance of the movement, in either direction, of the piston travel in an engine.

STRUT - A suspension element in which a reinforced shock absorber is used as one of the wheel's locating members, typically by solidly bolting the wheel hub to the bottom end of the strut.

SULFATION - A crystalline formation of lead sulfate on storage battery plates.

SUMP - The space in the engine block under the crankshaft into which the oil drains from its various applications.

SUN GEAR - In a planetary gear system, the central gear.

SUPERCHARGER - A device used in connection with engine fuel-air systems to supply more air at greater pressure to the engine, thereby increasing volumetric efficiency. The term is frequently applied only to mechanically driven compressors, but it actually encompasses all varieties of compressors - including turbochargers.

SUPPRESSION - In the electrical system, the elimination of stray electromagnetic waves due to action of ignition, generator, etc., so that they cannot be detected by radio.

SUSPENSION - The system of springs, etc. supporting the upper part of a vehicle on its axles or wheels.

SWAYBAR - A connecting bar placed between wheel supports, parallel to the axles, which prevents excessive vehicle roll or sway on turns.

SWITCH - In the electrical system, a device used to open or complete an electrical circuit.

SYNCHROMESH - A name designating a certain type of transmission which has the virtue of permitting gear-ratio shifts without gear clashing.

SYNCHRONIZE - To make two or more events or operations occur at the same time.

T

TACHOMETER - A device for measuring revolutions per minute.

TACTICAL VEHICLE - Vehicle designated primarily to meet field requirements in direct connection with combat, tactical operations, and the training of troops for combat.

TANDEM AXLES - Two axles one placed directly in front of the other.

TAPER - To make gradually smaller toward one end; a gradual reduction in size in a given direction.

TARGA - A removable-roof body style popularized by Porsche that is similar to a convertible except that it incorporates a fixed, roll-bar-like structure running from side to side behind the front seats.

TDC - Top dead center; the position of the piston when it reaches the upper limit of travel in the cylinder.

TEMPERATURE GAGE - An indicating device in the cooling system that indicates the temperature of the coolant and gives warning if excessive engine temperatures develop.

TENSION - A stress caused by a pulling force.

THERMAL EFFICIENCY - Ratio between the power output and the energy in the fuel burned to produce the output.

THERMOSTAT - A device for automatic regulation of temperature.

THIRD-BRUSH GENERATOR - An auxiliary brush which regulates the current output of the generator by increasing or decreasing the field coil current.

THREE-QUARTER TRAILER - Trailers, usually 2-wheeled; used for light loads. The load is practically balanced on the trailer suspension, although some of the load is thrust on the truck-tractor connection.

THROTTLE - A mechanism in the fuel system that permits the driver to vary the amount of fuel-air mixture entering the engine and thus control the engine speed.

THROTTLE-BODY - A housing containing a valve to regulate the airflow through the intake manifold. The throttle-body is usually located between the air cleaner and the intake plenum.

THROTTLE-BODY FUEL INJECTION - A form of fuel injection in which the injectors are located at the engine's throttle-body, thereby feeding fuel to more than one cylinder. Such an arrangement saves money by using fewer injectors; but because it routes both fuel and air through the intake manifold, it eliminates some of the tuning possibilities offered by port fuel injection.

THROTTLE VALVE PLATE - The disk in the lower part of the carburetor air horn that can be tilted to pass more or less fuel-air mixture to the engine.

THRUST - A force tending to push a body out of alignment. A force exerted endwise through a member upon another member.

TIE ROD - A rod connection in the steering system between wheels.

TIMING - Refers to ignition or valve timing and pertains to the relation between the actions of the ignition or valve mechanism and piston position in the cylinder.

TIRE - The rubber and fabric part that is assembled on the wheel rim and filled with compressed air (pneumatic type).

TOE-CONTROL LINK - A lateral link in a multilink suspension designed to control a wheel's direction as the suspension moves up and down.

TOE-IN - The intentional nonparallel orientation of opposite wheels. Toe-in is measured by subtracting the distance between the front edges of a pair of tires from the distance between the rear edges of the same pair of tires. The toe-in dimension is positive when the fronts of the tires are turned toward the center of the car.

TOE STEER - The changes in the direction of a wheel that occur without driver steering input. Toe steer can be caused by ride steer or by deflections in suspension components caused by the stresses of cornering, accelerating, and/or braking on smooth and bumpy roads.

TORQMATIC TRANSMISSION - A special type of transmission which includes a torque converter; it is designed for heavy-vehicle application.

TORQUE - A twisting or turning effort. Torque is the product, of force times the distance, from the center of rotation at which it is exerted. Measured in pound-feet.

TORQUE CONVERTER - A particular kind of fluid coupling with a third element added to the usual input and output turbines. Called the *stator*, this additional element redirects the churning fluid against the output turbine, increasing torque. This torque increase, however, is achieved at the expense of rpm and efficiency.

TORQUE ROD - Arm or rod used to insure accurate alignment of an axle with the frame and to relieve springs of driving and braking stresses.

TORQUE STEER - A tendency for a car to turn in a particular direction when power is applied. Torque steer is common in front-drive cars because reaction forces created in the half-shafts can generate uneven steering forces in the front tires.

TORQUE-TUBE DRIVE - The type of rear-end arrangement which includes a hollow tube that encloses the propeller shaft and also takes Up stresses produced by braking and driving.

TORQUE WRENCH - A special wrench with a dial that indicates the amount of torque in pound-feet being applied to a bolt or nut.

TORSION BAR - A spring consisting of a long solid or tubular rod with one end fixed to the chassis and the other twisted by a lever connected to the suspension.

TORSIONAL VIBRATION - Vibration in a rotary direction; a portion of a rotating shaft that repeatedly moves ahead, or lags behind, the remainder of the shaft is exhibiting torsional vibration.

TORUS - Rotating member of fluid coupling.

TRACK - The endless tread on which a tank rides.

TRACKLAYING VEHICLE - A vehicle that uses tracks instead of wheels for mobility.

TRACTION - The force exerted in drawing a body along a plane as when a truck-trailer pulls a semitrailer.

TRACTION CONTROL - An electronic control system that prevents wheelspin by detecting when a driven wheel is about to break traction, and then reducing engine power and/or applying the appropriate brakes to prevent it.

TRACTIVE EFFORT - The pushing effort the driving wheels can make against the ground, which is the same as the forward thrust or push of the axles against the vehicle.

TRACTOR - A motor vehicle (wheeled or tracked) especially designed to tow trailers.

TRAIL-BRAKING - A driving technique in which the driver begins to brake before entering a turn and then continues to brake as he eases into the corner. As cornering forces build, the driver gradually feathers off the brakes - trading braking power for cornering grip. By increasing the vertical loading - and thus the traction - at the front tires, trail-braking can improve a car's turn-in.

TRAILER - A vehicle without motive power towed by a motor vehicle, designed primarily for cargo carrying.

TRAILING ARM - A suspension element consisting of a longitudinal member that pivots from the body at its forward end and has a wheel hub rigidly attached to its trailing end. A sufficiently rigid trailing arm can provide all of a wheel's location. In that case, it is similar to a semi-trailing arm, except that its pivot axis is exactly perpendicular to the car's longitudinal center line.

TRAILING LINK - A suspension link that is aligned to resist longitudinal motions in a wheel; it is mounted to the chassis ahead of the wheel.

TRANSAXLE - A transmission and a differential combined in one integrated assembly.

TRANSFER - The auxiliary assembly for applying power to both forward and rear propeller shafts, and to front wheels as well as rear wheels.

TRANSMISSION - The device in the power train that provides different gear ratios between the engine and driving wheels, as well as reverse.

TRANSMISSION BRAKE - A brake placed at the rear of the transmission, usually used for parking.

TREAD - The design on the road-contacting surface of a tire which provides improved frictional contact.

TREAD SQUIRM - The flexibility in the tire tread between the surface of the tread and the tire carcass. Snow tires, with their small, deep, unsupported tread blocks, have a large amount of tread squirm. Slick racing tires, which have no tread pattern, have very little squirm.

TRUCK-TRACTOR - A motor vehicle especially designed to tow semitrailers.

TRUNNION - Either of two opposite pivots or cylindrical projections from the sides of a part assembly, supported by bearings, to provide a means of swiveling or turning the part or assembly.

TRUNNION AXLE - A supporting axle which carries a load with other axles attached to it. Its use as a part of a bogie permits independent wheel action in a vertical plane and within designed limits.

TUBE FRAME - A car frame made up of rigid tubing welded together. Tube frames are easier to manufacture in small quantities than unitized frames.

TUMBLEHOME - The term that describes the convex curvature on the side of a car body.

TUNED INTAKE AND EXHAUST SYSTEMS - Intake and exhaust systems that, by harnessing the pressure pulses and resonances inside the various passages and chambers of the intake and exhaust manifolds, increase the flow of intake charge into and out of the combustion chambers.

TURBINE - A mechanism containing a rotor with curved blades; the rotor is driven by the impact of a liquid or gas against the curved blades.

TURBOCHARGER - A supercharger powered by an exhaust-driven turbine. Turbochargers always use centrifugal-flow compressors, which operate efficiently at the high rotational speeds produced by the exhaust turbine.

TURBO LAG - Within a turbocharger's operating range, lag is the delay between the instant a car's accelerator is depressed and the time the turbocharged engine develops a large fraction of the power available at that point in the engine's power curve.

TURN-IN - The moment of transition between driving straight ahead and cornering.

TURRET TRAVERSING MECHANISM - A mechanism for rotating a tank turret on a horizontal plane.

TWO-STROKE-CYCLE ENGINE - An internal combustion engine requiring but two piston strokes to complete the cycle of events that produce power.

U

UNDERSTEER - A handling condition in which the slip angle of the front tires is greater than the slip angle of the rears. An understeering car is sometimes said to push, because it resists turning and tends to go straight.

UNITIZED CONSTRUCTION - A type of body construction that doesn'trequire a separate frame to provide structural strength or support for the car's mechanical components. A unitized body can employ monocoque construction, or it can utilize strong structural elements as an integral part of its construction.

UNIVERSAL JOINT - A joint that transmits rotary motion between two shafts that aren't in a straight line. Depending on its design, a universal joint can accommodate a large angular variation between its inputs and outputs. The simplest kind of universal joint, called a *Hooke joint,* causes the output shaft to speed up and slow down twice for every revolution of the input shaft. This speed fluctuation increases with the angular difference between the shafts.

UNSPRUNG WEIGHT - Weight of a vehicle that is not supported by springs.

V

VACUUM - A space entirely devoid of matter.

VACUUM ADVANCE - The mechanism on an ignition distributor that advances the spark in accordance with vacuum in the intake manifold.

VACUUM BRAKES - Vehicle brakes that are actuated by vacuum under the control of the driver.

VACUUM PUMP - A pump, used in a vacuum brake system (for example), that produces a vacuum in a designated chamber.

VACUUM SWITCH - In the starting system, an electric switch that is actuated by vacuum to open the starting system control circuit as the engine starts, producing a vacuum in the intake manifold.

VALVE - A mechanism that can be opened or closed to allow or stop the flow of a liquid, gas, or vapor from one to another place.

VALVE FLOAT - A high-rpm engine condition in which the valve lifters lose contact with the cam lobes because the valve springs are not strong enough to overcome the momentum of the various valvetrain components. The onset of valve float prevents higher-rpm operation. Extended periods of valve float will damage the valvetrain.

VALVE LIFTER - Also called a *valve follower* - the cylindrically shaped component that presses against the lobe of a camshaft and moves up and down as the cam lobe rotates. Most valve lifters have an oil-lubricated hardened face that slides on the cam lobe. So-called *roller lift-*

ers , however, have a small roller in contact with the cam lobe - thereby reducing the friction between the cam lobe and the lifter.

VALVE SEAT - The surface, normally curved, against which the valve operating face comes to rest, to provide a seal against leakage of liquid, gas, or vapor.

VALVE SEAT INSERT - Metal ring inserted into valve seat; made of special metal that can withstand operating temperature satisfactorily .

VALVE SPRING - The compression-type spring that closes the valve when the valve-operating cam assumes a closed-valve position.

VALVE TAPPET - The part that rides on the valve-operating cam and transmits motion from the cam to the valve stem or push rod.

VALVE TIMING - Refers to the timing of valve closing and opening in relation to piston position in the cylinder.

VALVE TRAIN- The collection of parts that make the valves operate. The valvetrain includes the camshaft(s) and all related drive components, the various parts that convert the camshaft's rotary motion into reciprocating motion at the valves, and the valves and their associated parts.

VAPOR LOCK - A condition in the fuel system in which gasoline has vaporized, as in the fuel line, so that fuel delivery to the carburetor is blocked or retarded.

VELOCITY - The rate of motion or speed at any instant, usually measured in miles-per-hour or feet-per-second or minute.

VENTURI - In the carburetor, the restriction in the air horn that produces the vacuum responsible for the movement of fuel into the passing air stream.

VIBRATION - An unceasing back and forth movement over the same path; often with reference to the rapid succession of motions of parts of an elastic body.

VISCOUS COUPLING - A particular kind of fluid coupling in which the input and output shafts mate with thin, alternately spaced discs in a cylindrical chamber. The chamber is filled with a viscous fluid that tends to cling to the discs, thereby resisting speed differences between the two shafts. Viscous couplings are used to limit the speed difference between the two outputs of a differential, or between the two axles of a car.

VOLATILITY - A measurement of the ease with which a liquid turns to vapor.

VOLT - Unit of potential, potential difference, or electrical pressure.

VOLTAGE REGULATOR - A device used in connection with generator to keep the voltage constant and to prevent it from exceeding a predetermined maximum. (One of the three units comprising a generator regulator.)

VOLUMETRIC EFFICIENCY - Ratio between the amount of-fuel-air mixture that actually enters an engine cylinder and the amount that could enter under ideal conditions.

VOLUTE SPRINGS - Helical coil springs made from flat steel tapered both in width and thickness.

V-TYPE ENGINE - Engine with two banks of cylinders set at an angle to each other in the shape of a 7.

W

WANDER - To ramble or move without control from a fixed course, as the front wheels of a vehicle.

WASTE GATE - A valve used to limit the boost developed in a turbo-charger. A waste gate operates by allowing some of the engine'sexhaust flow to bypass the turbocharger's turbine section under certain conditions.

WATER JACKET - A jacket that surrounds cylinders and cylinder head, through which coolant flows.

WATER MANIFOLD - A manifold used to distribute coolant to several points in the cylinder block or cylinder head.

WATER PUMP - In the cooling system, the pump that circulates coolant between the engine water jackets and the radiator.

WHEEL ALINEMENT - The mechanics of keeping all the parts of the steering system in correct relation with each other.

WHEEL BRAKE - A brake that operates at the wheel, usually on a brake drum attached to the wheel.

WHEEL CYLINDER - In hydraulic braking systems, the hydraulic cylinder that operates the brake shoes when hydraulic pressure is applied in the cylinder.

WHEEL HOP - An undesirable suspension characteristic in which a wheel (or several) moves up and down so violently that it actually leaves the ground. Wheel hop can be caused by many problems, including excessive unsprung weight, insufficient shock damping, or poor torsional axle control.

WINCH - A mechanism actuating a drum upon which a cable is cooled, so that when a rotating power is applied to the drum, a powerful pull is produced.

WOBBLE PLATE - That part of a special type of pump (wobble pump) which drives plungers back and forth as it rotates to produce pumping action. It is a disk or plate, set at an angle on a rotating shaft.

WORK - The result of a force acting against opposition to produce motion. It is measured in terms of the product of the force and the distance it acts.

WORM GEAR - A gear having concave, helical teeth that mesh with the threads of a worm. Also called a *worm wheel.*

Y

YAW - The rotation about a vertical axis that passes through the car's center of gravity.

Z

ZERO-OFFSET STEERING - A steering system whose geometry has a scrub radius of zero. This configuration minimizes the steering effects produced during acceleration (with front drive) or braking on varying traction surfaces.